Debating Women's Citizenship in India 1930–1960

In this amazingly comprehensive and confident history of women's enactment of citizenship in the struggle for and experience of Indian national independence, Annie Devenish has provided readers, historians of India and of women alike, with an entirely new investigation of the years of early nationhood and women's role as agents of change. This book goes a long way into solving the vexing problem of how the vigorous women's activism of the 1920s and 1930s did—or did not—flow into the creation of the Indian nation, and what historical resources contemporary Indian feminists can turn to in reviving their battle for women's dignity and rights.

Ellen Dubois
Distinguished Professor, History and Gender Studies
Department of Gender Studies
University of California Los Angeles

Women's organisations have made a significant contribution to women's development and empowerment in India. Yet, little scholarly work has so far been done to assess their contribution. This book, therefore, is a welcome addition to the existing literature on the subject. It explores the question of what the coming of independence meant to a generation of feminists and nationalists by focusing on the leading members of two prominent women's organisations of their time—the All India Women's Conference and the National Federation of Indian Women. It draws on autobiographies and oral interviews as well as archival records. It is a very well-researched book and should be read not only by scholars interested in women's studies but by all students of modern Indian history.

Aparna Basu
Former Professor of Modern History
University of Delhi

In this lucid account of the modern Indian women's movement, Annie Devenish invites us to consider the variety of ways that citizenship was conceptualised at the intersection of nationalist and feminist politics at key moments in the history of Indian democracy. Centring both the stories of individual women and the new imaginaries of and for gender that their words and work enabled, *Debating Women's Citizenship in India* argues for the role of a particularly energetic, strategic cohort of Indian women in shaping the contours of state practice, civil society and the post-war, postcolonial international order all at once.

Antoinette Burton
Professor of History
Department of History
The University of
Illinois, Urbana-Champaign

Debating Women's Citizenship in India 1930–1960

Annie Devenish

BLOOMSBURY
NEW DELHI • LONDON • OXFORD • NEW YORK • SYDNEY

Abbreviations

AIIMS	All India Institute of Medical Sciences
AISF	All India Students' Federation
AIWC	All India Women's Conference
CA	Constituent Assembly
CHR	the Commission on Human Rights
CPI	Communist Party of India
CSWB	Central Social Welfare Board
CSW	Committee on the Status of Women
ECOSOC	The Economic and Social Council
FPAI	Family Planning Association of India
ICCW	Indian Council of Child Welfare
INC	Indian National Congress
LGBTI	Lesbian, Gay, Bisexual, Transgender and Intersex
MARS	Mahila Atma Raksha Samiti
MCH	Maternal and Child Health
MNML	Madras Neo-Malthusian League
MP	Member of Parliament
NAACP	National Association for the Advancement of Coloured People
NCCW	National Council of Child Welfare
NCWI	National Council of Women in India
NFIW	National Federation of Indian Women
NPC	National Planning Committee
NWFP	North West Frontier Province
PC	Planning Commission
SEWA	Self Employed Women's Association
UDHR	Universal Declaration of Human Rights
UNICEF	United Nations International Children's Emergency Fund
WHO	World Health Organisation
WIDF	Women's International Democratic Federation

Preface

Citizenship in India today remains a highly contested terrain. There is ongoing lobbying for the re-categorisation of Scheduled Castes and Tribes (SCTs), as various communities seek access to state resources and entitlements. Civil society groups are challenging the National Register of Citizens (NRC), which effectively strips four million people, mainly Muslim Bengalis in the north-eastern state of Assam, of their citizenship because they are unable to prove that they came to the state before neighbouring Bangladesh declared independence in 1971.[1] LGBTI petitioners, while celebrating the September 2018 Supreme Court ruling decriminalising Section 377 of the Indian Penal Code, are also bracing themselves for the ongoing battle of changing conservative social attitudes, which continue to discriminate against queer communities. Meanwhile, people's movements across India carry on the fight with state governments and corporations over access to coastal fishing regions, forests, minerals and land in the face of development and dam building projects, asserting their right to local control over natural resources and economic livelihoods.

Indian women are prominently present in such struggles, as well as in many other specific campaigns that are seeking to apply and broaden the meaning of citizenship to their everyday lives. Women are speaking out in academia, the media and politics to demand their right to safety and bodily integrity with the recent arrival of the international anti-sexual harassment #MeToo movement.

At the beginning of 2019, women in the southern state of Kerala formed a 620-km human chain to demand equal access to the Hindu temple, Sabarimala Shrine, in the face of religious practices that have continued to deny them access, despite a recent Supreme Court ruling in

[1] 'Assam register: Four million risk losing India citizenship', *BBC News* online, India, 30 July 2018, accessed 4 February 2019, https://www.bbc.com/news/world-asia-india-45002549.

their favour.[2] In the nation's Lok Sabha, Muslim women activists continue to fight to have the arbitrary and instant Koranic divorce procedure of triple *talak* outlawed through The Muslim Women (Protection of Rights on Marriage) Bill, in the face of ongoing resistance.[3]

As these contemporary events suggest, there are many spaces in which the meaning of inclusive and substantive citizenship, based on the principles of gender justice, continue to be fiercely debated and contested.

This book takes us back to an earlier phase of this debate, focusing on the coming of independence in India and its meaning for a generation of Indian feminists and nationalists whose careers straddle this transition. It addresses some of the critical aspects of the encounter, engagement, and dialogue between the Indian State and its women citizens,[4] in particular, how this generation conceptualised the relationship between citizenship, equality and gender justice and the various spheres in which the meaning and application of this citizenship was broadened and narrowed, renegotiated and pursued. The aim is to provide a critical assessment of the contribution of this generation, documenting both their successes and failures in an effort to begin filling the void in the history of women's collective activism in India between the late 1940s and the 1960s.

Yuval-Davis emphasises that '[i]nclusion in the citizenship body and becoming entitled to the different kinds of citizenship rights is what much of feminism has been about', especially in the embryonic stages of the feminist movement. This encompassed not only the right to belong

---

2 'Sabarimala temple: Indian women form "620 km human chain" for equality', *BBC News* online, India, 1 January 2019, accessed 4 February 2019, https://www.bbc.com/news/world-asia-india-46728521.

3 See Mariya Salim, 'Muslim women will not misuse the 'triple talak' law', *Aljazeera* online, 6 January 2018, India, accessed 8 February 2019, https://www.aljazeera.com/indepth/opinion/muslim-women-misuse-triple-talaq-law-180103150031202.html.

4 K. Sharma and C.P. Sujaya (eds.), *Towards Equality: Report of the Committee on the Status of Women in India*, reprinted as part of V. Mazumdar (ed.), *Women, Equality and the Republic: Landmarks in the Indian Story* series (Pearson, Delhi, Chennai, Chandigarh, 2011).

but also the right to participate as equal adults in political communities.[5] It is not surprising, therefore, that the notion of citizenship, which has been contested and debated in political and sociological theory, has 'come to occupy the centre stage also in feminist debates during the last 15 or 20 years.'[6]

The State, Rights and Citizenship

Citizenship as a concept emerges out of and is closely associated with the rise of the modern nation-state and the transition from monarchy to that of parliamentary governance. T.H. Marshall, one of the key thinkers in contemporary citizenship theory, presents an evolutionary and dynamic model of citizenship based on a notion of rights. This commences with the emergence of civil rights concerned with ensuring citizens' freedom, their safety, their right to own property, earn a legal income and protection under the law in the eighteenth century. Political rights associated with the franchise, in the nineteenth century, and culminates with social rights in the twentieth century with the rise of the welfare state.

Socio-economic rights are concerned with ensuring an adequate standard of living through access to housing, education and healthcare.[7] Additional rights include security spatial rights, which give persons the right to enter the territory of a state, to remain there, to work and or study there, as well as cultural rights, which guarantee that people and communities can participate in a culture of their choice.[8] The idea of rights is, therefore, crucial to the notion of citizenship. As Niraj Gopal Jayal stresses, 'Claims, to rights are implicitly claims to citizenship, and often to an expanding conception of it.'[9]

---

5 N. Yuval-Davis, *The Politics of Belonging: Intersectional Contestations* (Sage, London, 2011), p. 87.

6 Ibid., pp. 60–61.

7 Ibid., p. 62, p. 65.

8 Ibid., p. 54, p. 64.

9 N.G. Jayal, *Citizenship and its Discontents: An Indian History* (Harvard University Press, Cambridge, Massachusetts, London, England, 2013), p. 109.
Mukhopadhyay, 'An Introduction', p. 5.

The first chapter of this book, entitled 'The Emergence of the Indian Woman as a Political Citizen' focuses on Indian women as rights-bearing individuals, exploring how Indian feminist identities and their claim to citizenship come to be expressed through articulations of various kinds of rights—political, economic and social in the 1930s and 1940s. It emphasises how this generation was able to develop a multifaceted conception of citizenship, which included new notions of equalities within the private sphere. It also looks at how a liberal conception of the universal abstract political citizen—divorced from the contexts of sex, caste, religion and class is accommodated within gendered notions of citizenship, through a duality of rights and duties.

Chapter two, 'Constitution Writing and the Sexless Citizen' explores Yuval-Davis's idea of citizenship as belonging to a political community. Following on from the previous chapter, which documents how Indian women were able to expand the meanings and possibilities of citizenship for their sex in two decades prior to independence, this chapter shows how the possibilities of this expanded conceptualisation of citizenship were diminished within the Constituent Assembly (CA) debates at the close of the 1940s. This was due to the fact that the liberal conception of the 'sexless citizen' took prominence in both constitution writing and electoral politics at this time, limiting the way in which women were able to 'belong' to the new nation-state, and the possibilities of various alliances and identities built on the recognition of community, class and caste differences.

Citizenship: the Social Contract versus the Sexual Contract

The claim to citizenship and its accompanying rights have provided a powerful rallying call for marginalised and oppressed peoples all over the world. Yet it is important to remember that the concept of citizenship is grounded within a particular worldview and that there are exclusions built into its very foundation. In light of this, feminist scholars from the Global South have drawn our attention to the importance of interrogating the assumed universalism of a concept such as citizenship, emphasising instead the situatedness and context-specific understanding and application of the term.

To do this, we need to return to the idea of the social contract. Social contract theory posits that individuals enter a social contract with the State, relinquishing certain freedoms and submitting to the authority of the State, in return for protection, law and order, and the acquisition of certain rights. According to Carol Pateman, however, the social contract—the very foundation of liberal democratic citizenship—is inherently masculine and patriarchal, as it is underpinned by a sexual contract, based on men's control over women in the home and family. Pateman argues that under a monarchy, subjects were governed by their ruler in the same way that fathers wielded patriarchal authority over their sons. With the evolution to parliamentary government, the social contract replaced this patriarchal authority of the monarch/father with the authority of civil government. A new kind of equality was established between men as a result, based on their authority as heads of the household, but it required that they surrender certain freedoms and submit to the power of the State. To make up for these losses, men were given control over women in the private sphere.[10]

This argument holds weight when the position of women in Europe and the United States over this period is considered, when their access to education and professions, to property ownership, the franchise and equal treatment under the law was denied outright or extremely limited (in many instances, women remained perpetual minors in law under the guardianship of their fathers or husbands), leading to the first wave feminist movement in the nineteenth and twentieth centuries.

Citizenship and the Colonial Project

Over the same period that the Enlightenment notion of rights was taking hold in Britain and giving birth to the idea of the citizen, the

---

[10] C. Pateman, *The Sexual Contract* (Stanford University Press, Stanford, California, 1988) pp. 32–36.

British government was expanding and consolidating its hold on the Indian subcontinent. In *Liberalism and Empire*, Uday Mehta argues that the ideology of liberalism, committed to political rights and self-determination in the West, contained within it the same propensity towards colonial domination.[11] Just as Pateman emphasises that there was a sexism underpinning the social contract, Mehta argues that there was a racism built into the concept of citizenship and its application within the context of Empire.

The imperial project was justified on the basis of the colonial subject being so different and culturally and socially backward that they were not entitled to self-governance or rights.[12] Division and heterogeneity in Indian society were used by colonialists to argue the impossibility of national consciousness and Indian citizenship, while 'attachments of Indians to these affiliations of family, caste and religion, were taken as evidence of a serious deficit of individuality', making these people unfit to be liberal citizens.[13] The perceived lack of space for the expression and rights of the individual in the context of culture and religion was especially evident in relation to colonial perceptions of the position of women in indigenous Indian societies. In the eyes of the colonist, the mistreatment of women under 'oppressive and barbaric customs' was key to the justificatory rhetoric of the colonial civilising mission in India. Producing and reinforcing the narrative of 'white men saving brown women from brown men', in the words of Gayatri Chakravorty Spivak.[14]

Colonial subjects were, of course, not without agency in this process. In India, the development of social reform movements at the beginning of the nineteenth century and an emerging Indian nationalism at its close, challenged the assumptions of this colonial discourse in several ways.

Colonial subjects also turned liberalism back on itself, claiming citizenship through belonging within and adherence to the values of

---

[11] See U.S. Mehta, *Liberalism and Empire: India in British Liberal Thought* (Oxford University Press, New Delhi, 1999)

[12] Mukhopadhyay, 'An Introduction', p. 12.

[13] Jayal, *Citizenship and its Discontents*, p. 121.

[14] G.C. Spivak, 'Can the Subaltern Speak?' in P. Williams and L. Chrisman (eds.), *Colonial Discourse and Post-Colonial Theory: A Reader* (Harvester Wheatsheaf, New York, London, 1993), p. 93.

the Empire. Until the early twentieth century, citizenship was conceived of by elite Indians as full and equal participation in the British Empire, and equality of status within the dominions and other colonies.[15] This was the reasoning behind Gandhi's appeal for the trading and residency rights of Indians in South Africa, at the turn of the century. It was also the basis for Indian suffragettes' claim to the franchise for educated and propertied Indian women in the first franchise campaign (1917) in India.[16]

This notion of imperial citizenship, which 'allowed for the recognition of particular classes of subject-citizens' was [b]ased on class as much as race'.[17] It was a citizenship available exclusively to an educated and cosmopolitan middle class and a wealthy Indian elite, and the illusion of its equality was ultimately shattered by the racism of Empire.[18] Indians were, therefore, subjects, rather than citizens under the British colonial regime. Indeed, feminist scholars have drawn parallels in the discourses used to exclude women in the West from citizenship in the eighteenth, nineteenth and first part of the twentieth centuries and those used to exclude colonial subjects in the nineteenth and twentieth.

This raises some problematic questions when it comes to thinking about the meanings, possibilities and applications of citizenship for postcolonial feminist agendas. It also poses the question of whether the very template of citizenship is inherently Western or Eurocentric. To what degree is it applicable in the postcolonial context?

In Europe, Yuval-Davis emphasises, the State—defined through a unified system of administration, territorial boundaries and an army—emerges first, followed by the idea of the nation, with the rise of nationalism. If the individual comes to prominence through the social contract, then by the time nationalism in Europe emerges, the notion of the individual in relation to the State has already been established. In India, in contrast, like in many formally colonised countries, the

---

15 Jayal, *Citizenship and its Discontents*, p. 36.

16 See Sumita Mukherjee, *Indian Suffragettes: Female Identities Transnational Networks* (Oxford University Press, New Delhi, 2018), p. 74.

17 Jayal, *Citizenship and its Discontents*, p. 50.

18 Ibid., p. 21.

postcolonial nation emerges through a national liberation movement before or at the same moment as the construction of a postcolonial State, which comes into being with independence.[19] In this context, the notion of the individual had not had time to take hold in the same way it had in Europe.

In Europe also, there tended to be greater homogeneity within the nation-state, allowing for an overlapping of State, territory, nation, culture and ethnicity. These were often mistakenly perceived as interchangeable.[20] In this context, it was easier, Yuval-Davis argues, to find a common sense of belonging and collective identity. Postcolonial societies, in comparison, tend to be defined by plurality and heterogeneity; this means that there can be many 'nations' within one State. In such societies, furthermore, these collective identities, defined by religion or ethnicity have continued to remain powerful.

This complicates the relationship between the State and the individual, and has led to much debate; to what extent should citizenship be seen as an individual contractual relationship between the person and the State in such societies—as liberal theory suggests—or should this relationship rather be seen as 'mediated by the national community within which the citizen has grown up'?[21] This has been a particularly vexing question for women in postcolonial India, coming to the fore through a number of issues, the most prominent being the reform of personal laws. Here arguments around personal law reform have pitted the legislative equality of the individual against community rights to cultural and religious identity and practices, a theme to which we shall return to later.

Citizenship and Indian Nationalism

The development of Indian social reform movements at the beginning of the nineteenth century and an emerging Indian nationalism at its close challenged the prejudicial assumptions of the colonial discourse

[19] Yuval-Davis, *The Politics of Belonging*, p. 102.

[20] Ibid., p. 42.

[21] Ibid., p. 61.

in several ways. It was within these movements that the seeds of an autonomous Indian citizenship first emerge. An 'imagined' nation-state, in the words of Benedict Anderson, had to be constructed first, as the foundation for the notion of liberal citizenship to be articulated and claimed. Responding to both indigenous pressures as well as external critiques, various communities of Indian social reformers began to reformulate a sense of themselves and their political and cultural identity in the world. Reformers emphasised the internal dynamism of their society to evolve with the times and to modernise. For Muslim and Hindu reformers, this was accompanied with maintaining a distinctive and superior cultural identity in the sanctity of the home. For other groups of reformers, such Self Respect Caste movements, it implied a more radical rejection of aspects of culture. Revivalist groups sought to reinvent a cultural identity, harking back to an idealised past.

Early Indian nationalism at the end of nineteenth century still worked with the idea of citizenship within the Empire, with an elite and educated middle class seeking expanded power-sharing with the Raj. Following the Government of India Act of 1858, India moved from Company to Crown rule, under a Viceroy. The Viceroy had an imperial council of state, which included nominated British and Indian representatives who provided advice on matters relating to government. Indians could not elect members to this council, but there were democratic structures at lower levels of government, which gave the educated middle class and elite Indians representation in municipal elections and village panchayats.[22] The system of Dyarchy introduced by the 1919 Government of India Act expanded the piecemeal representation and power-sharing between the Raj and these classes. Dyarchy left the colonial government of India in charge of foreign policy, the military, income tax, currency and criminal law, while devolving domestic matters, including public health, education, land revenue administration and 'law and order' to provincial governments, where an Indian electorate now had a say through an enlarged franchise.[23]

---

22 Mukherjee, *Indian Suffragettes*, p. 18.

23 Ibid., p. 67.

The first three decades of the twentieth century saw a shift in nationalist ambitions from a piecemeal broadening of representation towards *purna swaraj*, full independence from British rule, hastened by the rise of Gandhian nationalism in the 1920s.[24] With this shift, a notion of Indian citizenship grounded on equality and universal franchise, and underpinned by political and civic rights, as expressed through the Karachi Resolution of 1931, took hold.

Gandhian nationalism also introduced a fundamental reorientation of the meaning of citizenship in the Indian context, breaking with Empire and Western civilisation itself. Gandhi's political philosophy rejected the notion of progress; politically, in terms of an understanding of the development of British liberal thinking and economically, in terms of capitalism as a natural progression from feudalism, and its celebration of industrialisation, technology, consumerism and wealth. Gandhi's locus was the rural village, rather than the bustling metropole. He emphasised the local and the handmade, stressing the importance of self-sustainability, and the dignity and value of manual labour—famously symbolised by spinning khadi on a charkha. Reinventing himself as an Indian rishi in his loin cloth and walking stick, Gandhi sought to eschew the idea of private property ownership and institutions like marriage and the nuclear family, basic tenets upon which liberal citizenship is based. Instead, as a devotee of an ascetic life, he emphasised the idea of citizenship as freedom from material possessions, bodily desires and emotional connections.

Gandhian nationalism also revived the idea of duty, prominent in Hinduism, as an aspect of citizenship.[25] For the Mahatma, duty meant service to his fellow human beings as well as resistance to injustice. Duty had provided an important entry point for Indian women into nationalist activities, and continued to remain a fundamental way for organised women's groups to articulate citizenship post-independence, as explored in the third chapter, 'Citizenship through Struggle: The National Federation of Indian Women'. Here, duty was interpreted

---

[24] B.L. Shankar and V. Rodrigues, *The Indian Parliament: A Democracy at Work* (Oxford University Press, New Delhi, 2011), p. 11.

[25] Jayal, *Citizenship and its Discontents*, pp. 145–146.

as service in the field of social development, creating a gendered role for women's organisations post-independence and facilitating state recognition and access to state resources for such organisations.

Gandhian conceptions of citizenship co-existed with other competing and overlapping conceptualisations of citizenship in late colonial India. These included Marxist and Nehruvian visions of a secular, all-encompassing centralised State, driving the redistribution of resources and the elimination of class hierarchies in the former, and coordinating economic production and social modernisation in the latter. In both of these, the citizen was harnessed like a cog in the machine to work towards a greater collective good. These imaginings vied with other forms of political community and identity, such as anti-caste movements, expressions of ethno-nationalism, and many strong regional identities.

Postcolonial Citizenship

These competing and overlapping conceptualisations of citizenship form the background against which the postcolonial state came into being. India's new Constitution (1950) created a secular Republic, granted a universal franchise and guaranteed political rights and equality for all in the section on Fundamental rights. Social rights were placed in the Directive Principles of State section of the Constitution and were, therefore, promised, depending on State resources, rather than guaranteed.[26]

Within the CA debates, the liberal notion of the abstract universal citizen predominates, with only two exceptions that allowed for group-differentiated citizenship. These included the provision of cultural rights for religious minorities and positive discrimination for historically backward castes and tribal groups who had been disadvantaged.

Independence, however, was accompanied by the partition of the subcontinent, igniting large-scale forced migration and communal

---

[26] Jayal, *Citizenship and its Discontents*, p.21.

violence along the fault lines of Bengal, the Punjab and the Sindh, resulting in death and severe physical and psychological trauma. The nature of the violence was heavily gendered with rape and abduction employed to mark women as the sites of community identity and honour. As a result, 'tens of thousands of women were kept in the "other" country, as permanent hostages, captives or forced wives', while their families migrated.[27] These upheavals undermined the supposedly secular nature of the newly formed Indian state.[28] The impact of these events is investigated in the fourth chapter, The Reluctant Citizen: India's "Doubtful and Resisting" Women, which looks at how Indian women's citizenship came to be mediated through religious communities in the case of the Indian State's official programme initiated to rescue and recover such women, exposing 'the politics of religious identity' as central 'to the framing of citizenship in the political state' in India, 'even if distanced from the constitutional state'.[29]

Turning away from the subjugation of the colonial past and the painful trauma of Partition, the Indian government and people looked to the future: channelling their energies and hopes into the new nation-building project. Citizenship within this project was most clearly defined and articulated through two important concepts—the need for national unity and cohesiveness, and economic and social development through modernisation.

The need for national unity and cohesiveness assists in explaining the emphasis on the liberal notion of the universal abstract 'sexless' citizen, which took precedence in the CA debates at this time, where identity politics was perceived as a source of tension and division. Fostering national unity meant that the populace was encouraged to see themselves as 'Indian citizens' first and foremost, rather than as Brahmin or Dalit, Assamese or Tamil or Sikh or Hindu.

In Nehruvian India, where development and modernisation were to be achieved through increased economic productivity and output,

---

[27] Y. Khan, *The Great Partition: The Making of India and Pakistan* (Yale University Press, New Haven, London, 2007), p. 135.

[28] Jayal, *Citizenship and its Discontents*, p. 83.

[29] Ibid., p. 79.

Gopal Jayal emphasises that being a model citizen meant being a good economic citizen and contributing to the economy. A citizen of free India had to 'be a productive citizen' with civic duty being 'defined as contributing to making the nation strong and economically self-reliant'.[30]

Women, Citizenship and the Law

If the entitlement to rights defines the modern liberal citizen, then it is through the law that these rights are secured and exercised. The social aspect of modernisation in Prime Minister Jawaharlal Nehru's India focused on embracing and implementing legislative reform to advance the position of women and other marginalised groups in this society. In a liberal democracy, the law is seen to be the vehicle for the application of citizenship.[31]

Legislative reform was a vital component of the strategy pursued by this generation of nationalists and feminists who saw the law as a means to achieve equality and empowerment. Active lobbying in the 1950s and early 1960s saw the introduction of various statutes intended to give women greater equality and protection, especially in the private sphere of the family. These included the acts passed as part of the Hindu Code Bill between 1952 and 1956 and the Dowry Prohibition Act of 1961. This era also saw India's signing of several international treaties, including United Nations Convention on Political Rights of Women (1952) and the Convention on the Nationality of Married Women (1957).

However, without effective implementation, such legislative reform failed to change the socio-economic position of women, as revealed by the first comprehensive review since independence, the 1974 *Report on the Status of Women*. This study drew on nationwide statistical evidence in its analysis, which ultimately presented a damning conclusion that 'the vast majority of women in India were yet to realise their rights on the ground'. These findings proved a 'severe indictment of the first 25

[30] Ibid., pp. 171–172.

[31] N. Menon, 'State/Gender/Community: Citizenship in contemporary India', *Economic and Political Weekly* (*EPW*), 33:5 (31 January–6 February 1998), p. PE5.

years of independent India's achievements to ensure Indian women's rights to equality, justice, freedom and dignity'.[32] This shattered the confidence that had been placed in legislative reform as an effective tool for transforming society and achieving substantive equality and social justice.

Grassroots Citizenship: Socio-economic Rights and Livelihoods

Although concerned with legislation, this generation of women understood the complexity of the issues involved, which called for a comprehensive set of interventions. Forbes emphasises that they 'aimed at social change and understood that it would not come easily or quickly. Their writings and statements make it clear that their long-range goal was equality'.[33] Without state institutions to ensure effective implementation, together with an underlying transformation in social attitudes and women's equal economic participation, the promise of substantive equality would remain unfulfilled.

With this insight, it makes sense that the articulation of citizenship through the claiming of rights and through legislative reform formed part of a broader set of strategies pursued by this generation. These also included articulating citizenship through social welfare service provision and social policy development, through political participation, civic education and agitational politics; through challenging the new State to hold true on its commitment to the fulfilment of basic needs and livelihoods.[34] This is the focus of the fifth chapter, 'Citizenship through Struggle', which looks at how various local struggles around socio-economic rights contributed to new forms of collective organisation

---

[32] K. Sharma and C.P. Sujaya (eds.), *Towards Equality: Report of the Committee on the Status of Women in India*, reprinted as part of V. Mazumdar (ed.), *Women, Equality and the Republic: Landmarks in the Indian Story* series (Pearson, Delhi, Chennai, Chandigarh, 2011), 759–766.

[33] G. Forbes, 'Caged Tigers: "First Wave" Feminists in India' in *Women in Colonial India: Essays on Politics, Medicine and Historiography* (Chronicle Books, Delhi, 2005), p. 24.

[34] Jayal, *Citizenship and Its Discontents*, p. 93.

and identity amongst Indian women, resulting in the formation of the National Federation of Indian Women (NFIW) in 1954. It also looks at the intersection of two very different kinds of struggles, one for socio-economic rights and services at a municipal level, and the other for legislative equality at a national level, and how these come together through a cross-organisational campaign to agitate for the reform of Hindu personal laws in the 1950s.

Embodied Citizenship

Yuval-Davis draws our attention to the importance of belonging and equal participation in the body politic as a key objective of feminism. But what about the physical bodies that make up this body politic? Are they not in some way also significant in how one is perceived within the collective political body? The citizen of liberal parliamentary democracy is supposed to be abstract and universal. However, as Pateman and Mehta underline, this citizen is by default male and white.

In her groundbreaking study on gender dynamics and roles in Yorùbá society, Oyèrónké Oyěwùmí shows how the physical body has been fundamentally implicated in the way that Western social hierarchies are constructed, an ideology she refers to as biological determinism. Oyěwùmí argues that the privileging of sight in the West has meant that particular physical differences of the body, especially those associated with sex and race, have become the basis for constructing social differences.[35] 'Social categories like "woman" are based on body-type and are elaborated in relation to and in opposition to another category: man; the presence or absence of certain organs determines social position,' she emphasises.[36] Particular social attributes, such as intellect, temperament, personality and ability, come to be associated with particular physical attributes. In the Enlightenment worldview, which produced the liberal citizen, men tend to be defined by their

[35] O. Oyěwùmí, *The Invention of Women: Making an African Sense of Gender Discourses* (University of Minnesota Press, Minneapolis, London, 2001), pp. ix-xvii, 1-11.

[36] Ibid., p. x.

intellect and rationality; they are seen to be almost disembodied, rational thinking minds, whereas women are conceived appositionally, as emotional and intuitive, being driven by their bodies, in particular, their reproductive roles.

These physical differences are used to construct social hierarchies in society, which, in turn, form the basis for the exclusion of certain categories of people from positions of power and authority. For example, in the nineteenth and early twentieth centuries, opponents of female suffrage regularly cited the emotional nature of women, which was considered to make them unsuited to the rational judgement required of political citizenship, and used this as justification for their exclusion from the franchise. The body, therefore, becomes the basis for the construction of difference and inferiority, not with only regards to sex, but also in relation to exclusions of race and class. Furthermore, because biology is perceived to be the basis of these differences—and the social hierarchies that they underpin—these then come to be seen as natural rather than constructed.[37]

Whereas in the past women's bodies have often been the site of subjugation, feminist scholars today are claiming back the body as a site of power. Control over one's body is nowadays recognised as a fundamental articulation and expression of citizenship. This includes physical safety, bodily integrity, and control over one's physical and intellectual labour. Feminist epistemology has also urged us to think more critically about how we experience the world through our bodies. This is the starting point for the sixth chapter, 'The Embodied Citizen: Family Planning in Independent India', which explores the idea of citizenship as experienced and expressed through the body.

Women's bodies produce the nation-state, both literally through children bearing, as well as figuratively as the bearers of cultural identity and socialisation. This explains the State's interest in women's sexuality as a site of control. It also illuminates the gendered sexual violence that accompanied Partition. As both the physical and cultural bearers of the nation, a woman's sexuality was invested with the identity and honour of the community and was, therefore, especially vulnerable. Rape,

[37] Ibid., p. 8.

abduction, forced conversions and marriage targeted the sexuality of women, just as the Indian State's interest in the rescue and recovery of women was premised not 'upon their definition as citizens, but as sexual and reproductive beings. The honour of the nation was at stake because women as sexual and reproductive beings were forcibly held by the other side'.[38]

One of the most intimate ways in which the State is able to infiltrate and exercise control over the bodies of its citizens is through population control policies. These have a gendered element, as such policies tend to target women rather than men, and the interventions geared towards women tend to be more invasive. Population control policies also indicate the shifting of boundaries between the public and the private, legitimising new forms of State intervention in the spheres of family and reproduction.

It is through population control policies that women experience the powers and ideology of the State, but the technologies and knowledge that accompany such policies can also be harnessed, or subverted, for a more emancipatory agenda—to give women greater control over their own fertility. Chapter 6 explores the complexities of this generation's engagement with family planning policies in India, which shows an understanding of such policies as this two-edged sword; a tool for women's empowerment but equally a strategy for State authority and class control.

Global Citizenship and Human Rights

Through violation of the 'other', and the protection of 'our women', the discourse of Partition violence sought to mark out the boundaries of the communal nation-state on women's bodies, just as the Indian government's rescue and recovery of abducted women sought to police these boundaries by deciding who was a legitimate citizen and who was not, based on natal and community affiliations. This reinforced the

[38] V. Das, 'National Honour and Practical Kinship', in F.D. Ginsburg and R. Rapp (eds.), *Conceiving the New World Order: The Global Politics of Reproduction* (University of California Press, Berkeley, California, 1995), p. 68.

flawed conflation between territory, community and State that has been a haunting spectre of postcolonial India.

The ongoing mediation of citizenship through community identity has had enduring implications for Indian women as citizens. South Asian countries, including India, witnessed a rise of State-sponsored fundamentalism in the 1980s, which lead to a shift away from the liberal rhetoric of equal rights for women and the withdrawal of some of their hard-won legal and political rights in the name of preserving the traditions and fundamental tenets of religion. A case in point is the government's response to the 1986 Shah Bano judgement.[39] A good example of how the law in postcolonial India can be co-opted by religious fundamentalism to work against women's rights.[40]

Amrita Chhachhi suggests that the rise of religious fundamentalism as State ideology over this period provided a justification for controlling women's mobility, fertility and sexuality in response to the demands of the capitalist labour market, which had facilitated the wide-scale entry of women into the workplace and the world. Ruling parties also turned to religious fundamentalism to create ideological unity.[41] It is possible to see similar developments in recent years in India with the rise of the Bharatiya Janata Party (BJP) and the resurgence of the Hindutva movement.

To escape the problematic overlapping and mistaken conflation between territory, community and State, which has constrained some of the emancipatory possibilities and potential of citizenship for women in the Indian context, this generation of nationalists and feminists embraced the notion of global citizenship and human rights as an alternative framework upon which to ground rights, to claim a place in the body politic and to establish forms of collective solidarity.

---

[39] This Bill withdrew the right of Muslim women to appeal for maintenance under a special provision of the criminal code. See A. Chhachhi, 'The State, Religious Fundamentalism and Women: Trends in South Asia', *EPW*, 24:11 (18 March 1989), p. 567.

[40] Chhachhi, 'The State, Religious Fundamentalism and Women', p. 567; N. Menon, 'State/Gender/Community: Citizenship in Contemporary India', *EPW*, 33:5 (31 January–6 February 1998), p. PE5.

[41] Chhachhi, 'The State, Religious Fundamentalism and Women', pp. 572-3, 568.

The final and seventh chapter of this book, 'The Indian Woman as a Global Citizen: Vijayalakshmi Pandit, Hansa Mehta and the United Nations', explores the contribution of this generation to debates around the framing of the Universal Declaration of Human Rights and the mandate of the United Nation's Committee on the Status of Women, challenging the Western-centric orientation of international human rights history. It also shows how back at home, exposure to the ideas of global governance and social justice through the emerging concept of human rights, proved conceptually useful for this generation, offering ways of thinking about citizenship beyond territorial borders and religious community.

Acknowledgements

The journey of conceptualising, researching and writing a book like this would not be possible without the involvement and support of many people. First and foremost, I would like to thank my supervisors, Dr Faisal Devji and Prof. Judith Brown, who guided me through the process of initially conceptualising this research. I am also most grateful to my mentor in India, Prof Tanika Sarkar, and the Centre for Historical Studies at JNU in New Delhi, who hosted me as a visiting student while I conducted my archival research in 2011.

I owe a special debt of gratitude to my wonderful mentor, Prof. Crispin Bates, for his hands-on help in developing this research further into a book project, and for giving me the opportunity to learn from him in the archives. In addition, I would like to acknowledge The School of Law at the University of KwaZulu-Natal, who accommodated me as a post-doctoral fellow, providing the much-needed resources and time to add flesh and bones to this research. I would also like to thank Prof. Goolam Vahed and Betty Govinden who have generously shared their books and ideas with me.

None of this might have happened if I hadn't been inspired many years before as a history undergraduate at the University of Natal in the late 1990s. I would like to extend a very special thanks to Catherine Burns, Keith Breckenridge, Jeff Guy and Julie Parle who have shown me how powerfully history speaks to the present and the human condition. Together with my inspiring professors, I must thank the great cohort of fellow history students and friends who accompanied me on this journey, including Mandisa Mbali, Julian Brown, Bernard Dubbeld, Vashna Jagarnath, Prinisha Badassy, Stephen Sparks and Nafisa Essop.

This research would not have been possible without the valuable assistance of the leadership of the All India Women's Conference (AWIC) and the National Federation of Indian Women (NFIW), as well as the many veterans and workers of these two organisations who shared their stories with me. Many thanks to Anni Raja, Smt. Sarla

Sharma, Smt. Vidiya Munsi, Mrs Malabika Chatterjee, Mrs Sakhamuri Suguna, and Mrs Chennaboina Kamalamma of the NFIW, and Mrs Sham Mohini Pathak, Dr Sarojini Varadappan and Mrs Ranade of the AIWC. A special thanks also to Lakshmi and her colleagues in Hyderabad who helped me organise local interviews and translated for me.

I owe a great debt to the staff of the Bodleian Libraries; in particular, the Indian Reading Room, the History Faculty Library, the Social Science and the Radcliff Libraries, who helped me to locate many books and manuscripts over the years. In India, my particular thanks are extended to the staff and archivists at the Nehru Memorial Museum and Library, the National Archives, the Central Secretariat Library in New Delhi, the Joshi Archives at JNU, the CPI archives at Ajoy Bhavan and the Margaret Cousins Library.

In addition, I am very grateful to Mary John of the Centre for Women's Development Studies (CWDS) in New Delhi, as well Gargi Chakravartty, Janaki Nair, Aparna Basu and Devaki Jain who offered constructive feedback on my writing and ideas. In the UK, the Women's History Network has been a great source of support.

My time in India has been an adventure and an invaluable learning curve. My appreciation extends to the friends I met along the way. Madhuresh Kumar, Shibayan Raha, Anil Tharayath Varghese, Shalini Sharma and Gayatri Bhuyan helped me come to grips with the complexity of Indian politics and social movements. Equally, to my friends back at home in South Africa: Marisa, Juliette, Robert, Helge, Jen, Barry, Liz and Marc, and in the United Kingdom Kim, Anniken, Esme and Alberto, Jessica and Alfred, Margaret and Malcolm Yee, Pete, Vicky, Katie, Hannah and Gavin, for their unfailing support and encouragement. Finally, I would like to thank my parents, George and Patricia Devenish.

Introduction

'Does man make the age, or the age make the man?' asks well-known nationalist, socialist and feminist Kamaladevi Chattopadhyay at the start of her autobiography.[1] Chattopadhyay was a spirited teenager when Mahatma Gandhi launched his first Satyagraha campaign in 1920, marking the start of a crucial new phase in the Indian National Movement. She began her political career shortly after, as a volunteer in the Indian National Congress's Seva Dal and later as a member of the Congress youth movement, from where she launched into nationalist politics. Seeking an ideological language to critique the nature of colonial oppression and imagine an equitable future, she then turned towards socialism, becoming a leading figure in the formation of the Congress Socialist Party (CSP) in 1934. When political avenues were closed to her after independence, she found an alternative means of giving expression to her socialist ideology: by encouraging the development of a crafts cooperative movement, emphasising the value of labour and livelihoods in the production of traditional Indian arts and crafts. Throughout her life, she remained an outspoken advocate for women's equality.

Chattopadhyay uses the term 'man' in a universal sense to reflect on her own life and career as part of a generation of nationalists and social activists who steered India from late colonial rule to independence. This was a pivotal era of transition, marking the shift from colonial subjecthood to citizenship in the nation-state, defined by multiple and competing imaginings of this new State. There was considerable debate over the boundaries and possibilities of such citizenship, with Chattopadhyay and her colleagues participating energetically in this process. When Chattopadhyay contemplates the question 'Does man make the age, or the age make the man?', she could just as easily be asking 'Does the woman make the age, or the age make the woman?', to which her autobiography was to answer, that they make each other. Chattopadhyay's politics, like

[1] K. Chattopadhyay, *Inner Recesses Outer Spaces: Memoirs* (Navrang, New Delhi, 1986), p. 1.

those of her contemporaries, illustrates the complex ways in which the age and the individual were mutually constituted.

Kamaladevi Chattopadhyay was part of a cohort of nationalists and feminists who were leading members of two prominent women's organisations of their day: the All India Women's Conference (AIWC) and the National Federation of Indian Women (NFIW). This cohort of women was uniquely positioned at the moment of India's independence as both nationalists and feminists, and institutionally entrenched in Nehru's government with an unprecedented opportunity to contribute and experiment in the nation-building project. Their politics and careers provide a new framework that lets us analyse and understand the transition to independence. Drawing on life histories together with archival research, this book excavates 'the mental products of these women's lives, their ideas, their writings and their discourse'[2] to develop a deeper and more nuanced understanding of the feminist political personas of this generation, and how they negotiated the political and social terrains of their time. It addresses questions such as: How, as women and advocates of a gendered agenda, did this generation negotiate its way in the complex and competing politics of nation-building, and what scope did this give them to speak politically as women? Did their participation in this project bring various strands of their identity into conflict and could these be resolved? As part of a particular political milieu, caught up in a turbulent moment of history dominated by identity politics, to what extent were they able to imagine citizenship beyond the boundaries of the nation-state, and the barriers of religious identity, class and ideological affiliation? And finally, how did they grapple with the inheritance of colonial nationalism, endeavouring to give weight to this transition through the development of legislation, policy, institutions and social movements in the post-independence era? These questions are explored by documenting and analysing the voices of this cohort in some of the key debates around nation-building in Nehruvian India, and by tracing the range of activities and struggles engaged in by these organisations and individuals as expressions of citizenship in practice.

---

[2] G. Lerner, 'Introduction' in *The Challenge of Feminist Biography Writing the Lives of Modern American Women,* (eds.) Sara Antler et al. (University of Illinois Press, Urbana and Chicago, 1992), p. 5.

Rather than employing the idea 'of women as something to be framed by context', the theoretical approach adopted during the course of this research has taken inspiration from the work of feminist historians such as Kumkum Sangari and Sudesh Vaid. It attempts to 'rethink historiography as a whole' by analysing gender difference as both structuring and structured by a wide set of social relations.[3] To return to Chattopadhyay's opening question—'Does man make the age, or the age make the man?'—the objective of this research has been to explore how the age and the 'man', or rather 'woman', are mutually constituted. It is how they make each other that is of central interest. Drawing on Vaid and Sangari, gender is employed as an analytical tool or heuristic device, not as 'the endpoint of analysis, but rather as an entry point into complex systems of meaning and power.'[4] By applying such feminist historiography to this particular period of Indian citizenship-making, the scholar is able to expose some of the underlying power dynamics that have shaped its construction. But if this is not a contributory history, what is the justification for focusing on women? Is this not making the fatal mistake of equating subject matter with theoretical approach? The relevance of this cohort is not based on the fact that they were women, but rather that they were both nationalists and feminists, who brought their agenda of women's equality into the nation-building process. The intention of this research is to use the careers and voices of this cohort as an entry point into these larger sets of debates concerned with nation-building and citizenship-making, as well as the power dynamics and politics surrounding these.

Gender and Nation in India

Much of the theorisation on gender and nation in India has come to be informed by Partha Chatterjee's 1989 analysis of the 'Nationalist

---

[3] K. Sangari and S. Vaid (eds.), 'Introduction', *Recasting Women: Essays in Indian Colonial History* (Rutgers University Press, New Brunswick, 1990), pp. 2–3.

[4] K. Visweswaran, 'Histories of Feminist Ethnography', in *Annual Review of Anthropology*, 26 (1997): 616.

Resolution of the Women's Question.'[5] This analysis seeks to understand how gender is implicated in relations of political power, and consequently how women are brought into the imagination and construction of the nation-state. Chatterjee argues that a set of developments towards the end of the nineteenth century, in particular the conceptual separation of public and private, enabled the construction of a political identity for the modern Indian male nationalist through a particular reworking of gender relationships and identities.[6]

Reading back into earlier phases of the colonial encounter, subsequent scholarship has taken as its starting point, this close connection between the reworking of gender relationships and identities, and the development of new collective political identities. Lata Mani's analysis of the debate around sati in nineteenth-century India[7] illustrates the way in which colonial discourse functioned to construct a particular archetype of 'Indian woman' and the 'Indian man', and to define the dynamics of the relationship between the two in order to claim legitimacy for colonial rule through its civilising agenda.[8] Building on this, Mrinalini Sinha's work exposes the way

---

[5] S. Rege, 'Dalit Women Talk Differently: A Critique of "Difference" and Towards a Dalit Feminist Standpoint Position', *EPW*, 33: 44 (31 October to 6 November 1998), p. WS-39.

[6] I refer to the public and private spheres, not as innate and preconceived categories but rather as constructed concepts that have become influential in the analysis of other scholars such as Chatterjee. The construction of public and private, and their separation, must be historicised as, for example, Carole Pateman has attempted in her seminal work *The Sexual Contract* (Cambridge, Cambridge University Press,1988).

[7] See, for example, L. Mani, 'Contentious Traditions: the Debate on Sati in Colonial India' in Sangari and Vaid (eds.), *Recasting Women*, pp. 88–126.

[8] The British justified colonial rule by arguing that the 'barbaric' treatment of women within Indian society, expressed in cultural practices such as sati and child marriage was evidence of the 'uncivilised' nature of this society and, therefore, legitimised the civilising mission of colonial rule. Using this discourse, Britain was able to claim a 'moral responsibility' as the 'protector' of Indian women and claim the right to intervene in the private sphere of family and religion. Gayatri Spivak refers to this as 'white men saving brown women from brown men'. See, for example, Gayatri Chakravorty Spivak, 'Can the Subaltern Speak?' in P. Williams and L. Chrisman (eds.), *Colonial Discourse and Post-Colonial Theory: A Reader* (Columbia University Press, New York, 1994), pp. 66–111; R. Sturman, *The Government of Social Life in Colonial India: Liberalism, Religious Law, and Women's Rights* (Cambridge University Press, New York, 2012), p. 2.

in which constructions of masculinity and femininity were drawn into colonial administration and politics, to delineate difference and power amongst indigenous communities in India. The emergence of the stereotype of the 'effeminate babu' provided a way of checking the growing influence of a Western-educated Indian middle class, who were clamouring for a greater stake in the governance of the empire.[9] But this was not an exclusively colonial strategy. By the beginning of the nineteenth century, this very class of educated Indian elites was challenging British authority through their own reworking of gender identities and relationships. In order to articulate an alternative and affirmative identity for themselves within the context of the Indian social reform movement, reformers concerned themselves with the promotion of women's education and the change of social laws that determined women's status within the family. They inverted colonial discourse, arguing that their progressive treatment of women reflected their capacity for self-governance. Traditionalists challenged colonial domination by developing a strong and affirmative cultural, intellectual and spiritual identity for themselves as Indians.

As Indian political identities began to coalesce around the framework of an imagined nation-state, this reworking of gender relationships and identities became increasingly centred on the articulation and construction of the political identity of citizenship. The importance of the 'Indian woman' as the discursive site of this identity construction continued in this period and began to take on new significance. Late nineteenth-century Indian nationalist politics, according to Chatterjee, claimed the Indian woman as homemaker, mother and wife—symbolising culture and religion within the family—as the site for the construction of a revived cultural national citizenship. Simultaneously, as the 'empowered', 'new woman' of the late nineteenth century, she was claimed by social reformers as the site upon which a new refashioned identity of the Indian male as a progressive and legitimate citizen was crafted, becoming a powerful signifier of this new progressive

[9] M. Sinha, *Colonial Masculinity: The 'Manly Englishman' and the 'Effeminate Bengali' in the Late Nineteenth Century* (Manchester, Manchester University Press, 1995), pp. 1–5.

identity.[10] Chatterjee proposes that because culture and spirituality are traditionally associated with the private sphere, Indian women as the keepers of the home came to embody this Indian identity and its cultural and spiritual values. By the end of the nineteenth century, the separation of the public and the private, and the positioning of Indian women firmly within the sphere of the home, enabled nationalists to engage with the British on their own terms, in the public realm of politics, while maintaining a superior and unique identity untouched by Western values within the private sphere of the home.[11]

Uma Chakravarti argues in 'Whatever Happened to the Vedic *Dasi*?' that social reformers, such as the Arya Samaj who promoted women's education and the reform of social laws, were simply producing a new kind of restructured patriarchy. This patriarchy reflected and responded to the changing context, agendas and objectives of nineteenth-century nationalism, allowing them to represent themselves as progressive, but at the same time, doing this by continuing to anchor women firmly in the sphere of the domestic. Eleanor Newbigin, focusing on the Hindu Code Bill in the 1950s, reaches a similar conclusion. She emphasises that male politicians supported reforms to women's legal rights not so much out of a true conviction of gender equality, but rather because they wanted to display their credentials as a modern and progressive nation, grounded on particular notions of secularism, democracy and political economy. Such reforms, in fact, often advanced their own middle-class male interests within the family.[12] Lata Mani, in her analysis of the debate around the abolition of sati in early nineteenth-century India, coined an evocative and enduring phrase

---

10 See P. Chatterjee, 'The Nationalist Resolution of the Women's Question', in G. Caste (ed.), *Postcolonial Discourses: An Anthology* (Oxford University Press, Oxford, 2001), pp. 151–166.

11 Ibid.

12 See, for example, E. Newbigin, *The Hindu Family and the Emergence of Modern India: Law, Citizenship and Community* (New York, Cambridge University Press, 2013); E. Newbigin, 'The Codification of Personal Law and Secular Citizenship: Revisiting the History of Law Reform in Late Colonial India', in *The Indian Economic and Social History Review*, 46:1 (January–March 2009), p. 84.

for describing the place and function of women in this dynamic, as 'neither subjects nor objects, but rather the ground of the discourse'.[13] In their analysis, Chatterjee, Chakravarti and Newbigin identify the continuation of such a dynamic into the later nineteenth and twentieth centuries.

Although Chatterjee's analysis of the 'Resolution of the Women's Question' has encouraged the production of scholarship and research which has highlighted the important connections between the reworking of gender relationships and identities, and the development of new collective political identities, it leaves many questions unresolved. It also encourages new points of criticism arising from its representation of the 'Indian woman' as the 'ground of the discourse' for the reworking of political identity. One of the problems with framing colonial interaction and the subsequent development of nationalist identities in such terms is that it leaves little room for thinking about women as agents and active participants in such historical forces.

For Leela Kasturi and Vina Mazumdar, the major weakness of Chatterjee's analysis is the fact that it completely ignores the way women themselves responded to the challenges of colonial rule. Surely, they argue, 'the problem of an identity crisis is not the monopoly only of men.'[14] Women were not only acted upon in the private sphere, they were also active participants in this process of reworking. They engaged and responded to the dynamics of Indian nationalism, colonial domination, maternal imperialism and other indigenous movements, in attempts to redefine themselves, so that they could access new avenues of power and identity. The 'private sphere' was a site of negotiation, disruption and challenging of traditional relations of gendered power as much as it was a space for reinventing and consequently reinforcing these. As Tanika Sarkar illustrates in her insightful study on Rashsundari Debi, a housewife from an upper-caste landed Hindu family in East Bengal, who produced the first known published autobiography of an Indian

---

13 Mani, 'Contentious Traditions', p. 117.

14 L. Kasturi and V. Mazumdar, 'Women and Nationalism', Occasional Paper, Centre for Women's Development Studies (1995), p. 13.

woman in 1876, women could use the private sphere and the tropes of domesticity and religious devotion to critique and challenge their reinvention as 'the grounds of the discourse.'[15]

The work of Durba Ghosh on colonial interracial conjugality, like that of Tanika Sarkar, challenges Chatterjee's myth of the 'hermetically sealed' domestic 'spiritual space.'[16] In her case studies of various interracial sexual relationships between European men and indigenous women in India, Ghosh shows how the family, as much as the public sphere, was a crucial and constitutive part of early colonial state formation and governance in British India.[17] Furthermore, for the middle class and elite Indian women, the remaking of a political identity through the fashioning of the 'new Indian woman' created opportunities for them to move from the responsibilities of the home into the public sphere, through the professions of teaching and social work. In the case of Pandita Ramabai, one of the most admired role models of Chattopadhyay's generation, access to the language and mandate of social reform allowed her to build a career for herself as a social reformer, to travel the world, and ultimately to choose a new religion, that of Christianity, which she believed was able to offer greater personal and intellectual freedom. Women were defying imposed gender identities and prescribed gender relationships in the sphere of the domestic in a number of different ways before they began to do so in the public sphere. Not only this but by engaging in this process of the reworking of their domesticity, they were able to forge new bridges into the public sphere, contesting Chatterjee's neat separation of the home and the outside world.

Sharmila Rege's research shows how efforts to re-inscribe Dalit women's participation and voices in the nationalist struggle have

---

15 See, for example, T. Sarkar, *Hindu Wife, Hindu Nation: Community, Religion, and Cultural Nationalism* (Indiana University Press, Bloomington, 2001.)

16 D. Ghosh, *Sex and the Family in Colonial India: The Making of Empire* (Cambridge University Press, Cambridge, 2006) p. 250.

17 Ibid., p. 2. Ghosh shows how indigenous women in relationships with European men used the colonial encounter to engage with the institutions of colonial governance, in order to benefit and empower themselves; negotiating company pensions, gaining legal privileges, and expressing their cultural and religious affiliations. See Ibid., pp. 147–148, 252.

posed a further challenge to Chatterjee's analysis.[18] Chatterjee's reading mirrored colonial attempts to reclaim and reinvent a respectable domesticity by removing various categories of indigenous women, including colonial companions, who were considered non-desirable within the imperialist nationalist project in their imagining of the nation.[19] The subject of the 'new Indian woman' was class- and caste-specific, being generally middle or upper class, and higher caste and excluded Dalit women, peasants and workers. The latter groupings were at this time reworking the women's question in alternate areas of struggle, including those in the public sphere. The period Chatterjee identifies with the 'Resolution of the Women's Question' is the same era in which women's participation in the Ambedkarite movement reached its peak, Rege emphasises.[20]

The women's question re-emerges half a century later with history writing on the transition from late colonial rule to independence. In this instance, however, the question and its resolution, come to be framed through reading into the relationship between nationalism and feminism. Historians such as Jayawardeni Kumari, Geraldine Forbes and Gail Minault[21] might interpret the nuanced interaction of nationalism and feminism differently, but there tends to be a consensus amongst such scholars that in the playing out of this relationship, nationalist concerns of unity and political freedom ultimately triumphed over the priorities of a more directly feminist agenda. The resolution of this relationship in favour of nationalist priorities is often read forward into the early period of independence, through the 1950s and 1960s. Then it is used to explain the nation-state's failure to translate its commitment to constitutional equality into substantive socio-economic equality, a failing first brought to

---

18 Rege, 'Dalit Women Talk Differently', p. WS-39.

19 Ghosh, *Sex and the Family in Colonial India*, p. 250.

20 Rege, 'Dalit Women Talk Differently', p. WS-41.

21 See, for example, J. Kumari, *Feminism and Nationalism in the Third World* (Verso Books, London, 1994) and G. Forbes, 'The Politics of Respectability: Indian Women and the Indian National Congress' in D. Low (eds.), *The Indian National Congress: Centenary Highlights* (Oxford University Press, Delhi, 1988), pp. 54–91.

public attention by the findings of the 1974 Committee on the Status of Women India report.[22]

In the historiography of this period, the granting of constitutional equality is seen to lead to an era of complacency amongst women activists. Prominent individuals from the women's and the nationalist movement entered parliamentary politics, becoming part of the structures of power. Women's organisations such as the AIWC were understood to have been co-opted into the institutions of the State, and consequently integrated into the welfare machinery that reproduced and extended the paternalistic relationship of the family and community at a national level.

For many activists, particularly those on the political Left who came of age with the resurgence of women's activism in the late 1970s, even if the playing out of this relationship had been very different, with feminist concerns holding their ground, gaining recognition, and eventually transforming the political agenda of nationalist liberation itself, the end result would have remained unchanged. In this interpretation, it is, in fact, the consensus between feminism and nationalism that becomes the central problematic. By the mid- to late 1940s, communist women such as Renu Chakravartty felt that they were losing the battle in their attempts to transform the leading women's organisations of their day, such as the AIWC, into mass-based organisations able to represent the genuine interests of working-class and peasant women.[23] In their understanding, the middle class, urban and welfarist orientation of the feminism promoted by the women's movement shared the same class interests of the Congress-led nationalist movement. This meant that it was bound to fail before it even began, because of its inability to acknowledge the structural changes required for the true economic

---

22 The Committee on the Status of Women in India Report offered the first comprehensive quantitative and qualitative assessment of the limited socio-economic and political progress made by women in India since independence and brought into renewed focus the gap between laws and social context. See, for example, Committee on the Status of Women in India, 'Towards Equality: Report of the Committee on the Status of Women in India', Department of Social Welfare, Government of India, (New Delhi, 1975).

23 Renu Chakravartty provides a detailed account of her experiences working with the AIWC in the 1940s. See R. Chakravartty, *Communists in the Indian Women's Movement* (People's Publishing House, New Delhi, 1980).

and social empowerment of women. Class loyalty and identification are seen to win over gender loyalty in this interpretation.

Such conceptual understandings of the 'Resolution of the Women's Question' are weakened by the critiques discussed above, but they do remain valuable in that they draw attention to the close connection between the reworking of gender relationships and identities, and the development of new collective political identities. Rather than thinking about the 'Indian woman' as the 'fixed' discursive site of political identity construction, or her relegation to second-class citizenship due to triumphing of nationalism over feminism, this book takes as its starting premise the idea that these positionings, like identities, are neither fixed nor resolved. They are equally unstable, shifting and constantly requiring definition and re-articulation.[24] This enabled the discourse of social reform and nationalist envisioning—produced by this reworking of gender identities and relationships—to take on a life of its own, to be endowed with new meanings, and to be reclaimed and reinvented, creating an opening for a new kind of gender politics in Indian society. It gave activists, committed to a transformed society, access to a new set of discursive tools with which to talk about inequality between individuals and collective groups and to lobby for change within social institutions and relations. This enabled the development of new kinds of individual and collective identities for women. It also made new kinds of communication and mobilisation amongst women possible and socially acceptable.

This process continued into the era of Indian independence and indeed continues today. This dynamism made it feasible for activists and organisations of Chattopadhyay's generation to claim the debate over the boundaries, meanings and possibilities of postcolonial citizenship as their own set of 'grounds' for the reworking of a new civic and social identity for 'Indian woman' with the transition to democracy. As a consequence, the transition from the 1940s to the 1960s was never the

[24] Sinha emphasises that gender needs to be understood as one of 'multiple axes along which power was exercised in colonial India', operating to produce colonial identities which were themselves unstable, shifting and constantly requiring definition and re-articulation. See Sinha, *Colonial Masculinity*, p. 1.

quiet period that historiography tends to define it as. This was an active era with the crafting of new documents, such as the *Indian Woman's Charter of Rights and Duties*, the Mandate of the UN's Committee on the Status of Women, AIWC and NFIW civic education drives and the Campaign for the Hindu Code Bill. Collaboration between the AIWC, other voluntary associations and the State witnessed the conceptualisation and implementation of new welfare services and community development projects; the founding of new kinds of public-private institutions, and the formation of influential policy-making bodies. Renewed critical engagement and confrontation with the government was re-ignited with the growth of the communist women's movement in the 1950s, opposition to the reform of personal laws and the controversy over the Abducted Persons (Recovery and Rescue) Act (1949). Through these developments, this generation responded to the new spaces created to transform the Indian woman to a citizen.

Introducing this Generation

Both Gandhian and Nehruvian politics and developmental thinking provided a foundation for the gender politics and developmental praxis of this generation after independence. A range of other ideologies and philosophies, including social feminism, Western feminism, socialism, Marxism and various movements of international solidarity, also proved influential. What held Chattopadhyay and her colleagues together as a cohesive group was the fact that they saw themselves as agents of change. They believed they had a contribution to make to the nation-building project; they were committed to building the principles and practices of gender equality into this project. The Nehruvian era opened up an unprecedented set of opportunities to take part in the construction of a new political and social order in India, a set of opportunities that had been unavailable to any generation previously. With access to both state and philanthropic resources and political will, they were able to innovate and experiment with different developmental models. Constructive and social work during the latter phase of the nationalist movement had given them invaluable 'hands-on experience' of local problems and social inequalities, while an involvement at a leadership level in nationalist politics and the AIWC had given them opportunities to travel widely within India and even internationally. This enabled Chattopadhyay and her colleagues to contextualise struggles locally, as well as to see how they fit within a national, regional and global picture.

One of the features this generation shared with Jawaharlal Nehru, as a fellow architect of independent India, was a belief that the modern state must play a leading role in dismantling the structures of oppression in Indian society through economic development, legislation and education. There were, however, significant differences amongst this cohort with regard to the particular character they felt the State should assume, and the specific roles they envisioned for themselves within this picture. Like Chattopadhyay herself, some of her colleagues, such as Rajkumari Amrit Kaur, sought to adapt Gandhian values within a contemporary context. Others like Rama Rau, founder of the Family Planning Association of India (FPAI), placed greater faith in the technology and skills of the West to deliver socio-economic development. Communist women such as Renu Chakravartty and Sarla Sharma looked to the Soviet Union and communist China for developmental models, arguing that the Indian State must play a more proactive role in land redistribution and labour rights. There were those such as Sarojini Varadappan and Durgabai Deshmukh, founder of the Central Social Welfare Board (CSWB), who chose social service as an alternative to a political career, while others such as Renuka Ray sought to combine politics and constructive work.

Renuka Ray (1904 – 97) combined a successful career as a Congress Member of Parliament (MP), maintaining her autonomy, respect and influence in the party, while continuing to involve herself in social work activities, through her time as Minister of Relief and Rehabilitation in West Bengal, and as a governmental advisor on welfare subjects and policy. After committing herself passionately to the nationalist struggle as a teenager, Ray was sent by her father to study economics at the London School of Economics in the early 1920s. This was followed by her marriage to Satyen Ray, a civil servant whose job postings in rural India brought her into contact with village life and its problems. In the 1930s, she was able to apply this experience to the nationalist cause when

Gandhi asked her to volunteer for his village reconstruction programme, after which her career in social and constructive work took off.[25] For Ray, working within party politics as a Congress MP and a cabinet minister was a means to harness the resources and political will necessary for rehabilitation and constructive work in post-independence India.[26]

A number of Ray's colleagues in the AIWC, such as Sarojini Varadappan and Durgabai Deshmukh, chose social service as an alternative to politics.

Sarojini Varadappan (born 1921) is an AIWC stalwart based in Chennai who was interviewed for this research in December 2011. Although her father had been an influential Congress politician and Chief Minister of Madras, and her niece a Cabinet Minister, Varadappan stressed that, unlike these family members, her real interest had always lain in social service. In 1939, at the age of 18, she took up public work as a volunteer for Gandhi's visit to Madras.[27] Two years later, in 1941, she joined the Women's Indian Association (WIA), the Madras affiliate of the AIWC, and has been a member ever since.[28] Throughout her career, she has been involved in a wide range of social welfare and developmental initiatives for women and children, in the areas of education, employment and healthcare. She was also Chairperson of both the Madras State Social Welfare Board and the Central Social Welfare Board (CSWB), where she worked widely with other community and voluntary organisations.[29]

Muthulakshmi Reddi (1886 – 1968), a fellow Madras-based AIWC activist and nationalist, was a role model and mentor for Sarojini Varadappan. Reddi was born in 1886 in Pudukottah state and grew

---

[25] A. Devenish, 'Performing the Political Self: A Study of Identity Making and Self Representation in the Autobiographies of India's First Generation of Parliamentary Women' in *Women's History Review*, 22:2 (2013), p. 281.

[26] For a detailed account of the life and public career of Renuka Ray, see R. Ray, *My Reminiscences: Social Development During the Gandhian Era and After,* (Stree, New Delhi, 1982).

[27] 'Bio Data of Smt Sarojini Varadappan', unpublished booklet, (undated), p. 1.

[28] Varadappan also served a term as National President of the AIWC between 1980 and 1985.

[29] 'Bio Data of Smt Sarojini Varadappan', p. 1; Interview with S. Varadappan, 28 December 2011, Madras.

up to become a pioneer legislator and the first woman member of the Indian legislature in 1926. In this role, she used her skills to encourage the development of progressive social welfare legislation. As an activist, she was also involved in a number of social reform activities, including campaigning for the abolition of the *devadasi* system in Hindu temples and for the enactment of laws to prevent trafficking of women and children.[30] In 1937, she resigned from the Legislative Council in protest Gandhi's imprisonment and joined the nationalist movement.[31] Reddi's career brought together two professions, that of social welfare worker and activist, and of a trained doctor. This enabled her to combine her skills strategically, establishing the first children's hospital in India in 1927 and later, the Cancer Research Institute in Madras.[32]

Rameshwari Nehru (1886 – 1966), like Muthulakshmi Reddi, belongs to the cusp of an earlier generation of women activists. She was an enthusiastic social worker and campaigner against untouchability, and an active founder and organiser of the Delhi Women's League, another affiliate of the AIWC. She was involved in the campaign for women's franchise and a representative of women's interests as a committee member at the Round Table Conference.[33] Her post-independence work concentrated mainly on refugee relief and rehabilitation.[34] Nehru also had a deep interest and sense of solidarity with women's struggles in Asia and Africa, and helped to foster links between these struggles and the Indian women's movement back home.

Mridula Sarabhai (1911 – 74) worked together with Rameshwari Nehru in the Ministry of Relief and Rehabilitation, as a coordinator for the rescue and recovery of women who had been abducted during India's Partition in August 1947. She grew up in Ahmedabad and, like her contemporaries, was an outspoken feminist and a nationalist who

---

30 'Forward' in A. Basu (ed.), *The Pathfinder: Dr. Muthulakshmi Reddi* (Pune, AIWC, 1986), p. 8.

31 A. Basu and B. Ray, *Women's Struggle: A History of the All India Women's Conference 1927 – 2002* (Manohar Publishers, New Delhi, 2003), p. 224.

32 'Forward' in Basu (ed.), *The Pathfinder: Dr. Muthulakshmi Reddi*, p. 8.

33 Basu and Ray, *Women's Struggle*, p. 225.

34 Nehru was appointed Honorary Director of the Women's Wing of the Union Ministry of Relief and Rehabilitation.

participated in the Civil Disobedience Campaign (1930 - 34) and the Quit India Movement of 1942.[35] Sarabhai was a close associate of Jawaharlal Nehru, but lost her political influence due to her insistent support for Sheikh Abdullah, Prime Minister of Jammu and Kashmir state, in the face of Indian opposition.[36] Sarabhai's strengths—her conviction, outspokenness and her stubbornness—which had made her such a successful activist, ultimately also proved to be her greatest weaknesses, by preventing her from being able to adapt to the geopolitics of Indian independence.

Vijayalakshmi Pandit (1900 - 90), like Sarojini Varadappan and Durgabai Deshmukh, chose to forge a post-independence career beyond Congress politics in the sphere of international diplomacy. Between 1946 and 1962, she became an established figure on the international stage, serving as Indian Ambassador to Soviet Russia, the United States, Mexico, England, Ireland and Spain. She headed several Indian delegations to the UN in the 1950s, and in 1953 was elected President of the United Nations General Assembly.[37] Once her diplomatic career ended in 1962, she returned to India as Governor of Maharashtra and an MP. She later came to support the opposition movement against Indira Gandhi's prime ministership in the late 1970s.[38]

Hansa Mehta (1897 - 1995), a colleague of Vijayalakshmi Pandit, also earned an international reputation as an outspoken Indian representative at the United Nation's Commission on Human Rights. Mehta entered public life in the mid-1920s when she joined the Bombay branch of the AIWC, later moving up into the organisation's leadership and becoming its President in the mid-1940s. There she pioneered the AIWC's *Indian Woman's Charter of Rights and Duties*. She played a leadership role in the Congress party and became a member of the

---

35 Basu and Ray, *Women's Struggle*, p. 224.

36 See A. Basu, *Mridula Sarabhai: Rebel with a Cause* (Oxford University Press, Delhi, 1996), p. 144.

37 Pandit had built a name for herself in the pre-independence era as a Municipal Councillor and leader in both the nationalist movement and the All India Women's Conference.

38 Devenish, 'Performing the Political Self', p. 281.

CA, helping to draft the new Constitution whilst representing India at the United Nations, after which she moved on to play a role in the development of tertiary education as the Vice Chancellor of Baroda University (1949 – 58).[39]

Durgabai Deshmukh (1909 – 81) was born in Andhra Pradesh in 1909. Like many of her contemporaries, she became involved in nationalist activities at a young age; as a child, she had been a translator for Gandhi on his journeys to southern India. An early interest in promoting literacy encouraged her to set up the Balika Hindi Pathasala Kakinada at the age of 13, to provide literacy training to girls and women. Durgabai was an active nationalist, who participated in the Salt Satyagraha in 1930 and was imprisoned several times. As an adult, she campaigned around various social welfare issues affecting women, including the status of *devadasis*, and worked for the uplift of Muslim women and widows. She established the Andhra Mahila Sabha, a well-known welfare institute based in Chennai and Hyderabad, and also helped establish the Blind Relief Association in New Delhi and the Council for Social Development.[40]

Durgabai's post-independence career could have branched out in several different directions. She had already established herself as a successful lawyer in the High Court of Madras when she joined the CA in 1946 and intended to return to this job once her work there was complete. Nehru, however, had another position in mind and persuaded her to join the Planning Committee, after which she took on the chairpersonship of the CSWB.[41] Durgabai's legal training and background, combined with her experience and commitment to welfare, made for an interesting combination. As Chair of the CSWB, she sought to systematise and regulate social work activities and to

---

39 Between 1946 and 1948, Mehta was also Vice-Chancellor of Shreemati Nathibai Damodar Thackersey Women's University (SNDT). See Basu and Ray, *Women's Struggle*, p. 220.

40 'Durgabai Deshmukh: A Brief Life-sketch' in D. Jain, *What is Wrong with Economics? Can the Aam Aurat Redefine Economic Reasoning*, Durgabai Deshmukh Memorial Lecture, 15 July 2011, Council for Social Development, New Delhi.

41 For a detailed account of Durgabai's life, see Durgabai Deshmukh, Interview Transcript 16: Session I, recorded 5 January 1967, Oral History Project, Nehru Memorial Museum and Library.

enhance their impact through improved implementation of existing welfare legislation.

Rajkumari Amrit Kaur (1889 – 1964) was India's first Minister of Health between 1947 and 1957, and India's representative at the World Health Organisation (WHO) in the 1950s. She came from an affluent aristocratic family and underwent a cosmopolitan upbringing, including English schooling. This lifestyle was to change drastically when Kaur became politically conscious in the 1930s and joined the nationalist movement.[42] She went to live with Gandhi at his Wardha Ashram, and became one of his personal secretaries, as well as close friend and confidant. She continued to become a leading figure within Congress, and the AIWC, becoming a fellow drafter of the AIWC's *Indian Woman's Charter of Rights and Duties*, and also a member of the CA, guiding the birth of India's new constitution. After independence, in her role as Minister of Health, she worked to develop primary healthcare in India and to build infrastructure for medical research and training.

Although Rajkumari Amrit Kaur and Lady Dhanvanthi Rama Rau were colleagues within the AIWC, and both committed to 'equal rights and opportunities' for Indian women, they found themselves in disagreement over the question of a state-sponsored family planning programme.

Lady Dhanvanthi Rama Rau (1893 – 1987), with her colleague Avabai Wadia, was the founder of the Family Planning Association of India (FPAI), which played a leading but controversial role in family planning policy and institutions in independent India. Rama Rau was drawn to the women's rights activism of the AIWC when she was in her early twenties, campaigning for the franchise and for education.[43] Together with Wadia, a fellow colleague in the Bombay AIWC, she

---

42 Kaur was born in 1889 into the princely family of the Kapurthala state of Punjab. Her family lost the right to the throne when her father converted to Christianity, although they maintained their social status. See K. Kumar, 'Rajkumari Amrit Kaur: Her Life, Work and Ideology', and R. Ray, 'India's First Woman Cabinet Minister' in *Rajkumari Amrit Kaur*, Eminent parliamentarians monograph series: 15, (New Delhi, 1992), pp. 44, 71.

43 Basu and Ray, *Women's Struggle*, p. 219.

set up a number of local birth control and family planning initiatives, which ultimately led to the founding of the FPAI in 1952.[44]

Avabai Wadia (1913 – 2005) exemplified the multiple hats worn by many of this generation during the course of their careers. She was a social worker, barrister-at-law and international family planning activist who co-founded the Family Planning Association of India and played an influential role in shaping family planning policy in India during the 1960s and 1970s.[45]

Renu Chakravartty, Sarla Sharma and Vidya Munshi were all women activists who chose to pursue a professional interest in women's empowerment, together with a political career in the Communist Party of India.

Renu Chakravartty (1917 – 94) was born into a well-off Brahmo family in Calcutta. She was very active in student politics as a member of All India Students' Federation (AISF) before leaving to study at Cambridge University, which brought her into contact with Marxism in Britain. On her return, she played a leading role in building up the Mahila Atma Raksha Samiti (MARS), one of the parent organisations of the National Federation of Indian Woman (NFIW), and coordinated famine relief campaigns in the wake of the Bengal Famine of 1943.[46] In 1952, she was elected to the Lok Sabha as a representative of the Indian Communist Party becoming Deputy Leader of the CPI group in the House.[47] She combined her parliamentary work with building and leading the newly established NFIW, becoming as its first General Secretary.[48]

Sarla Sharma (born 1927) was born into a progressive Delhi family involved in girls' education, in 1927, and became a student

---

[44] Rama Rau was also President of the International Planned Parent Federation between 1963 and 1971.

[45] Basu and Ray, *Women's Struggle*, p. 219.

[46] Renu Chakravartty was also was a member of the Executive Committee of the AIWC before joining the NFIW.

[47] Interview with G. Chakravartty, NFIW leader and academic, 4 November 2011, New Delhi.

[48] For biographical details of the life and work of Renu Chakravartty, see Chakravartty, *Communists in the Indian Women's Movement: 1940-1950* (People's Publishing House, New Delhi, 1980).

activist for the nationalist cause as a teenager. Exposure to Marxism through her peers led her to join the Communist party-affiliated AISF in 1936, and the CPI three years later. Sharma was a member of the AIWC in Delhi, but she found herself frustrated in the 1940s by what she perceived as a neglect of working women's needs and struggles within the organisation. This frustration drew her to the NFIW, where she was a founding member, forging an association which she has maintained throughout her life. Sharma combined her leadership role in the NFIW with work as a local councillor for the CPI in Delhi.

Vidya Munshi (1919 – 2014) was a Calcutta-based contemporary of Sarla Sharma. She grew up in a Congress supporting family in Bombay. It was her mother's involvement in a women's organisation called Community of Sisters[49] that first sparked her interest in the cause of women. At 19, she went to England to study medicine, where she became a member of a Left-wing book club and avidly began reading the books that were banned in India. This experience brought her into contact with Marxist literature and led her to reach the conclusion that as an Indian, she would be able to do more to help her people as a communist than a doctor.

Munshi spent the war years in Newcastle upon Tyne, speaking to the local community about India on behalf of the India League Workers' Association. With her attention diverted from her studies, she failed medical college but decided to stay on after the War working for the AISF. She was fortunate to have the opportunity represent India at a number of international student conferences and to attend the first Congress of the Women's International Democratic Federation (WIDF) in Paris, the international parent organisation to which the NFIW affiliated when it was formed in 1954. When she returned to India, she was invited to cover the establishment of the NFIW as a journalist, joining the Federation shortly after.[50]

---

[49] Community of Sisters was a Bombay-based women's organisation which provided working women's hostels, indoor games and a moving library for the local community. Interview with Munshi, 2 December 2011.

[50] Ibid.

The Roots and Evolution of the Women's Movement in Colonial India

Contemporary activists working in the field of women's rights and gender studies tend to agree that India does not have a 'women's movement', as such, today.[51] The December 2012 Delhi rape case certainly galvanised women's rights activists into action, as has the more recent spread of the anti-sexual harassment MeToo movement, sparking discussions that the resulting public protest marked the beginnings of a third wave movement, but this remains speculative. Even if this was the case, it will take a number of years to develop. In India, issues that affect women, or 'gender-related' issues, are often addressed within other types of organisations and forums, such as human rights organisations, those that work in the informal economy, such as the Self Employed Women's Association (SEWA), and Lesbian, Gay, Bisexual, Transgender, Queer and Intersex (LGBTQI) collectives. These are organisations that have not necessarily been structured around women as a specific collective identity.

Equally significant is the observation that collective identity does not necessarily precede mobilisation and action. In fact, spontaneous action over local and immediate socio-economic needs has the potential to facilitate collective identity, rather than the other way around.[52] The potential of harnessing women's collective action to pursue a feminist agenda has also been problematised by the fact that women's rights have been claimed by other political communities, such as the Hindu Right for alternate agendas, which have often worked to undermine women's rights.[53] As Samita Sen stresses, it is crucial for the scholar to keep in mind that gender does not imply or offer an inherent set of common interests binding women together as a collective. However,

---

[51] I refer specifically to individuals interviewed during the course of this research, such as Anni Raja of the NFIW, economist and women's movement veteran Devaki Jain and Gargi Chakravartty.

[52] Here, I would like to acknowledge and thank Devaki Jain for bringing this important point to my attention.

[53] For a detailed analysis of this issue, see T. Sarkar and U. Butalia (eds.), *Women and the Hindu Right: A Collection of Essays* (Kali for Women, New Delhi, 1995).

women can be brought together as a constituency, through particular forms of political mobilisation.[54]

Coinciding with the rise of Gandhian nationalism in the 1920s and 1930s, a new set of all-India women's organisations, such as the Women's Indian Association (WIA) and the AIWC began to emerge. These facilitated forms of mobilisation and consciousness amongst women. This new all-India identity was closely woven into the larger political movement for independence, but it represented a significant evolution from the way in which women first became visible within earlier forms of nationalism.

At the beginning of the nineteenth century in response to colonial critiques and power dynamics, but also as a result of indigenous drives and motivations to reform and revive their culture and identity, male social reformers began to emerge across India and to establish social reform societies, such as the Brahmo Samaj and the Arya Samaj to promote their mission of reform.[55] Gender relationships and identities came to the fore in the mandate and focus of such reform societies through two central concerns: firstly, the problematic role of culture and tradition in determining the position of women within the family, through perpetuating practices such as polygamy, widowhood, sati and child marriage, and the question of how tradition and culture could be reformed, either through modernisation or purification. Secondly, through a dramatic change in attitudes towards education for girls and women. In the past, women in orthodox Hindu households were kept illiterate because educating them was believed to bring bad luck, and lead to widowhood.[56] As the educated and urban Indian middle classes reworked an identity and place for themselves in the new colonial order, however, education for women, and the idea of the Indian woman

[54] S. Sen, 'Towards a Feminist Politics? The Indian Woman's Movement in Historical Perspective' in K. Kapadia (ed.), *The Violence of Development: The Politics of Identity, Gender and Social Inequalities in India* (Zubaan, New Delhi, 2002), p. 511.

[55] G. Minault, *Secluded Scholars: Women's Education and Muslim Social Reform in Colonial India* (Oxford University Press, Delhi, 1999); See G. Forbes, *Women in Modern India* (Cambridge University Press, Cambridge, 1996), p. 19.

[56] T. Sarkar, *Words to Win: The Making of Amar Jiban: A Modern Autobiography* (Zubaan, New Delhi, 2013), p. 2.

as a companionate wife, became important markers of middle-class respectability and status.

Christian missionaries opened first schools for girls in 1819.[57] They were quickly followed by Indian reformers. Forbes emphasises, however, that there was little real progress in girl's education until the second half of the nineteenth century when the colonial government began to offer financial support. Women's education was given another boost towards the end of the century when the urban professional elite came on board to support reformers in promoting formal education for girls.[58]

Literature on social reform in India tends to focus on Hindu reformers. Gail Minault's scholarship on middle-class Urdu-speaking Muslims in Northern India, however, has shown a concurrent social reform movement, promoting women's education, emerging amongst certain Muslim communities as well. As in the case with Hindu reformers, the drive for Muslim women's education came from articulate and literate Muslim men.[59] Here, education for Muslim girls was pioneered by Muslim reform associations known as *anjumans*.[60]

This reform movement encouraged the creation of the first schools for girls, which were funded through private patronage and networks of kinship and association. These schools were established in such a way to accommodate the demands of purdah and more relaxed forms of seclusion. Specific educational curricula and programmes were developed for girls and women's education, many of these drawing upon Islamic intellectual traditions. This movement culminated in the late 1930s when a number of girls' schools that had been established earlier became degree colleges.[61]

Along with education for girls came efforts to improve the social position of women, through legislative reform relating to marriage, widowhood and inheritance. In 1829, the Sati Abolition Act was passed, outlawing this practice. Through the lobbying of reformer Ishwar

---

57 Sarkar, *Words to Win*, p. 93.

58 Forbes, *Women in Modern India*, pp. 33–34.

59 Minault, *Secluded Scholars*, p. 9.

60 Ibid., p. 158.

61 Ibid., pp. 9–12.

Chandra Vidyasagar, the 1859 Hindu Widows Remarriage Act legalised the remarriage of Hindu widows, whose status, especially as upper-caste women, often condemned them to a life of austerity and social ostracism. In 1891, The Age of Consent Act raised the age consent for girls both married and unmarried from 10 to 12.

Outside of the sphere of education, one of the other ways in which women began to claim a sense of autonomy and selfhood within the changing world of the colonial encounter was through using such laws, and the judicial system introduced by the British, to claim certain protections and rights. The most well-known example of this is the famous case of 22-year-old Rukhmabai who refused to consummate her marriage and to live with her husband, Dadaji Bhikaji.[62]

Rukhmabai had married Dadaji Bhikaji at the age of seven, but had remained within her father's home, even after she reached puberty. Here, she had continued to study and had eventually matriculated. When her husband demanded that now, well past the age of maturity, she should come to live with him, she refused. He proceeded to sue for the restitution of conjugal rights in the Bombay court.[63]

Rukhmabai, who had developed a strong dislike for her husband based on his reckless behaviour and indebtedness, argued that because she was married at an age where she was unable to give intelligent consent, the marriage should be considered invalid. This was a courageous and radical stance for a woman of her time, drawing widespread public attention to her case. There were both supporters, and detractors, who argued that Rukhmabai's challenge posed a threat to the sanctity of Hindu marriage and the family.[64]

The Bombay court found in favour of Rukhmabai, with Justice Pinhey, the presiding judge, interpreting consummation as essential for the completion of the Hindu marriage. Dadaji, however, then took the case on appeal resulting in a series of litigation between 1884 – 88.[65] In 1887, under Justice Farran, Rukhmabai was tried and sentenced to

---

[62] S. Chandra, *Enslaved Daughters: Colonialism, Law and Women's Rights* (Oxford University Press, Delhi, 1999), p. 1.

[63] Ibid., p. 1.

[64] Ibid., pp. 1,5.

[65] Ibid., pp. 73–75, 102–104.

prison for refusing to have conjugal relations with her husband.[66] She was fortunate to escape imprisonment though, when Queen Victoria issued a decree dissolving Rukhmabai from the marriage. Rukhmabai had attempted to employ the law for an emancipatory purpose, but its ultimate interpretation was 'used to force women to submit to the most onerous of patriarchal customs'.[67] Nonetheless, Rukhmabai had set a precedent, showing that it was possible for Indian women to exercise agency, and to articulate an independent sense of self in a changing world.

In their discourse and efforts to uplift and reform the position of women in Indian society, social reformers and nationalists used Indian women as the sites, symbols and canvases for the making of bourgeois nationalist modernity. Yet, as the case of Rukhmabai, and that of Rashsundari Debi suggests, women were also claiming and subverting discourses of reform for more emancipatory and subversive agendas.

In the first half of the nineteenth century, social reformers were largely men working for the upliftment and enlightenment of their womenfolk. However, by the second half of the century, the practices of social reform and the new opportunities for women's education enabled pioneers such as Pandita Ramabai, Anandibai Karve and Parvatibai Athavale to enter the public sphere. There they built professional careers for themselves as practitioners of social reform and women's education. Education also opened up other professional opportunities for women. Take, for example, Maharashtrian Anandibai Joshee, who enrolled in the Women's Medical College of Pennsylvania in the United States in 1883, as the first Indian women to train as a doctor. Joshee was followed by others, including the young Rukhmabai, who was finally released from her marriage and trained as a doctor in England. She then returned to India where she practised medicine between 1895 and 1948.[68]

---

66 Forbes, *Women in Modern India*, p. 49.

67 Ibid., p. 69.

68 M. Allen, 'Crossing Thresholds: Feminist Essays in Social History by Meera Kosambi'. *Australian Feminist Studies*, 24:59 (2009), p. 139.

Cornelia Sorabji, the first female graduate from Bombay University and the first woman to study law at Oxford, went on to become the earliest female advocate in India, where she consulted and gave legal advice to *purdahnashin*, women living in seclusion. Despite her entry into the professional world through the new possibilities created by reform, Sorabji herself did not support the work of male and female social reformers. She argued that these efforts at reform had only reached a small elite group of women, while the vast majority continued to live in ignorance and illiteracy. These women were not ready for modern Western educational institutions, or for liberal rights and the franchise; rather they needed paternal protection.[69] The case of Sorabji is an important reminder that the educated middle class and elite women themselves held a diversity of views with regards to the social position and emancipation of their sex, and that simply being women did not mean that they shared the same ideals and aspirations for women.

The movement for the education of girls and women provided an opportunity for women to begin breaching their chains of seclusion and domesticity, and give voice to their restrictions and their aspirations. By the late nineteenth and early twentieth century, with the first generation of educated women came the emergence of a flourishing literary culture that 'brought new ideas and new role models to women who had never gone to school'.[70] These created a forum for literate women to communicate with each other, to share information, viewpoints and opinions, and to develop a collective voice.

In 1863, Umeshchandra Datta started publishing *Bamabodhini Patrika,* a journal for the education of women. What was significant about the journal was that it was published in new vernacular Bengali, which meant that it was accessible to women who had not had a classical education or been taught English.[71] A new postal system in Bengal also made it possible to bring newspapers and journals, such as *Bamabodhini Patrika* to remote village areas for the first time.[72]

---

[69] Forbes, *Women in Modern India*, p. 98–99.

[70] Minault, *Secluded Scholars*, p. 158.

[71] Sarkar, *Words to Win*, pp. 81–82.

[72] Ibid., pp. 81–84.

It was not only in Bengal that these developments were taking place; Padma Anagol's work documents the emergence of regional women's presses in Maharashtra over the same period, which produced materials, such as the independent women's magazine *Arya Mahila Samaj,* founded by Pandita Ramabai.[73] Gail Minault's research on Muslim reformers attests to the emergence of a concurrent Urdu women's literary culture in North India, where the growth of Urdu speaking women's literary magazines encouraged women to contribute their writings for publication.[74]

As Tanika Sarkar emphasises, women themselves were now writing about the question of their own education and their social position within society, adding another important set of voices to the social reform debate.[75] Women's writings of the nineteenth and early twentieth centuries broadened the women's question as it had been posed by social reform, giving it new feminist possibilities and potential.[76]

With this flourishing literary culture, women also began to publish poetry, autobiographical writings, short stories and novels. In 1876, upper-caste Bengal housewife Rashsundari Debi (1809 – year of death unknown) published *Amar Jiban,* the first autobiography written by a Bengali woman, and probably also the first full-scale autobiography in Bengali. The publication was well received by a readership who were 'keenly interested in the life and self-reflections of an ordinary woman', leading to the publication of a second edition.[77]

Rashsundari came of age prior to supporting the education for girls in Bengal. She never went to school, however, when she was 25, the desire to read a particular sacred text led her to secretly teach herself how to read, and later how to write, a process which ultimately resulted in the creation of *Amar Jiban*. Sarkar emphasises that Rashsundari was very strategic in how she framed the story of how she came to write

---

[73] P. Anagol, *The Emergence of Feminism in India 1850-1920* (Routledge, Ashgate, 2005), pp. 72–80, 61–62.

[74] Minault, *Secluded Scholars*, p. 10.

[75] Sarkar, *Words to Win*, p. 81.

[76] J. Nair, 'On the Question of Agency in Indian Feminist Historiography', *Gender and History,* 6:1 (April 1994), p. 89.

[77] Sarkar, *Words to Win*, p. 4.

her autobiography, by couching it in religious or devotional terms, to undermine the transgression of her act and to give it legitimacy. In her account, 'She was the chosen instrument of God, who worked a miracle on her, the fruit of which was her wonderous mastery over the written word.'[78] Like many women of her generation, and those after her, she worked within traditionally accepted social and religious conventions of her time, but simultaneously subtly subverted them in such a way to give herself a voice in the world. In so doing, she created 'a space of her own, as well as a space in public view'.[79]

What makes *Amar Jiban* unusual for its time is the fact that the text is not merely descriptive or emotional, but that the author also reflects upon the events of her life, as well as her state of mind. In this discursive and reflexive turn, Sarkar identifies something strikingly new and modern. 'This is a modern articulation about the inwardness of an individuated self. It is also a way of experiencing and reacting to an old condition in new words'.[80]

Amar Jiban would have been circulating in Bengal at the end of the nineteenth century when another woman writer, educationalist and social activist Rokeya Sakhawat Hossain (1880 – 1932), was growing up. While this new literary culture had provided Rashsundari with a forum for articulating an emerging sense of self in the world, for Rokeya, a Muslim Bengali, the consolidation of this literary culture provided an opportunity to express and share a new kind of feminist consciousness.

Like Rashsundari, Rokeya taught herself to read and write in Bengali, in secret, and against the wishes of her father, in this instance with the help of her older sister who also became a poet. Later in life, she went on to learn English. She married when she was 16, but fortuitously her older husband, Sakhawat Hossain, proved to be a progressive and supportive partner and it was through his encouragement that she began publishing her essays in various literary magazines.[81]

---

[78] Ibid., p. 3.

[79] Ibid., p. 13.

[80] Ibid., pp. 6, 257.

[81] 'A Bibliographical Essay'. *The Essential Rokeya: Selected Works of Rokeya Sakhawat Hossain* (Leiden, Boston, Brill, 2013), pp. xviii-xxii.

Rokeya carried on writing poetry, several novels, various articles and essays, giving voice to her ideas, opinions and frustrations on the position of women in Bengali society. In 1905, she published *Sultana's Dream* in *The Indian Ladies Magazine,* an original and thought-provoking story which presented a feminist utopia where gender roles were subverted, and 'where women ruled and enjoyed freedom in its fullest sense'. *Sultana's Dream,* which also contains elements of satire, science fiction and ecofeminism, is set in Ladyland, a society in which men are kept in seclusion and where women roam freely and control society, studying at universities, and developing and harnessing science and new technologies to live in harmony with nature.[82]

This was not Rokeya's first foray into feminist writing. In 1904, she had published *Morichur,* a text which provides a critique of religion as a tool of the patriarchy.[83] After *Sultana's Dream,* she went on to publish several other pieces of writing that commented on the position of women in society, including *Zenana Women* (1931), anecdotal stories about purdah among Bengali Muslim and Hindu women, and an essay, entitled 'Women's Downfall'. At the time of her death, Rokeya was working on a piece on 'The Rights of Women'.[84] The 'intensity, ingenuity and depth' of her writing has earned her the title of the best female writer of the Bengal Renaissance.[85]

Rokeya's life reflected the complexity and intersectionality of her subject position. She herself practised a moderate form of purdah as a Muslim Bengali woman, and supported sex segregation in the schools she established, but spoke out against the excesses of the practice, which kept women caged at home and prevented them from being able to go out into the world. Rokeya was not just a mirror image of Western feminism, nor was she merely the product of a cohort of male Muslim

---

82 Mohammad A. Quayum, 'A Bibliographical Essay' in M. Quayum (ed.), *The Essential Rokeya: Selected Works of Rokeya Sakhawat Hossain* (Leiden, Boston, 2013), p. xxiii; F. Hasanat, 'Sultana's Utopian Awakening: An Ecocritical Reading of Rokeya Sakhawat Hossain's Sultana's Dream' in Quayum and Hasam (eds.), *A Feminist Foremother: Critical Essays on Rokeya Sakhawat Hossain* (Orient BlackSwan, Hyderabad, 2017), pp. 223–225.

83 Hasanat, 'Sultana's Utopian Awakening', p. 224.

84 Mohammad A. Quayum, 'A Bibliographical Essay', pp. xxvi-xxvii, xxi, xxxi.

85 Ibid., p. xxvii.

reformers. She worked with, and within, her own cultural identity, claiming but also subverting, challenging and adapting it.

The Emergence of Local and Regional Women's Organisations

Together with women's regional presses, came the development of local and regionally based women's societies at the end of the nineteenth century. In the 1870s, Pandita Ranade established the Hindu Ladies Social club in Mumbai. There was also the Community of Sisters, which Vidya Munshi's mother had been a member of, and the *Striyancha Sabha*, both based in Maharashtra. Although many of these societies focused on women's position within the family and home, together with access to education, Padma Anagol argues that in places such as Maharashtra, some of these societies reflected the growth of an early collective feminist consciousness predating Gandhian nationalism.[86]

In 1904, the Bharata Mahila Parisad Indian Women's Social Conference was inaugurated as a ladies auxiliary to the National Social Conference, which had been established 1887. The yearly meetings of this auxiliary brought together between 300 and 700 women. Working within a larger male-dominated reform organisation presented its own set of problems and, Forbes emphasises, it was out of this experience that women began to see the need and value of separate women-only organisations, which would give them a space of their own.[87]

In 1910, Saraladevi Chaudhurani established the Bharat Stree Mahamandal in Allahabad, which concentrated on educating women who lived under purdah.[88] And in 1916, Rokeya Sakhawat Hossain founded the Muslim Women's or Calcutta Mohamedan Ladies Association committed to social work activities. The Association

---

86 Anagol, *The Emergence of Feminism in India*, pp. 60–68, 10.

87 G. Forbes, 'Caged Tigers "First Wave" Feminists in India'. *Women in Colonial India: Essays on Politics, Medicine and Historiography* (Chronicle Books, Delhi, 2005), p. 14.

88 Ibid., p. 15.

offered financial assistance to poor widows, provided rescue and shelter for abused wives and promoted literacy amongst slum women in the city.[89]

In the early twentieth century, these trends continued until the First (1917) and Second (1927) Franchise campaigns, which represented an important step in the evolution of the women's question from the perspective of uplift within a traditional framework, to that of women's equality, by expanding the demands of women beyond the home and into the public sphere through a claim to civic rights.[90] This shift was accompanied by the development of the first national Indian women's organisations.

Women's Indian Association (WIA)

The Women's Indian Association (WIA) was established in Madras in 1917, by Annie Besant and several Indian women activists and reformers.[91] Combining nationalist and feminist agendas, the WIA was recognised as one of the first all-India women's organisations to bring women together as a political community.[92] Its initial activities were dedicated to Besant's Home Rule movement, together with an emphasis on the self-development and education of members.[93] In 1921, the WIA campaigned for Dr Gour's Civil Marriage Bill, and took an interest in the cooperative movement. The Association was also the first all-India women's association to take up the demands of women workers; it unionised and lobbied the government for the introduction of

---

[89] Quayum, 'A Biographical Essay', pp. xxvii–xxviii.

[90] See Kasturi and Mazumdar, 'Women and Nationalism'.

[91] Including Dorothy Jinarajadasa, Malati Patwardhan, Ammu Swaminathan, Mrs Dadabhoy and Mrs Ambujammal. See R. Kumar, *A History of Doing: An Illustrated Account of Movements for Women's Rights and Feminism in India 1800–1990* (Zubaan Books, New Delhi, 1993), p. 54.

[92] Ibid.

[93] This was encouraged through the reading of particular texts and discussion of subjects, such as domestic economy, physiology and religion. See Kumar, *A History of Doing*, pp. 54, 67.

maternity leave and benefits for women workers.[94] The WIA continues to function today as an affiliate of the AIWC.

The All India Women's Conference (AIWC)

The All India Women's Conference (AIWC), the second all-India women's organisation to pioneer this new politics of collective belonging, was established in Poona in 1927 as a group devoted to the promotion and expansion of education for girls and women. The Conference quickly realised that this could not be achieved until the social, cultural and political constraints that prevented them from being able to take up new educational opportunities were addressed. In a short period of time, the organisation began to expand its activities. The AIWC understood women's oppression to be multifaceted and rooted in an interconnected web of culture (or society), economics and politics. In accordance with nineteenth-century nationalists and social reformers, they saw the corruption of Hindu culture as perpetuating traditions and practices that were harmful to women and which reinforced their oppression. Such a cultural environment created a context where women lived in ignorance, lacking education and, consequently even awareness of their own oppression. But the AIWC understood that there was an economic and political component to Indian women's oppression as well. This economic component was articulated in *The Women's Role in the Planned Economy Report* (1939), drafted in close consultation with the AIWC leadership at the time, which drew attention to the double burden of women's work in the home and in the field or factory.

Because many AIWC members were also involved in nationalist politics and sympathetic to the nationalist cause, they identified with their male colleagues in the Congress and Socialist Congress as fellow oppressed colonial subjects and articulated a discourse which saw women's emancipation and political freedom as interconnected. Veteran activists

[94] Ibid.

and nationalists, such as Renuka Ray, Hansa Mehta, Rajkumari Amrit Kaur and Kamaladevi Chattopadhyay, argued that true empowerment of women was not possible in a context of political oppression. Political freedom was, in fact, a prerequisite for women's emancipation.

The solution for the AIWC lay in access to civic and constitutional citizenship. This included the right to vote, to equality in terms of legislation, to access the health, education and welfare services offered by the democratic government, as well as social empowerment through welfare services, which would conscientise women to exercise their new constitutional rights. At a national level, the AIWC concerned itself with lobbying for the female franchise and campaigns for the reform of social laws relating to women's status in the family. At regional and local levels, its branches were involved in education, and in creating public opinion and interest around social reform issues, such as polygamy, purdah, the trafficking of women, the position of *devadasis*, drinking and gambling, untouchability, the universal demand for free and compulsory education and the propagation of 'scientific birth control'. Branches were involved in the running of various welfare activities, including the provision of medical relief, maternity and child welfare facilities, the training of indigenous midwives or *daias*, the establishment of crèches, sanitation education, rescue homes for women and campaigning for the rights of women and child labourers.[95]

One of the strengths of the AIWC, particularly in the pre-independence era, was its flexible structure. This accommodated a spectrum of existing structures and a range of attitudes amongst women concerning gender roles and expectations. It was crucial in enabling the organisation to develop an all-India character. In addition to developing new branches from scratch, local groups of women that were already established could affiliate to the Conference. The WIA based in Madras was one such affiliate and continued to maintain its identity as the WIA together with its attachment to the AIWC. The Delhi Women's League, founded by Rameshwari Nehru, was another

---

[95] AIWC, 6th Annual Conference Report, 28 December 1931 to 1 January 1932, pp. 30, 110.

such affiliate. In addition to national campaigns initiated by the head office, the Conference was able to accommodate a diversity of activities and interests, which were locally or regionally grounded and relevant. The representative structure of the AIWC also meant that the voices of local branches were heard in its decision-making forums. For every 50 or 100 members, a branch was entitled to send a representative to the annual national conference to represent the views and interests of their colleagues back at home. This was the forum where the agenda of the Conference was decided, and where policy was finalised by voting on resolutions.

Although the official policy of the AIWC was non-affiliation with party politics, many of its members also belonged to the Congress, the Congress Socialist Party or the Communist Party of India, and were actively involved in nationalist politics. In practice, this policy was not adhered to, as the AIWC participated in a number of nationalist activities, which were generally Congress-led. The principle of inclusivity underpinning the policy did achieve a degree of success in the 1920s and 1930s, with the AIWC using its claim to impartiality to bring together communities of women, across religious, class and caste lines. By the late 1930s, however, cracks were beginning to emerge within the organisation. Communities of socialist and communist women were becoming increasingly frustrated with what they saw as the elitist and middle-class orientation of the AIWC and its welfare focus, which they argued did not address the economic and political causes of gender and class oppression.[96] Simultaneously, rising communal tensions in nationalist politics were beginning to be felt within the organisation and were leading to the alienation of some of its Muslim members.[97]

As Geraldine Forbes observes, the 1940s marked a turbulent decade in the fight for women's rights in India, with growing communal and class divisions undermining the claim of the AIWC to speak as the

[96] Many of these women went on to establish the National Federation of Indian Women in 1954 as an autonomous women's organisation, but with a strong membership of communist women. See Chakravartty, *Communists in the Indian Women's Movement.*

[97] See G. Forbes, *Women in Modern India* (Cambridge University Press, Cambridge,1996), pp. 196–203.

legitimate voice and representative of 'Indian women'. These tensions were exacerbated by emerging struggles, highlighting class and ideological differences within the nationalist movement, and exposing a range of competing economic and political pathways towards emancipation. By the mid-1940s, the AIWC had lost its hegemony as a representative of women's interests.[98]

Independence in August 1947, with its immense and exciting nation-building project, offered the Conference new possibilities for reclaiming hegemony as the representatives of women's interests, and as the inscribers and defenders of women's equality and rights. With the coming of independence, the AIWC embarked on a dual strategy of pursuing citizenship through the theory of rights and the practice of service.

Independence also brought with it the possibility of other forms of collective being and belonging. The newly established NFIW, equally concerned with questions of inclusivity and legitimate representativeness, took an alternative route to the AIWC. It attempted to claim this hegemony by building an identity for itself and for the working class and peasant Indian women through constructing and articulating a conceptualisation of citizenship defined through the claim to socio-economic rights and a presence within civil society.

National Federation of Indian Women (NFIW)

Drawing considerable leadership from communist women and a mandate from an emerging international women's movement, the NFIW was launched in Calcutta in 1954 as an affiliate to the Women's International Democratic Federation (WIDF). Banners decorating the University Institute Hall, where this first Congress was held, proclaimed the vision of the Federation in short, succinct sound bites: 'We want a prosperous and free India in a peaceful world,' and 'Equal economic, social and political rights for women.' This vision was more

98 Ibid., pp. 189–191.

fully elaborated in the Congress's printed report, which stated that the Federation stood 'for a sovereign, democratic and prosperous India, a peaceful world where freedom is guaranteed to all nations and there is an end to all discrimination on the basis of colour, sex, religion and political belief'.[99] This was to be achieved through a commitment to the Federation's aims and objectives: the winning of equal rights, ensuring the welfare and protection of children and securing peace on the international stage as well as with Pakistan.[100]

Developments both within India and internationally facilitated the establishment of this new Federation. A common agenda of peace brought Indian women activists into increasing contact with an emerging international women's movement. The WIDF was one of the key players within this community. In 1953, the WIDF invited Indian women activists to form a nationwide federation affiliated to them. This invitation came at a moment when women activists were increasingly feeling the need for a new platform through which they could represent their interests and a new way to come together on a national scale.

The Federation's programme of action included a combination of agitational activities (both intra and extra-parliamentary) together with day-to-day welfare to uplift women, and to 'build' the new organisation. The NFIW saw itself as playing a crucial role in uniting women's voices to lobby for equality in law, but also to act as enablers and watchdogs to ensure the required transformation of social attitudes and institutional structures. 'Laws must, of course, be enacted by the government, but creating necessary conditions for their application, is our job,'[101] reminded Smt. Urmila Devi to Federation delegates during her inaugural address in 1957.

The Marxist influence meant that the NFIW leadership positioned women's oppression within larger systems of economic exploitation and saw the struggle for women's equality as intricately interconnected

---

99 NFIW, 'Indian Women Meet in Conference': The Report of the National Congress of Women, June 1954, New Delhi, pp. 2, 60.

100 Interview with Chakravartty, 4 November 2011.

101 NFIW, Report of the Second National Conference, June 1957, Vijayawada, pp. 29, 20.

to these larger struggles. Part of the NFIW's strategic programme included collaboration with unions around workers' rights, organising women workers for strikes and agitations, organising protests with the working class and middle class housewives around food security, and working with peasant women in their struggles for livelihoods and land rights. Welfare activities conducted by the Federation's affiliated organisations in the early years included the provision of milk schemes, the running of adult literacy programmes for women, schools, libraries and crèches, as well as the creation of employment and livelihood opportunities for women through various kinds of vocational training, the establishment of industrial and handicraft centres and the running of cooperatives.[102]

A total of 17 resolutions were passed during the course of the first Congress in 1954, revealing the broad range of concerns and interests of its members and leaders.[103] Among these were resolutions on working women demanding equal wage for equal work, the removal of all discrimination in terms of employment, a maternity home for every 10,000 women, social rights with special reference to the marriage laws, as well as a Bill for the Abolition of Dowry.[104] There were also resolutions on the right to education, the improved working conditions for nurses, the rights of Muslim women, the introduction of a ban on the Hydrogen Bomb and an end to the Pak-US Military Pact.[105]

---

[102] NFIW, Third National Conference: Report and Resolutions, 4–7 October 1959, Benares, pp. 21–24.

[103] Many of these overlapped with resolutions passed at the AIWC's Annual Conference of the previous year. See for example AIWC, 23rd Annual Conference Report (Silver Jubilee Session), 2–5 May 1953, Poona, pp. 46–48. These included resolutions on the Hindu Code Bill and ensuring equal inheritance and custody rights for women, the provision of family planning services, universal education, the creation of jobs to tackle unemployment, support for cottage industries, relief for famine victims, ensuring coordination between the government and voluntary organisations in the implementation of welfare work, health outreach to the rural areas and objections to the representation of Indian women in film and advertising.

[104] S. Munsi, 'National Conference of Women in Calcutta', *New Age*, 13 June 1954, copy located in CPI offices, Ajoy Bhavan.

[105] NFIW, 'Indian Women Meet in Conference', June 1954, p. 6.

Like the AIWC, the NFIW aspired to build an identity for itself grounded on inclusiveness and plurality. This reflected the political milieu of the time where Partition and communal violence called for a sensitive and encompassing approach to nation-building. The narrative of the birth and early years of the Federation cultivated such an identity. A *New Age* article reporting on the first Congress session describes delegates travelling from every corner of India to attend, 'from Manipur and Tripura in the East to Rajasthan in the West, from Kashmir in the North to Travancore-Cochin in the South'.[106] Not only was this inaugural gathering representative of the geographical diversity of India but encompassing of its socio-economic spectrum too. The Congress Report informs us that amongst the representatives from Bengal hailed 'every cross section of toiling, struggling women, women in professions, refugee women. Workers, peasants, Hindus, Muslims, Christians, Parsis were present including tribal women and Harijans'.[107] In this Report, an emphasis was placed on the consultative and democratic nature of the Federation's formation. 'The Constitution, which united various organisations in a broad federation, is discussed till the long hours of the night before it is finally adopted,' it states.[108] This stress on inclusivity and diversity at the heart of the Federation was again reinforced in the Second Congress Report, which described 'the galaxy of languages being spoken in the delegates' camp'. It recurred in the Third Congress Report, which informed readers that the opening speech of Aruna Asaf Ali, the Federation's President, had to be translated to six languages.[109]

The NFIW adopted a broad federal structure, which meant that, as with the AIWC, existing organisations could affiliate rather than be initiated and grown from scratch. A provision was made in its Constitution for individual members to join as well. At the time of the founding Calcutta conference, the NFIW claimed a

[106] 'Over 1,000 Delegates Will Attend the Women's Congress', *New Age*, 6 June 1954.

[107] NFIW, *For Equality: For a Just Social Order* (New Delhi, 1984), p. 18.

[108] NFIW, 'Indian Women Meet in Conference', June 1954, p. 6.

[109] NFIW, Report of the Second National Conference, June 1957, pp. i, iv, 5.

membership of a 1,20,000 through affiliation from 13 provinces.[110] It drew its strongest support from West Bengal, Tripura, Andhra Pradesh, Punjab and Tamil Nadu.[111] Any women or organisation who agreed with the aims and objectives of the Federation could join. The Federation initially claimed that the bulk of this membership consisted of 'peasant women in rural areas'.[112] By 1957, it acknowledged, however, that its regional leadership had in effect lost touch with some of these groups. Manikuntala Sen, one of the founding members of Federation, describes the majority of founding members, certainly in West Bengal, as teachers.[113] Sen's description of the profile of founding members makes more sense, particularly as we know that the early leadership of the Federation[114] was mainly teachers, lecturers and principals.[115]

Working across the spheres of party politics, state bureaucracy, international relations and civil society, this generation of women within the AIWC and NFIW continued to build on the foundations laid by the Women's Movement in the 1930s and 40s. They were aiming to clarify, strengthen and implement the principles of equality promised by Indian nationalism. The impact of their work was mixed, but one thing is undeniable: they left an indelible imprint on the form of the State today. Their legacies range from their construction of the problematic category of 'women and children' in policy and planning to the crucial contribution of non-governmental organisations (NGOs) in the delivery of social welfare services, the contested role of family planning in independent India, and the ongoing debates around the impact of women's reservations in panchayats and Parliament.

---

110 Ibid, p. 28.

111 Ibid., p. 28; *For Equality: For a Just Social Order*, pp. 13, 18, 14.

112 NFIW, Report of the Second National Conference, June 1957, p. 28.

113 M. Sen, *In Search of Freedom: An Unfinished Journey* (Bhatkal & Sen, Calcutta, 2001), p. 227.

114 By leadership, I am referring to the National Coordinating Committee, which was established in 1953.

115 Sen, *In Search of Freedom*, p. 227; NFIW, 'Indian Women Meet in Conference', June 1954, p. 25.

The second half of the nineteenth century had paved the way for these latter developments. It opened up the professional sphere of social work and enabled access to education, which facilitated new forms of communication and the founding of local women's organisations. The first three decades of the twentieth century saw vital developments in terms of collective gender politics for Indian women, culminating in the 1920s and 1930s with the creation of the first all-India women's organisations and the entry of women into Indian nationalism. By the time of the drafting of the Karachi Resolution in 1931, to which we turn next, Chattopadhyay's generation was able to bring a coherent and determined call for equal rights, and equal treatment under the law, to the negotiating table.

Chapter 1

The Emergence of the Indian Woman as a Political Citizen

The struggle for egalitarian politics in India is a complex story with deep historical roots. It is a narrative that continues to unfold against the contemporary political landscape, as fierce parliamentary debate rages over the potential of caste and gender reservations to fulfil the constitutional promise of inclusive citizenship. This chapter returns to an earlier phase in this struggle, analysing the participation of Kamaladevi Chattopadhyay and her generation in the making of three crucial documents; the Karachi Resolution of 1931, the 1939 Report titled *Women's Role in Planned Economy* and the 1945 AIWC's *Indian Woman's Charter of Rights and Duties*. These were to set the parameters for the drafting of India's democratic constitution.

In their efforts to construct a constitutional identity for women as citizens in a future democratic nation-state, these documents sought to rework the social contract. The Karachi Resolution marked a key moment in the emergence of a political identity for the Indian as a citizen, divorced from social citizenship or social identity. The 1939 *Women's Role in Planned Economy* Report created space for the articulation of economic citizenship within this political identity, while the AIWC's *Indian Woman's Charter of Rights and Duties*, through a duality of rights and duties, reconciled tensions between liberal conceptions of the abstract political citizen and social belonging and being.

In regard to all three of these documents, the analysis here is concerned not only with the text itself but equally with the context out of which this text emerges, and the interaction between text and context. This relationship exposes the multiplicity and instability of the subject positions from which this generation of women activists 'spoke' in their efforts to remake the social contract. In opening up new spaces for conceptualising and defining the boundaries, meanings and implications of citizenship and equality, the embeddedness of these documents in the worldview and politics of their drafters also foreclosed alternate spaces and forms of collective being and belonging.

The Social Contract

The work of political theorists such as Carole Pateman and Christine Keating is central to exploring the gendered dynamics in the making of the social contract.[1] Pateman argues that the development of liberal constitutional democracy, the framework out of which the concept of modern citizenship emerges, is itself inherently patriarchal and gendered because it is grounded on a subordinate relationship between men and women, and on an abstract understanding of the individual who is, by definition, masculine.

Social contract theory explains how and why individuals allow themselves to be grouped together and for their freedoms to be curtailed in exchange for order and security. It is premised on the idea that in a state of nature, humans are free; however, life is unsustainable and insecure.[2] In the words of Thomas Hobbes, as quoted in his famous treatise, *Leviathan*, the life of humanity in a state of nature 'without a common power to keep them in awe' is 'solitary, poor, nasty, brutish, and short'.[3] In an attempt to seek security for both their bodies and their property, people consensually join together in political communities.[4] In moving from a state of nature into such political communities, humans agree to live together under a mutual contract, which counterbalances security and freedom. Grouping together within civil society requires the introduction of 'a variety of civil arrangements

---

[1] See, for example, Carole Pateman's seminal work *The Sexual Contract* (Stanford University Press, Cambridge, 1988) and Christine Keating, *Decolonising Democracy: Transforming the Social Contract in India* (Penn State University, Pennsylvania, 2011).

[2] S. Welch, *A Theory of Freedom* (Palgrave Macmillan, New York, 2012), p. 3.

[3] T. Hobbs, *Leviathan* (Cambridge, 1991), pp. 88–89.

[4] A.C. Grayling, *Ideas that Matter: A Personal Guide for the 21st Century* (Weidenfeld & Nicolson, London, 2009), p. 381.

necessary for regulating peaceable interactions between people, which culminate in some form of authority—typically the State'. Individual freedoms are, therefore, managed and curtailed within the 'domain of permissible interventions by the identified authority'.[5]

Pateman is concerned with the transition from the more traditional form of authority, that of monarchy, to that of parliamentary governance, which forms the foundation of the modern State today. In her book *The Sexual Contract*, she explains how the social contract is inherently patriarchal because it is underpinned by a sexual contract—an agreement in which the paternalism of the old system (articulated through a father's control over the son) was replaced by fraternalism (equality between men as individuals, which is based on their authority as heads of the household). In the transition from monarchy to parliamentary democracy, the social contract replaced the patriarchal right of the father with that of civil government. This created a new kind of equality, a fraternity of men, but was itself dependent on the exclusion of other communities, such as women, and slaves in the United States. In fact, Pateman argues, men's loss of power in the public sphere was compensated for by granting them authority in the private sphere, as the male head of household. One of the central reasons why men, who were ostensibly equals as political brothers, agreed to be governed, was to preserve and enhance their power over women. To resolve the contradiction between democracy's ethos of equality and assertions of masculine power, Western political theorists separated the public and private spheres.[6]

In her recent analysis of the making of the social contract in postcolonial India, Christine Keating argues that the CA, the body responsible for writing India's new Constitution, operated as a site for the reworking of both the racial and the sexual contracts that had underpinned India's colonial domination, ushering in a new kind of 'inclusive democracy'.[7] This book is premised on an understanding of the drafting of the Indian Constitution as a point of culmination,

[5] Welch, *A Theory of Freedom*, pp. 3–4.

[6] Pateman, *The Sexual Contract*, pp. 32–36.

[7] Keating, *Decolonising* Democracy, pp. 64–69, 91.

rather than a starting marker in this process. The Indian women's movement began engaging in efforts to rework the social contract prior to independence, with the first franchise campaign for women running in 1917, and continued in its efforts with the entry of Chattopadhyay and her peers into the Indian nationalist movement in the 1920s and 1930s. In order to fully understand the efforts of Chattopadhyay's generation to rework the social contract, and in doing so to renegotiate the gendered dynamics of power in the construction of the nation-state, let us return to the three documents that set the terms of the debate around citizenship and equality in the Indian CA—the Karachi Resolution of 1931, the 1939 Report on *Women's Role in Planned Economy* and the 1945 AIWC's *Indian Woman's Charter of Rights and Duties.*

The Karachi Resolution of 1931

By the time of the Karachi Congress in 1931, the question of the constitutional future of India had become one of the central concerns within the Congress, and between nationalist leaders and the British Raj. The Karachi Congress envisioned an independent and democratic India and sought to position Indians as citizens within such a future. In 1931, when the Karachi Resolution was drafted, it represented a definitive break with the compromise of colonial power-sharing with an Indian elite.

In 1927, the British government appointed the Simon Commission to discuss the constitutional future of the country, but failed to include any Indian representation on this Commission, which alienated the leaders of all parties and communities in India. In response, the Congress urged parties to boycott the Commission and decided to form its own all-India committee to draft a constitution.[8] The result was the Nehru Report of 1928, the first Congress document to lay out a broad constitutional framework for a future independent India, advocating

---

[8] S. Tejani, *Indian Secularism: A Social and Intellectual History 1890-1950* (New Delhi, Permanent Black, 2007), pp. 185–186.

dominion status.[9] Many leaders within Congress, including Jawaharlal Nehru and Subhas Chandra Bose, however, advocated a more radical break with Britain. At its 1929 Lahore Session, Congress agreed that its goal was *purna swaraj*, complete independence, and that this was to be achieved through civil disobedience rather than discussion and collaboration with the British Raj.[10] In alignment with this, Congress embarked, at the beginning of 1930, on the first phase of its 1930 – 34 Civil Disobedience Campaign. This campaign was to commence with the Salt Satyagraha, a protest against the British imposition of taxes on Indian-manufactured salt. Gandhi's famous Salt March, through Gujarat to the coastal village of Dandi, that took place in March and April 1930, kicked off proceedings and was followed by groups of volunteers across the country breaking salt laws, picketing legislatures and boycotting alcohol and imported cloth.[11] Clashes between those participating in the Satyagraha and the authorities led to the arrest of many, including Congress leaders, such as Nehru and Gandhi.

While all of this was unfolding, other nationalist leaders, including the Muslim League, agreed to participate in discussions with Britain through a series of round table talks in London. Congress, leading the resistant campaign back home, did not participate. However, the Viceroy Lord Irwin's release of Gandhi and the members of the Congress Working Committee in January 1931 prompted the Mahatma to meet with the Viceroy in a reconciliatory gesture, at the close of this first series of talks. Both men discovered that they had an accord and this initial meeting resulted in a series of informal talks between the two, culminating in the signing of the Gandhi-Irwin Pact at the end of March 1931. Through this pact, Congress agreed to a range of conditions, including the cessation of civil disobedience, while the colonial government agreed to lift repressive measures against Congress. However, members of Congress were divided over their endorsement of the Gandhi-Irwin Pact. Many leaders were highly critical of the pact, including Nehru and Patel,

---

9 D.A. Low, *Congress and the Raj: Facets of the Indian Struggle, 1917-1947* (Oxford University Press, New Delhi, 2006), p. 139.

10 J. Brown, *Modern India: the Origins of an Asian Democracy* (Oxford University Press, New York, 1994), p. 272.

11 R. Kumar, *The History of Doing*, p. 74.

and the Karachi Congress held between March and April 1931 was, according to Low, dominated by this question, rather than that of the Resolution on Fundamental Rights, which was drafted at this session.[12]

Scholars today recognise the Resolution of the Karachi Congress on Fundamental Rights and Economic Changes as a landmark document in the development of Indian nationalist ideology. For its time, it provided the most concrete and specific policy brief on economic and political transformation. The mid- to late 1920s had been troubled years for the Congress party, with internal divisions and disorganisation marring the development of a clear vision. The return of Gandhi to Congress politics in 1928 played a positive role in pulling the organisation together. But, as Judith Brown observes, it was only two years later, under Gandhi's leadership of the Civil Disobedience Campaign, that Congress began to make the transition to becoming an all-India movement.[13] The Karachi Resolution as a document reflected this important transition.

The Karachi Resolution reflects the coexistence of a Gandhian worldview with the rational and modernist approach of Congress leaders like Nehru. The resolution included 20 clauses. Clause 1, with sub-clauses (a) to (i), covered Fundamental Rights. Clauses two to four advocated religious neutrality on the part of the State, universal adult suffrage and free primary education. Clauses five to nine focused on the rights and protections of workers, while Clauses ten to twelve covered the terms of agricultural tenure, taxation and ownership, as well as inheritance tax. Clause 13 detailed terms for military expenditure, Clause 14 set terms for civil department expenditure. Clauses fifteen to twenty revealed a clear Gandhian agenda, including the protection of indigenous cloth, prohibition of alcohol, a ban on the placement of duty on Indian manufactured salt, control over exchange and currency policy, control over usury, and State control over key industries and mineral resources.[14]

---

[12] Low, *Congress and the Raj*, p. 139.

[13] Brown, *Modern India*, p. 267.

[14] Copy of the Original Resolution of the Karachi Congress on Fundamental Rights and Economic Changes with suggestions received from various organisations and individuals, 17 April 1931, File G75/1931, AICC Papers (hereafter AICC), Nehru Memorial Museum and Library (hereafter NMML).

The Fundamental Rights section of the document was most significant for the Indian women's movement, in particular, the following sub-clauses:

a. All citizens are equal before the law, irrespective of religion, caste, creed or sex

and

b. No disability to attach to any citizen by reason of his or her religion, caste or creed or sex in regard to public employment, office of power or honour, and in the exercise of any trade or calling

Not only was the Karachi Resolution of 1931 recognised as a landmark in the development of a clear egalitarian nationalist ideology, but it was also retrospectively seen as an important moment in the struggle for gender equality in colonial India. It is the first nationalist document to offer a clear definition and commitment to equality between the sexes, as a foundational principle of the Congress policy. The Karachi Resolution was significant furthermore because it signalled a distinct break with the rhetoric of social feminism in preference for a liberal conceptualisation of belonging to the nation-state.

Kamaladevi Chattopadhyay participated in the Salt Satyagraha, which launched the first phase of the Civil Disobedience Campaign, defiantly auctioning salt in the markets, and even the local courthouse, in violation of the British monopoly on this essential and basic commodity. In her autobiography, she describes the mass participation of women in the campaign, and the sense of agency, solidarity and collective identity that this experience fostered in her consciousness: 'The whole air became so surcharged, every nerve in the body tingled. I felt elated as part of one of the most spectacular dramas in India's political history.' In setting the scene, she writes that although India had a long 'illustrious tradition of women warriors', the Salt Satyagraha marked 'their first appearance in any modern militant political campaign'. She goes on to recall that while signing her name on the campaign pledge, 'It seemed such a stupendous moment in my life, in the life of the women of my country. I felt I was tracing not the letters of my name but recording a historic event'.[15] The first phase (1930 – 31) of Congress's Civil Disobedience Campaign witnessed the unprecedented participation of Indian women in protests and boycotts. Four thousand women were arrested and went to jail for the nationalist cause.[16]

The research of historians such as Suruchi Thapar-Björkert indicates that it was not only the elite and educated middle-class women who were involved, but that the call to action drew in new groups from Indian society, including working-class and peasant women. The campaign was also strengthened by the informal participation of many women involved in Indian women's organisations, such as the WIA and the AIWC. The Karachi Resolution, framed against the backdrop of the first phase of Civil Disobedience, therefore, marked an important moment in the recognition of women as active participants in the nationalist struggle. The report containing the Karachi Resolution, in fact, begins with the Congress congratulating all those who underwent great sufferings during the late Civil Disobedience Campaign, especially the women of India who rose in their thousands and assisted the nation in its struggle for freedom. This respectfully assured them that no constitution will be acceptable to the Congress that discriminated against the (their) sex in the matter of franchise.[17]

The narrative of the Salt Satyagraha might well have been different had it not been for the persistence of energetic, young activists, such as Chattopadhyay, as Gandhi's initial vision of the Satyagraha did not include a direct role for women. Gandhian nationalism is presented as a movement that facilitated the entry of Indian women into nationalist politics en masse. Chattopadhyay's recollection of events leading up

---

[15] K. Chattopadhyay, *Inner Recesses, Outer Spaces* (Niyogi Books, New Delhi, 2014), pp. 152–157.

[16] See S. Thapar-Björkert, *Women in the Indian National Movement: Unseen Faces and Unheard Voices* (Sage, New Delhi, 2006); Brown, *Modern India*; Forbes, *Women in Modern India*, p. 129. Forbes emphasises that women's participation in this later campaign was quantitatively and qualitatively different from their participation in the campaigns of the 1920s.

[17] 'Resolutions recommended by the Subject Committee', Draft programme of the 45th Session of the INC at Karachi, 29 March 1931, File 25/1931, AICC Papers, NMML.

to the Salt Satyagraha suggests that the new opportunities created by their participation in the struggle for independence were not simply facilitated by the strategy and approach of Gandhian nationalism, but that they were equally the product of individual efforts to push, challenge and expand the openings that Gandhian nationalism created. In her autobiography, Kamaladevi Chattopadhyay described her excitement on hearing about the Salt Satyagraha, followed by her disappointment on being told that she could not participate: 'As batches for the first Satyagraha were to be selected, I asked that women be included. I was told that Gandhiji did not want them, as he had other programmes reserved for them. I was flabbergasted.' She decided to travel to Surat specifically to visit Gandhi and to persuade him to change his mind. When she confronted Gandhi over his exclusion of women in the Satyagraha, he reassured her that his decision was not based on discrimination, but rather due to the fact that he had reserved specific and alternative activities for them, including the promotion of *swadeshi*, the picketing of foreign goods and the elimination of liquor, which he felt were more appropriate for their nature. 'The tasks reserved for them are a tribute to the high qualities they possess,' he explained patiently to her. 'The call for them was not for slogan shouting or marches, but utter dedication, which was a natural quality of women.' Chattopadhyay did not challenge Gandhi's logic that women were endowed with specific feminine qualities; in fact, she very cleverly made a counter-argument using this logic but turning it back on itself. She argued that it was the unique nature of Satyagraha, as a form of moral protest, that enabled it to accommodate women as the weaker sex. 'The significance of a non-violent struggle is that the weakest can take an equal part with the strongest and share in the triumph, as you have yourself said.'[18] This exchange was indicative of the way in which women activists often had to negotiate between a set of abstract ideals and a set of socially acceptable norms, within the nationalist movement.

In her argument, Chattopadhyay had used the language of social feminism to argue her case for her fellow female activists' right to participate on equal terms in the Salt Satyagraha. This generation of

---

[18] Chattopadhyay, *Inner Recesses, Outer Spaces*, pp. 149–151.

women nationalists and gender activists, however, did not consider their ideology and organisational activities as feminism, in the Western sense of the term. They practised what Geraldine Forbes defines as a form of social feminism, an ideology which acknowledged that women were physically and psychologically different from men, but argued that it was because of the value and significance of their special qualities that they should be able to contribute equally to society.[19] Social feminism was based on the principle of recognising women's equality, and hence their inclusion in the body politic, through an identity of difference. It acknowledged the unique and valuable contribution their gendered roles were able to make to the nationalist struggle and the envisioning of a new nation-state. It was, however, a broad and multifaceted ideology with the capacity to encompass a range of interpretations, positionings and constructions of gendered identities, depending on the context and the group articulating it. One strand of social feminism articulated an identity and role that could be defined as paternalistic and protectionist. Emerging out of the nineteenth-century Indian social reform movement, and the practices and discourses of maternal imperialism, this strand sought the inclusion of women within the State through a policy of protectionism and guardianship. But there were other strands of social feminism that were grounded on notions of women's moral and spiritual power, as well as the power of sacrifice, as, for example, women revolutionaries invoking the destructive power of Hindu goddesses, such as Durga and Kali.

Social feminism fulfilled a strategic function by providing an ideological base that was broad enough to embrace women from a range of political and social views: from the more conservative, to those with a more liberal politics, such as Vijayalakshmi Pandit, those with a Gandhian worldview, such as Rajkumari Amrit Kaur, as well as socialist and communist women, such as Renu Chakravartty. It also functioned strategically, enabling Indian women to carve out an independent identity as advocates of women's equality, as distinct from that of their Western sisters, and to walk the tightrope between feminism and nationalism. It allowed Indian women activists to pursue

[19] Forbes, *Women in Modern India*, pp. 90–91.

a commitment to the empowerment and equality in a way that was less overtly challenging to the social structures of Indian society and, hence, more accommodating to many of their male colleagues in the movement.

Up until this point of time, the language of social feminism which acknowledged the equality and inclusion of women in the freedom struggle on the basis of their unique and valuable gendered roles was the language employed by Congress and many of Kamaladevi's colleagues in the women's movement. However, when it came to debating the terms of belonging in the Karachi Resolution, the representatives of the women's movement resisted such a claim to belonging, indicating that the terms of inclusion were shifting.

The first draft of the Karachi Resolution was produced at the Congress's annual conference over March and April 1931. At this conference, the working committee appointed another committee, the Fundamental Rights and Economic Programme Committee, 'to invite opinions and suggestions from Provincial Congress Committees and other bodies and persons' on the terms of the Resolution and suggest changes and revisions.[20] The WIA was one of the organisations that engaged in this process of discussion and revision, submitting a series of suggested amendments. While with social feminism, difference formed one of the bases for inclusion within the imagined future nation-state, points (e) and (f) in Clause 1 of the Resolution implied an understanding that viewed difference on the basis of sex or other social identities, such as religion and caste, as barriers to inclusion and equality. This implied that the claiming of political rights by women, and their inclusion in the nation-state would necessarily be as the 'sexless' citizen.

The WIA's engagement in the crafting of the Karachi Resolution clearly shows a move towards this particular identity through the removal or rephrasing of any clauses intended to 'include' women in the realm of State protection and jurisdiction, and through any reference to

[20] Congress Secretary to Prakasa, informing him that he has been made convenor of this committee and explaining the duties required, 2 April 1931, Camp Karachi, File G75/1931, AICC Papers, NMML.

their social identity, in particular their specific needs as a predefined social category. For example, responding to clauses five to nine, all of which dealt with issues around labour regulation and the protection of workers' rights and worker unions, the WIA argued that 'the phrase "protection for women workers" should not be used', because 'placing women in a condition of "protection" is writing down women publically as in a state of weakness which is not desirable for our whole sex.'[21]

Within the political language of Chattopadhyay's generation, a strand of rhetoric was gaining ground that was increasingly resistant to women being seen and identified as a specific socially defined category, in the sphere of party and parliamentary politics, although this was not the case in other spheres like social welfare and constructive work. The reasoning behind this rejection was based on an understanding that it encouraged paternalism, which denied women equality and inclusion on the basis of an identified weakness and consequent need for protection. Social identity operated in this context as the basis for exclusion on the grounds of discrimination. The next chapter illustrates the logic that led this generation to reject this particular framing of social identity, not only as a marker of weakness and discrimination but in the case of reservations, on the basis of its use to grant special privilege and advantage. This rejection, under both pretexts of discrimination and privilege, required making social identity irrelevant or invisible in the eyes of the State, and points (e) and (f) of the Karachi Resolution were embraced by the Indian women's movement precisely for this reason—because they were interpreted as facilitating such an invisibility or indistinguishability.

This invisibility could, however, become a two-edged sword. The issue around labour legislation is an example of how in certain contexts it became necessary to make women invisible, in order to claim a particular conception of equality. In other contexts, as the example below demonstrates, it became imperative to name them as a specific community, to ensure that they were not excluded because of this

---

[21] 'Original Resolution of the Karachi Congress on Fundamental Rights and Economic Changes with suggestions received from various organisations and individuals', undated, File G75/1931, AICC Papers, NMML.

invisibility. So, for example, in reference to Clause 3 on Adult Suffrage, the WIA recommended that 'adult suffrage should be expressed explicitly as meaning the right of every man and woman of the age of 21 and above to vote'.[22] In being made visible or invisible, the principle or intention was the same—to ensure inclusion in the body politic.

Together with the identity of the Indian woman as the sexless citizen, more traditional ideologies of gender politics can be identified vying for recognition in the debate around the framing of citizenship in the Resolution. Bans Gopal of Fatehpur recommended that 'No conversion of minors or women without their guardian's consent'[23] be added to Clause 1 (c), thereby reinforcing a conception of the legal status of women as defined by their familial relations, and trapping them as perpetual minors in law. This recommended change positioned the authority and identity of the family over the authority of the individual. In this context, it operated as a means to deny the power and the ability of a woman as a citizen to act as an independent agent. In other suggested inclusions and changes to the Resolution, the social difference was emphasised. However, in these instances, it was not done to deny women agency, but rather to facilitate it and to enable them to participate in the nation-state. For example, Shah Ozair requested that in Clause 3 on suffrage, 'with special arrangement of Pardah' be added, in order to ensure that women were able to exercise their right to vote without any violation of their privacy.[24]

The claim to citizenship through social feminism, as articulated in Chattopadhyay's passionate argument for women's participation in the Salt Satyagraha, versus the political feminism of the sexless citizen, expressed in the WIA's amendments to the original Karachi Resolution, should not necessarily be seen as inherently opposite or contradictory. They both coexisted as two streams of ideology within gender politics over the period from the 1930s to the 1960s, and produced various sub-streams, at times reinforcing each other, and on other occasions existing in tension.

---

22 Ibid.

23 Ibid.

24 Ibid.

Some of the recommendations made by the WIA reveal a drive towards pushing the jurisdiction of citizenship, based on equality before the law, beyond the public and into the private sphere of the home and family. For example, the WIA recommended that 'Equal rights for both men and women in laws relating to marriage, to the guardianship of children, inheritance rights and nationality rights' be inserted at the end of clause (e), in the section on Fundamental Rights.[25] By this stage, the reform of social laws, in particular, Hindu Law, had become a pivotal concern for the Indian women's movement. It was, therefore, expected that this would be suggested for inclusion within the Resolution. What is significant, however, is the WIA's insistence that this be positioned within the section on Fundamental Rights. In doing so, the intention was to build equality before the law into the foundational principles of an imagined future nation-state. Such efforts indicate, furthermore, an attempt to rewrite the social contract by destabilising the accepted legal boundaries between civil and private law.

The Karachi Resolution provided a strategic tool which this generation of activists used to hold the Congress, and later the independent Indian government, to account in their struggles and arguments for inclusion within the body politic. In 1938, when Polygamy and Divorce Bills were introduced into Parliament, Rajkumari Amrit Kaur wrote to Congress President Subhas Chandra Bose, referencing the Karachi Resolution, to remind the party of the necessity of its undivided support for these bills: 'You will understand,' she wrote, 'how much we rejoice at the Congress declaration of Fundamental Rights at Karachi in which this organisation proclaimed themselves in favour of the equality of the sexes in every department of life.' Continuing, she referred to the 1937 Congress Election Manifesto, quoting the exact section of 'A Call to the Nation' where the organisation declared that it stood 'for the removal of all sex discrimination whether legal or social or in any sphere of public activity'. She explained that her letter had been prompted by the AIWC's experience that despite 'these declarations, we are grieved to find that remedial legislation, which strives to remove the social disabilities under which women suffer, does not receive the united support of the

[25] Ibid.

Congress Party either in Provincial or the Central Assemblies'. Kaur then requested Bose to reassure the AIWC of the Congress's support for 'the ideal of monogamy', divorce and of the reform of social laws 'in order to give their just rights to women' and 'whether the Congress Working Committee through their Parliamentary Board will be willing to direct Congress parties in the various provinces and legislatures to support adequate measures relating to the above as well as all social legislation.'[26]

The AIWC's support for, and use of, the political language of the Karachi Resolution, which presented an identity for women as the sexless citizen, stemmed from an understanding that equality depended on the capacity of the State to see people first and foremost as political citizens, rather than social beings. This was grounded on experience; being identified as a woman in the political sphere, being defined in terms of one's gender often resulted in exclusion, marginalisation or the imposition of double standards, which hindered incorporation and full participation in a political fraternity. The Karachi Resolution of 1931 drew on the modern democratic and liberal conception of citizenship concerned with regulating the relationship between the individual and the State, to ensure equal treatment for all by blinding the State to social difference. It was also deeply rooted in the notion of the individual as the unit for engagement with the State. The statement, 'All citizens are equal before the law, irrespective of religion, caste, creed or sex' was not intended to discard the womanliness of this generation, but rather to prevent this social identity from being used as a barrier to 'promoting and encouraging respect for human rights and for fundamental freedoms without distinction as to race, sex, language or religion'.[27] It sought to make this social identity invisible in terms of the individual's interaction with the State. But did this imply a need for the invisibility of all other social and collective identities? And did a call for the sexless citizen equally demand the religion-less and caste-less citizen too?

---

[26] Kaur to S.C. Bose, 2 August 1938, File 42, AIWC Papers, NMML.

[27] Document 1, Charter of the United Nations, signed 26 June 1945 (extract) in United Nations, *The United Nations and the Advancement of Women 1945-1995*, Blue Book Series, Vol. VI (New York, 1996), p. 93.

Politics in India has shown the scholar that collective or social identity can be a source of strength and solidarity and that the claim to such collective identities can be crucial in struggles for State recognition and rights. Women have often chosen to mobilise under other categories of identity, standing not specifically as women, but, for example, as part of anti-caste movements. For Dalit women, understanding and challenging their position of subordination was dependent on being seen and recognised by the State as subjects burdened by both caste and gender. Such group identity provided a source of strength and leverage in such struggles. However, the inflexibility of the political identity articulated by the Karachi Resolution did not always allow for such malleability in the construction of identity as a channel into power.

Sharmila Rege's research on the agency and participation of Dalit women in anti-caste movements illustrates how the particular needs, struggles and contributions of Dalit women have been overlooked in the historiography of mainstream Indian feminism. This was because they did not fit the framework of the 'sexless citizen'.[28] Just as Pateman argues that the social contract reconfigured the political identity as masculine, Rege argues that the Karachi Resolution reconfigured the sexless citizen as inherently Brahmin and middle-class. It consequently functioned to silence other 'contentious non-Brahmin images' and identities for women, marginalising the articulation of other ways of being and other forms of collective belonging.[29]

The situated-ness and subjectivity of the 'sexless' and 'religion-less' citizen as articulated in the Karachi Resolution was brought into renewed focus by the experience of Muslim women. In her work on the emergence of feminism among Indian Muslim women, Azra Asghar Ali emphasises that Muslim women often felt that they had greater recourse to justice and to equal treatment within the legal systems

---

[28] See, for example, S. Rege. 'Dalit Women Talk Differently: A Critique of "Difference" and Towards a Dalit Feminist Standpoint Position'. *EPW* 33, no. 44 (1998): WS39-S46. http://www.jstor.org/stable/4407323.; S. Rege, *Writing Caste/ Writing Gender: Narrating Dalit Women's Testimonies* (Zubaan Books, New Delhi, 2006).

[29] Rege, 'Dalit Women Talk Differently', p. WS-42.

of Islam, in comparison to other personal codes of law.[30] A claim to a communal identity for Muslim women in this context operated as a means of empowerment, whereas for Hindu women activists it was interpreted as a tool of oppression. When lobbying Congress in support of the 1937 Monogamy Bill, Rajkumari Amrit Kaur used the Karachi Resolution to hold Congress to account in terms of its commitment to equal treatment, and as a benchmark for what such treatment entailed in practice. Instead, she exposed the underlying modern middle-class Hindu or Christian family identity underpinning the supposed neutrality of the Fundamental Principles equality clause.

The Karachi Resolution addressed the issue of political equality, but what about economic equality? Communist and socialist women activists, together with their male colleagues, also found themselves critical of what they perceived as the 'bourgeois vision' of the new nation-state, and of citizenship, put forward by the Karachi Resolution on Fundamental Rights. The Resolution implied a belief in a neutral State, and in such a State's capacity to administer justice by engaging with its subjects as 'sexless', 'casteless' and abstract citizens. For communists, the root cause of inequality lay not in the relationship between the State and individual, but rather between individuals and between classes. In a capitalist society based on the ownership of private property, inequality was created due to the exploitative nature of relationships between workers and employers, and between the working class who sold their labour and those who owned the means of production. In order to rectify such a dynamic, it was these relationships that needed to be reformed, rather than the interaction between citizen and State. Treating all citizens equally in the law would merely perpetuate inequality between them because it would not address the underlying economic structures of property ownership that facilitated such inequality in the first place. With the Karachi Resolution, however, the 'political contestations between competing political visions of how various national subjects would be related to each other were thus levelled out.'[31]

[30] See A. Ali, *The Emergence of Feminism Among Indian Muslim Women 1920-1947* (Oxford University Press, Oxford, 2000).

[31] Oxford, 'Dalit Women Talk Differently', p. WS-42.

The Report on Women's Role in Planned Economy 1939 – 40

There was greater scope for communist and socialist women activists to address economic inequalities within the Report on *Women's Role in Planned Economy* (WRPE), the second document to be analysed here. While the Karachi Resolution, which had provided the terms of reference for the 1939 Report, was concerned with opening up political citizenship to women, the Report on *Women's Role in Planned Economy* concerned itself with what it would mean to translate the possibilities of political freedom, equality and empowerment into the economic sphere.

The Report was researched and written between 1939 and 1940[32] as one of a series of 29 reports commissioned by the National Planning Committee (NPC) to provide recommendations for the social, political and economic strategy required to achieve the removal of 'all obstacles or handicaps in the way of realising an equal status and opportunity for women'.[33] The scope of the research was comprehensive, covering agriculture, industrial development, cottage industries, population, health and education, with all 29 reports then informing the compilation of an overall document which was to provide a broad blueprint for 'a planned economy on which the future structure can be built.'[34]

The NPC, established in October 1938 under the chairmanship of Jawaharlal Nehru, reflected two things. The first of these was the influence of a Soviet-style macroeconomic planning model as the mechanism for achieving 'the comprehensive economic development of the new nation', and the second was the presence of industrialists

---

32 A 1940 draft version of the Report was produced. However, the finalised report was only printed after World War II in 1949.

33 K.T. Shah (ed.), '*Women's Role in Planned Economy: Report of the Sub-Committee*', National Planning Committee (Bombay, 1949), p. 29 quoted in L. Kasturi, 'Development, Patriarchy and Politics: Indian Women in the Political Process 1947-1992', Occasional Paper 25 (1995), Centre for Women's Development Studies, p. 13.

34 K.T. Shah (ed.), Being an abstract of the Proceedings and other particulars resulting to the National Planning Committee No. 1, Bombay, National Planning Committee Series, undated, p. 82.

and businessmen within the Congress party. These men saw centralised planning as essential for harnessing the technical expertise and investment necessary for industrial development. From its emergence, the project of national planning was expected to satisfy various interests and agendas. On 16 June 1939, the NPC appointed the Sub-Committee on Women's Role in the Planned Economy, to guide the development of the WRPE Report. This committee consisted of prominent women in public life and Indian nationalism, including freedom fighters from various political parties, social workers, office-bearers of women's organisations, such as the AIWC and the WIA, and lawyers.[35] Rani Laxmibai Rajwade, the founding president of the AIWC, headed the Sub-Committee as its Chairperson, while Mridula Sarabhai was assigned the role of Secretary. The Sub-Committee was tasked with producing a comprehensive framework for 'envisaging the part women should be enabled to play in the planned society of the future',[36] taking into consideration 'her social, economic and legal status, her right to hold property, and carry on any trade, profession or occupation'.[37]

National planning was premised on the belief that social justice was achievable through the 'the organisation of economic life'. The 'well-being of the community' and a 'decent standard of living' could be secured through 'intensifying the economic development of the community concerned on an all-round basis, in an ordered systematic manner.'[38] Data collection was an important process in this national planning exercise; planning recommendations were to be supported by an accurate socio-economic picture of the country. This called for the extensive surveying of available statistics and opinion.[39] Much of the data and many of the opinions presented in the WRPE Report were gathered through the membership networks of the AIWC.

---

[35] L. Kasturi, 'Development, Patriarchy and Politics', pp. 12–13.

[36] K. Khandwalla, 'Smt Khandwalla's Note on The Report of the Sub-Committee on Women's Role in Planned Economy', undated, File G-23/1940, Vol. II, AICC Papers, NMML.

[37] Kasturi, 'Development, Patriarchy and Politics', p. 13.

[38] Shah (ed.), 'Being an abstract of the Proceedings and other particulars resulting to the National Planning Committee', p. 15.

[39] Ibid., pp. 7–8.

Each of the 27 members of the Report Sub-Committee was responsible for organising a research working group in their home state or province. These working groups collected whatever statistical information they could find and circulated an extraordinarily detailed questionnaire.[40] Close to 2,000 of these questionnaires were translated into Assamese, Bengali, Hindi, Gujarati, Marathi, Urdu as well as English, and sent out to individuals and institutions, including Central and provincial government departments, district Mahila Sanghs, welfare organisations and trade unions. The information gathered through this process was then consolidated into the Report.[41]

The experience of collecting this information revealed some of the frustrations and shortcomings encountered in attempts to amass qualitative and quantitative data on gender discrimination and the lived reality of women within Indian society. It also exposed some of the inherent class biases of those gathering this material. In Gujarat, the working group complained that the 'investigation was mostly amongst middle classes'. There was 'no information from the poorer classes in towns and villages. Response from organisations of labour, etc., was not satisfactory'. The working group from Assam concurred, stressing that they had experienced 'difficulty in gathering information' with 'the number of educated women being few' and those that did exist being 'all in government service'. In the North West Frontier Province (NWFP), those administering the questionnaire complained that 'owing to few educated women and purdah, little interest taken by ladies. Men have their own point of view about the questionnaire.'[42] Taking into account these specific biases, the Report remains a valuable reflection of the opinions of educated, organised and literate women across India at this time, and as such provides a rich historical source.

[40] The research methods employed showed the beginnings of an effort towards evidence-based social policy, a methodology that the AIWC and the Central Social Welfare Board (CSWB) were to promote as the basis for policymaking in independent India.

[41] Appendix IV: Method of Work, The Report of the Sub-Committee on *Women's Role in Planned Economy* (1940 Draft), undated, File G-23/1940, Vol. II, AICC Papers, NMML.

[42] Ibid.

The time, effort and detail taken by this network of AIWC members and other related women, to gather the research for the *WRPE* Report, appears to have made a considerable impression on the Planning Commission (PC). Nehru, observing a meeting of the Sub-Committee in Bombay, was impressed with the 'earnestness and ability of members' in tackling the research problems of the Report. Later, he wrote to the organisation in his capacity as Chairman of the NPC to thank the membership for their assistance in gathering the necessary material. 'I feel that of all the sub-committees of the National Planning Committee, the sub-committee which has done the most work, and built up almost a movement for the purpose has been the women's sub-committee,' he wrote.[43]

After a preface and introduction by K.T. Shah, editor for the Report series, the report was divided into three sections. Section one focused on the individual status of women and included four chapters on civic rights, economic rights, property rights and education. Section two addressed the social status of women in the family through two chapters entitled 'Marriage and its Problems' and 'Family Life'. The third section included a chapter covering what was described as miscellaneous issues; it included caste, widows, widow remarriage, widows' inheritance, unmarried mothers, abortion, illegitimate children, prostitution and the trafficking of women and children. The Report concluded with a summary statement of policy and a summary of recommendations.[44] The *WRPE* Report envisaged a 'new social order', whereby '[w]hatever be the form of society as emerges out of the plan, the woman shall have equal status and equal opportunities with man'.[45] It identified the obstacles that were inhibiting women's full participation as economic citizens, and their social equality, and gave recommendations for the required reforms in

[43] The Sub-Committee, in fact, requested an extension of time to work through all the material in these questionnaires, in order to get their interim report into the NPC. See J. Nehru to Begum Hamid Ali, 25 March 1940, in *Selected Works of Jawaharlal Nehru*, Vol. 11 (B.R. Publishing Corporation, New Delhi, 1973 – 82), p. 283.

[44] M. Chaudhuri, 'Citizens, Workers and Emblems of Culture: An Analysis of the First Plan Document on Women' in P. Uberoi (ed.), *Social Reform, Sexuality and the State* (Sage Publications, New Delhi, 1996), p. 214.

[45] 'Report of the Sub-Committee, *Women's Role in Planned Economy*, National Planning Committee Series (1947)' in M. Chaudhuri (ed.) *Feminism in India* (Zed Books, New Delhi, 2004), p. 139.

realms of legislation, workplace conditions and familial relations, with a strong emphasis on recognition of the equal value of women's paid and unpaid labour. The need for propaganda to break down social customs, and education to modify backward social attitudes was also stressed upon: 'Propaganda...has to destroy and eradicate all superstitions and customs that hamper the advance of woman, break the old traditions that train boys to authority and girls to dependence.'[46]

Significant emphasis was placed on women as workers; as industrial workers, homemakers or agricultural workers, although as Leela Kasturi has emphasised, the lack of detail around the context and conditions of rural women meant that their experiences and voices remained largely neglected.[47] Work was put forward as a right, and citizenship was conceptualised not as something endowed, but rather as something earned through economic participation. Citizenship was to be claimed through the identity of the Indian woman as a productive worker. In this respect, the report sought to rework gender identities and roles in the economic sphere, by calling for the kinds of social and economic changes that would allow women to enter this sphere as equals, and for the value of their work to be recognised on the same basis. Equal wages for equal work were demanded, as were provisions for adequate maternity benefits, crèche facilities and childcare, which would enable women to combine work and family responsibilities. For women working in family businesses, the report recommended that they be made co-sharers in the collective income of the family. Financial security, in case of illness or maternity, was to be covered through the provision of a scheme of social insurance intended to cover housewives, as well as the women going out into the workplace.[48]

Although the report has been validly criticised by both Leela Kasturi and others for its internal inconsistencies in terms of the framing of women as citizens, it is nevertheless acknowledged as being a pioneering and progressive document for its time. Firstly, it acknowledges the economic value of women's unpaid domestic labour and secondly, it calls

---

[46] Shah (ed.), *Women's Role in Planned Economy*, p. 194.

[47] See Kasturi, 'Development, Patriarchy, and Politics'.

[48] Shah (ed.), *Women's Role in Planned Economy*, p. 198.

for a common moral code for both men and women in society. 'Society today ostracises women for the same moral lapse for which the man goes free. An identical standard of morality should be insisted upon for both man and woman', proclaims the report, emphasising that such a standard required that the harmonising of 'social welfare with individual freedom should be accepted for both man and woman, and should guide legislation and social convention'.[49] The report was potentially revolutionary in its recognition of domestic work in the private sphere of the household, or agricultural labour in the field, as an equal form of economic participation.[50] This destabilised the traditional boundaries between the public and private by extending the rights and protections of economic citizenship into the home. These boundaries were further destabilised by the report's stress on transforming social and cultural attitudes towards the responsibility of housework. In households where both men and women worked, the report recommended that the husband and wife should share the domestic workload equally. And in households where women were principal homemakers, the equal value of their domestic labour was to be recognised:

> A great many women will confine their activities to the home, and in any event, a great part of their work will be done in the home. This homework, though not recognised in terms of money value, is an essential contribution to the social wealth of the State and should be recognised as such. The aggregate of social wealth under [a] planned economy will include all kinds of work, whether rewarded in money value or not.
>
> We feel that this work, which at present receives no recognition either from the State or society, should be recognised as having an economic value and that work in the home should not be considered in any way inferior to the other type of work done outside the home.[51]

---

[49] See Extract from 'Women's Role in Planned Economy', pp. 198–199, 227 quoted in Chaudhuri (ed.), *Feminism in India* (Zed Books, New Delhi, 2004), p. 139; N. Banerjee, 'Whatever Happened to the Dreams of Modernity? The Nehruvian Era and Woman's Position', in *EPW*, 33:17 (25 April to 1 May 1998), pp. WS2–WS7; Kasturi, 'Development, Patriarchy, and Politics'.

[50] Shah (ed.), *Women's Role in Planned Economy*, pp. 102–105.

[51] *Women's Role in Planned Economy*, pp.199–201 quoted in Chaudhuri (ed), *Feminism in India*, p. 145.

The focus of the *WRPE* on embedded forms of labour practice as the cause of inequality meant that it indirectly addressed the intersection between social and economic inequality. The report was groundbreaking in its efforts to expose how the creation of hierarchies of labour was used to maintain women's social subordination. In doing so, it preempted more contemporary research, which has exposed the relationship between the feminisation of certain forms of work, and their devaluing (as in the case of unequal wages paid to women factory workers), or the removal of women's work from the economic sphere entirely (as with housework). However, the Sub-Committee drafting the report missed the opportunity to make the same connection between labour and caste. Instead, caste is relegated mainly to section three, revealingly entitled 'Miscellaneous', where it is approached as a cultural and social issue, rather than something having an economic basis.

The report is not without its tensions. It makes regular references to the individual as 'the unit in national planning',[52] advocating the freeing of women from their social identities as wives and mothers, and their recognition as 'a separate and independent unit in the economic structure with equal rights and equal status'.[53] However, simultaneously, there are repeated allusions to the specific and unique function that women played within their homes through the creation of a 'cultural environment...for the proper nurture of children'.[54] This reflects the friction between the Marxist and the Socialist feminism in the *WRPE*, with both ideological perspectives vying to rewrite the social contract according to their particular vision of this new 'social order'.

The critique of Kapila Khandwalla, one of the Sub-Committee's members, brought these tensions to the fore. Inserted into both the 1940 draft version and the final published version in 1949 is a note by Khandwalla criticising the authors for producing a document that, she argued, fundamentally departed from the agreed upon core issues

---

52 Shah (ed.), *Women's Role in Planned Economy*, p. 198.

53 *Women's Role in Planned Economy*, pp.199–201, quoted in Chaudhuri (ed.), *Feminism in India*, p. 145.

54 Shah (ed.), *Women's Role in Planned Economy*, p. 104.

and principles of a 'Socialist Planned Society'. One of the areas of divergence between Khandwalla and the rest of the Sub-Committee arose over the role of the family in planning for, and building, the new 'social order'. For Khandwalla, the authors had not taken the principles underpinning a 'Socialist Planned Society' to their logical conclusion, which was the complete dissolution of the family as a unit of policy and planning. In her note of dissent, Khandwalla described her vision of this 'new social order' in which 'all the various rights the Sub-Committee has laid down in the list of fundamental rights of citizenship, as affecting women, shall be completely divorced from any taint of relationship of any kind'.[55] Rights were to be conferred, and the status of citizenship to be granted, on the basis of the identity of the abstract 'sexless citizen' or rather the 'sexless' worker. The road to empowerment and equality for women was to be achieved by the inclusion of these groups within a democratic fraternity of workers. Khandwalla's claim here pushes an identity for women as the 'sexless citizen' further than that of the woman as an independent economic agent, as articulated by the other authors of the Sub-Committee. 'The only social status to be recognised in [a] planned society will be that of the individual worker...The social status, therefore, which today presents the most serious question of social reform, will not, I take it, matter at all in planned society.' Khandwalla condoned a materialist approach, stressing that the transformation of the economic structure of society would automatically lead to the positive transformation of social inequalities:

> If the right to work is guaranteed in the manner mentioned above, the disabilities now resting upon the woman in her civic or social position would be comparatively negligible.
>
> Neither motherhood, nor wifehood, and a fortiori widowhood matter at all. Every requirement of all these and similar positions will be provided for in consideration or in virtue of the individual concerned being a citizen and worker and on no other ground.[56]

---

[55] Ibid.

[56] Khandwalla, 'Note on The Report of the Sub-Committee', (*Women's Role in Planned Economy*), File G-23/1940, Vol. II, AICC Papers, NMML.

Although the *WRPE* repeatedly drew on the rhetoric of the individual as the unit for economic planning, many of its policy recommendations were actually based on the modern nuclear family as the basic unit. Reference to the specific and unique function that women played in the home through the creation of a 'cultural environment...for the proper nurture of children'[57] sat uneasily together with the emphasis on the importance of freeing women from their social identities as wives and mothers, and of planning through the individual. Rather than discarding the family completely, which is what Khandwalla demanded, the framers of the report sought to reinvent it by applying the principles of the nationalist movement's egalitarianism to the domestic sphere. The traditional extended Indian family was targeted as holding women back by preventing them from entering the world as workers, and by exploiting their productive and reproductive labour in the home. The proposed solution was a reworking of gender relationships and identities while moving towards the modern nuclear family.

In discussing the drafting of the *WRPE* Report, Khandwalla's was not the only voice of criticism. Muslim women members of the Sub-Committee were also negative in their assessment of the debate surrounding the report's final recommendations. Begum Hamid Ali, one of the few Muslim members of the Sub-Committee, and an active leader in the AIWC, felt that the Sub-Committee did not make an effort to fully investigate and understand women's rights within marriage and family relations under Islamic systems of law. As a consequence, she thought that these were largely overlooked or misrepresented in the report's recommendations. Her dissatisfaction led her to withhold her name from the interim report produced by the Sub-Committee in 1940, and it was only with the intervention of Nehru that she was prepared to reconsider.[58]

The report stressed the identity of the 'sexless' and 'religion-less' citizen claimed in the Karachi Resolution through the implementation of a uniform civil code. This was to be introduced incrementally and initially optional. In the interim, certain 'immediate changes'

[57] Shah (ed.), *Women's Role in Planned Economy*, pp. 198, 104.

[58] Forbes, *Women in Modern India*, p. 199.

were to be made, granting daughters the same rights to succession, inheritance and the acquiring of property as sons. Furthermore, 'All properties belonging to husband and wife respectively at the date of marriage' were to remain their separate properties, while 'the income or acquisition from any source' acquired during coverture was be owned by husband and wife jointly.[59] But as Azra Asghar Ali's research on the emergence of feminism among Muslim women has suggested, the demand for a uniform civil code inadvertently undermined the strategy pursued by some Muslim women activists of seeking reform and gender equality within systems of personal law. From this perspective, it is possible to empathise with the alienation experienced by Begum Hamid Ali and her Muslim colleagues over this issue.

Despite the effort and resources involved in its production, the ideas and recommendations put forward in the report were largely overlooked in the development planning documents of early independence.[60] The first Five-Year Plan adopted a clear 'welfarist' approach to women's needs and concerns, mentioning them in the sections concerned with services, such as education and health, but ignoring them in the sections on agricultural and industrial development. Where they were acknowledged, they tended to be positioned largely as dependants and as the beneficiaries of State services and protection, not as workers, producers and consumers.[61] The *WRPE* Report was very progressive for its day and for this reason, perhaps too idealistic and impractical for a Congress-led government accommodating a wide coalition of interests, from socialists to conservatives, from Gandhian social workers to businessmen and industrialists. A 'welfarist' approach in this context is likely to have offered greater consensus. The rhetoric of

[59] '*Women's Role in Planned Economy*', p. 201, quoted in Chaudhuri (ed.), *Feminism in India*, pp. 150–151.

[60] N. Buch, 'State Welfare Policy and Women, 1950-1975' in *EPW*, 33:17 (April 25 – May 1998), p. WS-19.

[61] For example, Chapter 34 on Labour includes a discussion on wage differentials in general but does not make any mention of the differences in wages between men and women's work. Nor is there any discussion of how the absence of childcare facilities hinders women's ability to participate with a greater degree of equality in the economy.

gender equality was easily accepted as an abstract theory and principle within the nationalist movement, translating it into practice, however, was to prove far more challenging and controversial.

The Indian Woman's Charter of Rights and Duties 1945

> During the past 18 years of its existence, the AIWC has adopted many resolutions with the object of improving the status of the Indian woman and helping her to attain her rightful place in society which is by the side of man. The object of this charter is to crystallise these resolutions with a view that they may form a basis for future legislation and also give a clear picture of what we stand for and wish to realise.[62]

With these ambitious words, the AIWC's *Indian Woman's Charter of Rights and Duties*, the third and final document to be discussed in this chapter, begins. The charter and its accompanying twin, a *Memorandum on Planning for National Welfare*, were introduced at the eighteenth annual session of the AIWC, held in Hyderabad in 1945. There, they were voted upon and published a year later in the June 1946 issue of the AIWC's journal, *Roshni*.[63] Conceptualised and drafted by the organisation's executive leadership—Rajkumari Amrit Kaur, Hansa Mehta, Lakshmi Menon, Kamaladevi Chattopadhyay, Renuka Ray, Kitty Shiva Rao and Hannah Sen—these documents were an expression of the organisational ideology and gender politics of the AIWC at this particular moment.[64] Written in the format of a constitution or social contract, the charter used the terms 'we think' and 'we believe' setting itself up as a legitimate 'voice of the people'. It built on the principles of the Karachi Resolution of 1931 and the

[62] 'Draft of the Indian Woman's Charter of Rights and Duties'. *Roshni: Journal of the All India Women's Conference*, 1:5 (June 1946), p. 12.

[63] Foreword to the Woman's Charter of Rights and Duties (Draft version), undated, File. 7, Hansa Mehta Papers, NMML.

[64] Rajkumari Amrit Kaur, Hansa Mehta and Lakshmi Menon signed their names under the Charter in the *Roshni* version, while Kamaladevi Chattopadhyay, Renuka Ray, Kitty Shiva Rao and Hannah Sen appear as authors of the Memorandum.

Report of the Sub-Committee on *Women's Role in Planned Economy*,[65] combining these with the AIWC's mandate for 'equal rights and opportunities'.

The charter's frequent reference to 'rights' revealed the growing influence of a rights-based discourse within the AIWC at this time, a discourse where the claim to rights provided the basis for the Indian woman-citizen to engage with the emerging new nation-state. Drafted at the close of the Second World War, the charter also sought to situate itself within an emerging international arena defined by the United Nations and the terminology of human rights, which it adopted and used. The charter claims the term 'human being' as an inclusive category, and with it, the concepts of equality and inclusion based on the shared claim to 'human rights':

> Whereas we believe that freedom and equality are essential to human developments and whereas woman is as much a human being as man and, therefore, entitled to share with him.
>
> Whereas in a democratic society, no citizen can be denied the fundamental rights which are founded on the basis of human equality.[66]

In addition to being expressions of organisational ideology and gender politics, the charter and memorandum were also working documents drafted as part of the AIWC's strategy to secure the inclusion of its mandate of 'equal rights and opportunities' in the new Indian Constitution and the development of national economic and social policies.

These documents indicated awareness, amongst AIWC leadership, of the necessity of translating the agenda and accumulated efforts of the organisation into an appropriate format, so that these could be effectively channelled into the building of a new State and society.

[65] The Charter Preamble was followed by a section on Fundamental Rights, which reiterated sub-clauses e and f from the Karachi Resolution. Next was a section on Civic Rights. This was followed by an extensive segment on Education, then Health, one on Women and Work, Woman as Homemaker, Woman and Property Rights, Woman and Marriage, Woman's Place in the Family, and finally one on the Duties of Woman. The Charter also contained a section on an equal moral code drawn from the Report of the Sub-Committee on *Women's Role in Planned Economy*.

[66] 'Draft of the Indian Woman's Charter of Rights and Duties', *Roshni*, pp. 12–13.

Abstract principles would require a clear spelling out of the meanings and implications of 'equality' and the process called for active lobbying on part of the women's movement in order to translate these into substantive equality. '[T]ake up the Charter and educate women with regards to their rights and duties,' urged Hansa Mehta in the President's Circular to standing Committee Branch leaders. 'Now that the Indian states are introducing some constitutional changes, women should see that they get the same rights as men. They must bring it to the notice of the conference where political rights are denied to women,' she continued. Once these documents had been ratified at the annual AIWC Conference, they were sent to the interim Indian government and the provincial governments at the end of 1946.[67] They were also translated into Marathi and Gujarati, and circulated to other AIWC branches and members by April 1947, with the instruction that they were to 'be studied and explained to women' and 'given as much publicity as possible'.[68]

While the charter was a statement of principles and values intended to guide the development of the newly independent nation-state, the memorandum laid out the Conference's economic and social policy recommendations for the future government of independent India. This was an ambitious set of recommendations combining Gandhian principles, in terms of its preoccupation with the development of rural industries, holistic education, public health, and service as human capital, with a Nehruvian model of development, through its emphasis on the central coordinating role of the State in policy implementation and service delivery. 'Because the problems in India are many and onerous, a national government alone can successfully and effectively rally the people to the swift and organised action that the Indian situation demands,' its preamble states, but, it adds, this government must simultaneously enjoy 'the fullest cooperation and confidence of the people'.[69]

[67] Hansa Mehta, AIWC President's circular to the Standing Committee, September 1946, File 58, Hansa Mehta Papers, NMML.

[68] Ibid. Vimal Ranadive (Secretary, AIWC Bombay) to Mehta, September 1946, File 58, AIWC Papers, NMML (See Mehta's handwritten notes on this letter); Mehta, Circular to AIWC Branch Representatives and Standing Committee, undated, File 58, AIWC Papers, NMML.

[69] Draft Memorandum, *Roshni*, 1: 5 (June 1946), p. 26.

The memorandum commenced by reiterating the Fundamental Rights of citizens, moving on next to tackle economic policy in a section entitled 'Economic Security'. Here, the influence of socialist principles was evident in the memorandum's call for a system 'governed entirely by the principle of social justice', and the adoption of a 'policy of levelling incomes' through the development of industry, co-operatives, the maximisation of employment and the rebuilding of the rural economy. Universal, free and compulsory basic education, with progressively free nursery and higher education, were demanded together with free adult education. The memorandum's health policy placed emphasis on universal primary healthcare, and the development of medical infrastructure, calling for every citizen to be entitled to medical care, including outreach rural healthcare.[70]

The charter and memorandum reveal an accommodation between the liberal feminism of the abstract 'sexless' citizen, claimed in the Karachi Resolution, with the social feminism underpinning Chattopadhyay's argument for women's participation in the Salt Satyagraha. Within both these documents, rights which ensure equality are counterbalanced against duties and obligations, which allow for a particular gendered and social identity for women as mothers, homemakers, social and community workers, and citizens. These duties and obligations reveal the clear influence of Gandhian thinking on the drafters of these documents. The memorandum offers several examples of how women could fulfil their responsibilities. Firstly, as voluntary workers, assisting in the running of local welfare services, secondly, as described in the section titled 'Woman as Homemaker', through their unique contribution as mothers and homemakers. Thirdly, the charter also stressed that educated women could fulfil their duties by educating their sisters about their civic and personal duties: 'Today our country-women are entirely oblivious of their duties as citizens. Woman as an individual and as a citizen has duties to perform not only to herself and her family but to society of

[70] Draft Memorandum, *Roshni*, p. 32. Drawing from the *Women's Role in Planned Economy* Report, the Memorandum called for the provision of special childcare for women having to go to a hospital and social insurance for the elderly and sick.

which she is a member.'[71] It was through performing these duties in the form of service, work, family and civic participation and education that women were seen to be able to claim their 'rightful place in society', 'by the side of man', and to contribute their 'legitimate share to the general reconstruction of the life of this country'. This accommodation between the social identity of a woman and her civic identity as a sexless citizen did not, however, accommodate a coexistence with other forms of social identities. One of the weaknesses of the 'sexless citizen', as it was interpreted in these documents, lay in the fact that its notion of equality was dependant on a particular type of uniformity.

With regards to the long-standing demand for the reform of personal laws for Indian women, the 1945 charter called for 'legal equality [and] no half measures'[72] and the memorandum emphasised that '[e]very effort should be made' to make such legislation 'applicable to all parts of India'.[73] This uniformity, while claiming neutrality grounded on 'universal' rights and civic identity, in fact, alienated Muslim women through its positioning of Hindu law reform as the norm, revealing a continuation of the trends identified in the Karachi Resolution and the *WRPE:*

> Whereas we believe that woman should have the same rights as man to hold, acquire, inherit and dispose of property; and whereas some of those rights are denied to women or if given are given on an unequal basis; the All-India Women's Conference demand that:
>
> a. The sex disqualification by which Hindu women, in general, have hitherto been precluded from inheriting in various parts of India be removed;
>
> b. Woman shall inherit in her absolute right and the Hindu Woman's limited estate be abolished...[74]

This reflected the legal developments and debates going on within the emerging nation at this moment. Earlier demands articulated in terms of a uniform civil code had now been narrowed down to a

---

[71] Woman's Charter of Rights and Duties, *Roshni*, pp.12–13.

[72] Ibid, pp. 19–25.

[73] Draft Memorandum, *Roshni*, p. 35.

[74] Ibid, p. 22.

more specific focus on certain reforms to Hindu law, as they related to women's position in the family. In this way, the AIWC, through the demands in its charter, became complicit in a process that reinforced the middle-class Hindu woman as the focus and target of legislative and social change, while inadvertently marginalising other communities of women and their needs in this process.

The Karachi Resolution of 1931, the 1939 Report of the Sub-Committee on *Women's Role in Planned Economy* and the 1945 AIWC's *Indian Woman's Charter of Rights and Duties* represented an attempt on the part of Chattopadhyay's generation to rewrite the social contract for a democratic and independent India. These documents demanded entry for Indian women into the male-dominated body politic of the new Republic. They did so by endeavouring to give Indian women a political identity based upon a claim to equal rights and opportunities, and by offering a set of recommendations to facilitate the removal of all socio-economic and legal barriers that prevented their participation in the public sphere on equal terms. But the most revolutionary contribution of these documents lay in their efforts to challenge the theoretically constructed division between public and private. They introduced the egalitarian principles that had been committed to in the public sphere of nationalist politics, into the space of the home economy and the relationships between the sexes, challenging the 'sexual contract' underpinning the social contract of liberal democracy.

These texts clearly signal the emergence of a rights-based discourse as a tool in the struggle for egalitarian politics, revealing the idealistic and ambitious vision of Chattopadhyay's generation. However, they are equally a reflection of some of the theoretical and practical difficulties encountered by this generation, as they sought to speak on behalf of the interests of all Indian women and to develop a working concept of citizenship that accommodated the needs and struggles of diverse communities. They expose the problematic relationship between rights and identity, particularly the 'fixing' of rights to notions of identity grounded on the individual. The difficulty of reconciling 'difference' with equality is evident, particularly in the Indian context where collective identity has continued to remain a dominant feature of politics, and 'where attempts at homogeneity have often been made in the absence of a social consensus between many heterogeneous groups which live here'.[75] Although there were significant points of agreement, the debate surrounding these documents, in particular, the Report of *Women's Role in Planned Economy*, reveals the multiple visions of a new social order held by this generation, and the multiplicity and instability of the subject positions from which they 'spoke'. How could this generation lay claim to a citizenship that incorporated multiple layers of identity, both individual and collective? As the following chapters reveal, this was a challenge that Chattopadhyay and her contemporaries continued to grapple with, in the drafting of the Indian Constitution and the crafting of the new nation-state.

---

[75] Kumar, *The History of Doing*, p. 5.

Chapter 2

Constitution Writing and the Sexless Citizen

When the Indian CA gathered for their first session on 9 December 1946, Hansa Mehta and Rajkumari Amrit Kaur, two of the principal architects of the AIWC *Indian Woman's Charter of Rights and Duties*, were amongst the 210 nationalists, community leaders, businessmen, constructive workers and professionals gathered in the parliamentary buildings of New Delhi.[1] This group of individuals faced the exhilarating yet formidable task of translating the hopes and values of the nationalist movement into concrete principles. Over the course of three years and several drafts, a new Constitution was given form by the Assembly, which also acted as the provisional national government.[2]

This body of representatives included 15 women.[3] Twelve of them were official representatives for the Congress, the remaining three, Shah Nawaz, Shaista Suhrawardy Ikramullah and Aziz Rasul, represented the Muslim League.[4] Austin Granville emphasises that although the

---

[1] At this initial meeting, 210 of the 296 invited members were present. See Constituent Assembly (CA) Debates of India (Procedural), Vol. II, Monday, 20 January 1947, accessed 14 September 2010, available online: http://parliamentofindia.nic.in/ls/debates/vol2p1.htm

[2] The CA operated as the provisional national government of India between August 1947 and January 1950, See A. Granville, *The Indian Constitution: Cornerstone of a Nation* (Oxford University Press, Bombay, 1972), p. xii.

[3] For a list of these women representatives and the regions of India they came from, see B. Shiva Rao et al., *The Framing of India's Constitution: Select Documents* Vol. I (IV), (The Indian Institute of Public Administration, New Delhi, 1966 – 68), pp. 296–297. According to an account by Renuka Ray, there were 14 women in the CA. See Renuka Ray, 'India's First Cabinet Minister' in *Rajkumari Amrit Kaur*, Eminent Parliamentarians monograph series: 15 (New Delhi, 1992), p. 45. It is not clear how many out of the 210 were present at the initial meeting on 9 December.

[4] Shiva Rao et al., *The Framing of India's Constitution: Select Documents* Vol. I (IV), pp. 296–297.

CA was chosen by the Congress, and was essentially a 'one-party assembly', the Congress made an effort to ensure it was representative of the whole country.[5] The Assembly incorporated the voices of 30 Scheduled Caste representatives, five Sikh representatives, six members of the Christian faith, five representatives of the Backward Tribes, three Anglo-Indians, three Parsis and four Muslims.[6] Hansa Mehta was the official representative of the AIWC in the CA. Her name and her affiliation are listed under the subheadings 'Party Leaders' and 'Important Personalities Elected by the Constituent Assembly', suggesting that the AIWC was, by this stage, being seen as an organisation prepared to engage and participate 'officially' within a partisan politics context. Other prominent AIWC members included Vijayalakshmi Pandit, Sarojini Naidu, Renuka Ray and Begum Shah Nawaz. There were also several other women who made a mark on these proceedings, who were not members of the AIWC, such as Sucheta Kripalani who went on to lead one of the earliest opposition parties, the Praja Socialist Party.[7]

Although Mehta, Kaur and their AIWC colleagues constituted only a small percentage of the representatives in the CA, they collaborated closely and consciously. They drew on the Karachi Resolution, the *WRPE* Report and the principles laid out in the AIWC's *Indian Woman's Charter of Rights and Duties* to ensure their voices as advocates for equality were heard. This was not an easy task, nor one that could be taken for granted. As Renuka Ray recalled, 'During those days, the 14 women who were members of the Constituent Assembly met very often'

---

[5] Granville, *The Indian Constitution*, p. 2.

[6] CA Debates (Legislative), Vol. II, no. 1, Monday 20 January 1947, p. 251. In total, 80 representatives of the Muslim League had been selected. However, due to the fact that the League boycotted the Assembly, the actual representation of this group was much lower.

[7] See, for instance, S. Kripalani, *Sucheta: An Unfinished Biography* (Navajivan Publishing House, Ahmedabad, 1978), which offers insight into the life story and political career of Sucheta Kripalani. She initiated the Congress Women's Wing. She was not a member of any specific Indian women's organisation, however, her political engagement reveals an awareness of the importance of the gendered needs of Indian citizens. For example, she plays a leading role in a number of price rise and food security campaigns. As Chief Minister of UP, she established the first factory in India manufacturing intra-uterine contraceptive devices. See Kripalani, *Sucheta*, p. 243.

and, under the guidance of Rajkumari Amrit Kaur, 'put up a united and concrete stand in regard to women's rights'.[8] They did, however, have a number of powerful allies supporting them in their cause, including Congress leader Jawaharlal Nehru and B.R. Ambedkar, Law Minister and Chair of the Constitutional Advisory Committee. For Nehru, who was deeply invested in a modernising agenda for India, the principle of gender equality was a necessary precondition for enabling socio-economic progress, while for Ambedkar the struggle for women's equality formed an important component of the struggle for equality between the castes and the empowerment of untouchables.

The end of British rule and the creation of the Republic was a pivotal moment for Indians, marking the shift from colonial subjecthood to citizenship in the nation-state. The early years of independence were defined by considerable debate over the boundaries, meanings and possibilities of postcolonial citizenship, with various political constituencies, including women's organisations, participating energetically in this process. This chapter focuses on the participation of these women and their allies in this discourse, exploring how the Indian woman as a political citizen, who first emerged through the crafting of earlier nationalist documents, was developed and embedded in the reworked 'social contract' of the new Constitution, and shaped and constrained by the particular national context of the moment.

Rejecting Reservations for Women: the Logic of the Sexless Citizen

Although 75 per cent of the new constitution was drawn from the 1935 Government of India Act, its focus and intention differed completely. While this Act was primarily concerned with maintaining the old colonial order through a measure of power-sharing with the Indian elite and middle classes, the new Constitution was tasked with a social revolution.[9] This, however, had to be balanced with much-needed

---

[8] Ray, 'India's First Cabinet Minister', in *Rajkumari Amrit Kaur*, p. 45.

[9] Granville, *The Indian Constitution*, p. xi.

unity and stability at a time of delicate transition when many interest groups were competing for alternate 'visions' of the nation-state.[10] A democratic federal government with a strong centre was eventually agreed upon as the most viable structure for achieving this.

The Karachi Resolution of 1931 provided the heart of the new Constitution. The Resolution's conception of equality and Congress's commitment to social justice were prominently positioned in the Fundamental Rights section of the Constitution in Article 15, which stated that 'The State shall not discriminate against any citizen on grounds only of religion, race, caste or sex, place of birth or any of them.'[11] Economic citizenship was also acknowledged in Article 39 (a), where the Constitution proclaimed that 'The State shall, in particular, direct its policy towards securing [t]hat all citizens, men and women equally, have the right to an adequate means of livelihood', and (d), which demanded 'equal pay for equal work

[10] Members of the CA were in agreement on the need for radical change in the old colonial order. This desire for change was a point of commonality shared amongst CA members, and articulated as a desire for a 'Social Revolution'. A working definition of Social Revolution and how exactly it was to be put into practice, however, remained contested. Congress itself composed a wide coalition of groups and interests which had to be brought together, and the Constitution sought to advance multiple agendas, which came into tension with each other. For example, social and land reform versus treatment in law and right to property. Furthermore, a significant gap existed between legal and constitutional arrangements, and social practices and norms. See S. Saberwal, 'Introduction' in Z. Hasan (ed.), *India's Living Constitution, Ideas, Practices, Controversies* (Anthem Press, London, 2005), p. 10. Many important debates over the Indian Constitution dealt with the conflict between using legal powers of State to bring about change in social institutions and practices, while simultaneously constraining political authorities to act within the law. See P. Chatterjee, *State and Politics in India* (Oxford University Press, Delhi, 1998), p. 90. For a detailed analysis of the articulation, debate and meanings of social transformation in the Constituent Assembly, see Z. Hasan, E. Sridharan and R. Sudarshan (eds.), *India's Living Constitution: Ideas, Practices, Controversies* (Anthem Press, London, 2005); P. Chatterjee, *State and Politics in India* (Oxford University Press, Delhi, 1998), and S. Sarkar, 'Indian Democracy: The Historical Inheritance' in A. Kohli (ed.), *The Success of India's Democracy* (Cambridge University Press, Cambridge, 2001).

[11] The Constitution of India, 1st Edition (Delhi, 1950), with a detailed commentary by O.P. Aggarwala and S.K. Aiyer, accessed 15 July 2013, available online at https://archive.org/stream/constitutionofin029189mbp#page/n3/mode/2up, p. 28.

for both men and women'.[12] Along with the principles of equality articulated in the Karachi Resolution, the AIWC brought the concept of the 'sexless' citizen developed in the Karachi Resolution, into the CA, as the model for political identity. This, in turn, was to have implications for the way in which this cohort responded to the idea of reservations for women as a political constituency.

This generation of women experienced and perceived particular kinds of social identities as barriers to equality and inclusion in the body politic (see Chapter One). It was not social identities in themselves that were problematic, but rather how they created differences and divisions amongst the political or nationalist community, and were employed as the basis for justifying discriminatory treatment. The appeal of the 'sexless' citizen lay not in denying social identity, but in making India a place where 'caste, creed or sex' would not be recognised as barriers to 'progress'[13] and where 'there should no longer be any sex consciousness or sex separation in the service of the country'.[14]

Whether or not to grant reservations for various minority communities was one of the questions over which there was extensive debate in the CA. It required not only agreement on this matter, but also a consensus on how such minority communities were to be defined and constituted in the first place. In January 1947, the CA appointed an Advisory Committee on Minorities under the Chairmanship of Vallabhbhai Patel to garner opinion on the position and rights of minorities, and consider options for their place in the Constitution. The Committee presented its findings in the Interim Report on Minority Rights, submitted to the CA on 8 August 1947.[15] This report recommended the abolition of separate electorates, but supported reservations of seats for various minorities in

---

[12] Ibid, pp. 61–62.

[13] V.L. Pandit, Speech delivered at the United Nations, 25 October 1946, File 4: Speeches and Writings, Vijayalakshmi Pandit Papers (hereafter V.L. Pandit Papers), 1st Instalment, NMML.

[14] CA Debates (Procedural), Vol. IV, Tuesday 22 July 1947, accessed 15 June 2012, available online: http://parliamentofindia.nic.in/ls/debates/vol4p7.htm

[15] J. Kananaikil, *Scheduled Castes in the Constituent Assembly: Rebirth in a New Nation* (Indian Social Institute, New Delhi, 1982), p. 14.

the legislatures on the basis of their population.[16] The interim report had not, however, considered the implications of granting minority rights in the context of the violence and upheaval unfolding in the Punjab and West Bengal, before and after Partition. Towards the end of 1947, the Advisory Committee appointed a sub-committee to study what was happening in these areas.[17] The communal tension between Hindus, Muslims and Sikhs reflected and inflated by the violence, and the consequent need for cohesion and national unity in the face of these disturbances, led the Advisory Committee to reconsider its position on minority rights for religious communities.

With religion considered a source of extensive division within the nation, the Advisory Committee decided to withdraw its suggestion for reservations for religious minorities.[18] Initially, the Advisory Committee had recommended the removal of reservations for all minority groups. However, representatives of the Scheduled Castes and Sikhs advocated for their continuance.[19] Some minorities such as the Christian community voluntarily relinquished their special rights in the name of national unity and were applauded for what was considered to be a sacrifice; an act that laid faith and trust in the capacity of the State to facilitate a genuine democracy. But the CA also recognised the insecurity and vulnerability of minorities and was prepared to concede in certain cases, by reframing such reservations as safeguards and protections. As Rochana Bajpai argues, this was because the ultimate goal was integration through trust and an environment

---

[16] Ibid. See, for example, the agreement reached by the Minority Committee which was presented in the Report on Minority Rights, CA Debates (Legislative) Vol. V, No. 8, 27 August 1947, p. 213.

[17] Kananaikil, *Scheduled Castes in the Constituent Assembly*, p. 16.

[18] R. Bajpai, 'Recognising Minorities: A Study of Some Aspects of the Constituent Assembly Debates 1946-1949', MPhil Book, Faculty of Social Sciences, University of Oxford, 1997, p. 26. Bajpai has subsequently expanded her MPhil book into a book on this subject matter. See R. Bajpai, *Debating Difference: Group Rights and Liberal Democracy in India* (Oxford University Press, New Delhi, 2011). For further analysis of the development of minority rights as a category in the CA, their conceptual boundaries and how these shift over the course of the CA debates, also see section III: Secularism in S. Tejani, *Indian Secularism: A Social and Intellectual History 1890–1950* (Indiana University Press, Bloomington Indiana, 2008.), pp. 199–297.

[19] Kananaikil, *Scheduled Castes in the Constituent Assembly*, pp. 17–19.

of safety (as was the case with the initial support of reservations for religious minorities) or through assisted development (in the case of Untouchables, Backward and other Scheduled Castes and Tribals).[20] Reservations conceptualised as 'special privileges' or as markers of communal identity were rejected because they were seen to reinforce difference and disunity.

Growing awareness of the communal violence that had accompanied Partition led to a re-evaluation of the implications of reservations for national unity. Yet, Rajkumari Amrit Kaur, Hansa Mehta and the other female CA members remained constant in their strident opposition to women's reservations throughout the course of constitutional negotiating, on the grounds that these undermined the principles of equity and fair play.[21] Hansa Mehta reminded Assembly members that:

> ...we have never asked for privileges. The women's organisation to which I have the honour to belong has never asked for reserved seats, for quotas or for separate electorates. What we have asked for is social justice, economic justice and political justice.[22]

However, Mehta's claim that the 'women's organisation to which I have the honour to belong has never asked for reserved seats, for quotas or for separate electorates' was not entirely accurate. There was no clear consensus amongst women within the AIWC, with regard to the issue of reservations and separate electorates, as Forbes shows. The WIA and the AIWC had changed their position on this issue, moving from initial support for reservations in the first phase of the First Round Table discussions—as an interim measure to enable more women to access political power—to opposition, due to the broader context of the nationalist movement. What led them to alter their position was not a change of mind, but rather a reorientation of priorities.[23] The question of whether to accept or reject reservations for women was linked to the broader strategy deemed to be

[20] Bajpai, 'Recognising Minorities', pp. 27–36.

[21] Ibid.

[22] CA Debates (Procedural), Vol. I, 19 December 1946, accessed 9 September 2010, available online: http://parliamentofindia.nic.in/ls/debates/vol1p9.htm

[23] Forbes provides an account of the Second Campaign for Female Franchise in *Women in Modern India*, pp.107–112.

most effective in the struggle for equality. Were incremental change and political expediency to be favoured over broader long-term ideological vision and solidarity? What was best for women's interests? And who was to define these interests in the first place?

As Wendy Singer explains, separate electorates in the context of the 1937 elections defined women as a constituency, linking them to support within urban areas and to 'specific' women's concerns such as welfare and health. It led to a definition of 'women's interests' as minority interests.[24] In rejecting reservations, this cohort sought to resist the categorisation of women as a minority, and the separation of their interests from the broader body politic, even when they were certainly striving to make women a coherent political constituency. What then happened to groups of women who were minorities themselves? The condemnation of reservations in the CA by AIWC leaders, such as Mehta, further contributed to the alienation of Muslim members, such as Begum Shah Nawaz. The rejection of reservations sought to dismiss the application of paternal citizenship to women as political actors and sought to articulate a sense of political belonging and equality based on the idea of the individual, and of merit and fair play. In this respect, the rejection of reservations offered a way for these women to define a particular kind of equality and inclusion in the new nation-state, one which sought 'invisibility' on the basis of sex difference in order to claim visibility and recognition on the basis of political agency and participation. However, criticism by subsequent scholars, such as Sharmila Rege and Geraldine Forbes, has highlighted how the inability to see the potential benefits of reservations as a channel into power for marginalised groups, such as Muslim women and untouchables, reveals the blinkered vision of this collective even while they claimed to speak on behalf of all.

Claiming the Language of Rights

Building on the *Indian Woman's Charter of Rights and Duties*, an emphasis on rights was one of the defining features of the emergence

---

[24] W. Singer, *'A Constituency Suitable for Ladies': And Other Social Histories of the Indian Elections* (Oxford University Press, New Delhi, 2007), p. 56.

of the Indian woman as a political citizen in these debates. In order to claim belonging to the new political fraternity, Mehta, Kaur and their colleagues in the AIWC drew extensively on the language of rights, and their inheritance of such rights through citizenship. Women's inequality and disempowerment were understood as a denial of rights, as Hansa Mehta explains in her response to the *Resolution on Fundamental Rights* moved by Jawaharlal Nehru during her discussion of the aims and objectives of the Constitution:

> The average woman in this country has suffered now for centuries from inequalities heaped upon her by laws, customs and practices...There are thousands of women today who are denied the[ir] ordinary human rights. They are put behind the purdah, secluded within the four walls of their homes, unable to move freely.[25]

The use of the term 'human rights' was significant here; it facilitated inclusivity, ensuring that women's rights and equality were taken as part of a collective package of rights and statuses that were indivisible.

This rights discourse percolated outwards from the AIWC's Charter, into CA debates, and then back into the organisation's constitution during the early years of independence, influencing the AIWC's subsequent expression of its role and responsibility in relation to the nation-building project. Over the same period of the CA, the AIWC appointed a reorganising committee to consider updating its mandate, strategy and organisational functioning. In response to the recommendations of this committee, the Conference redrafted its constitution.[26] The aims and objectives of the original AIWC constitution had remained unchanged from the time of the Conference's establishment in 1927 to 1951, the year in which the revised constitution first appeared in print in the annual conference report.

The original set of organisational aims and objectives of the Conference were expressed as follows:

---

[25] CA Debates (Procedural), Vol. I, 19 December 1946.

[26] For a detailed discussion concerning the restructuring of the AIWC post-independence, see File 159, AIWC Papers, NMML.

i. To work actively for the general welfare and progress of women and children.
ii. To inculcate in women and children the ideals of true citizenship.
iii. To promote education along right lines.
iv. To work and press for social reform.
v. To strive to establish equal rights and opportunities for all.
vi. To work for a united India.
vii. To set and demand a high moral standard in all departments of life.
viii. To stand for international goodwill and peace.[27]

These were then reformulated and rephrased under the recommendations of the reorganisation committee as follows:

i. To work for a society based on the principles of social justice, personal integrity and equal rights and opportunities for all.
ii. To secure recognition of the inherent right of every human being to work and to the essentials of life, such as food, clothing, housing, education, social amenities and security, in the belief that these should not be determined by accident of birth or sex but planned by social distribution.
iii. To support the claim of every citizen to the right to enjoy basic civil liberties.
iv. To stand against all separatist tendencies and to promote greater national integration and unity.
v. To work actively for the general progress and welfare of women and children and to help women to utilise to the fullest the fundamental rights conferred on them by the Constitution of the Indian Union.
vi. To cooperate with peoples and organisations of the world for the implementation of these principles which alone can assure permanent international amity and world peace.[28]

---

27 AIWC, 17th Annual Conference Report, 7–10 April 1944, Bombay, p. 125.
28 AIWC, 22nd Annual Conference Report, 28–31 January 1951, Bangalore, p. 93.

In the set of reformulated aims and objectives, the terms of 'welfare' and 'social reform' are replaced with the concepts of 'equal rights', 'inherent rights' and 'fundamental rights'. The earlier priority of the Conference had been 'to work actively for the general welfare and progress of women and children' and 'to inculcate in women and children the ideals of true citizenship'.[29] In this revised constitution, the organisation's foremost mandate is 'to work for a society based on the principles of social justice, personal integrity and equal rights and opportunities for all', and 'to secure recognition of the inherent right of every human being to work and to the essentials of life, such as food, clothing, housing, education, social amenities and security, in the belief that these should not be determined by accident of birth or sex but planned by social distribution'.[30]

The new AIWC constitution ensured equality and the removal of untouchability, committed itself to the achievement of socio-economic justice through universal education and the right to work, offered protection from various forms of exploitation, and guaranteed freedom of the press and practice of religion. Perhaps most crucially though, it granted universal adult franchise. This opened up an important avenue for Indian women to speak and act as political citizens. Participation in elections as both voters and candidates was quickly adopted by this generation of women nationalists and feminists as a means of voicing their active citizenship. Women's organisations such as the AIWC and WIA had been demanding the franchise on the same terms as their male colleagues and partners since the first Franchise Campaign of 1917. It could not, however, be taken for granted that Indian women would be able to harness this new tool without education and support.

The Indian Woman as a Voter

The AIWC's 1945 *Indian Woman's Charter of Rights and Duties* had been specifically designed as pedagogical text to supply necessary education and awareness. Teaching women about the importance of claiming their rights and fulfilling their duties as citizens formed part of

---

29 AIWC, 17th Annual Conference Report, p. 125.
30 AIWC, 22nd Annual Conference Report, p. 93.

a broader civic programme promoted by the AIWC during the period of political transition from the mid-1940s. It took on added significance in the face of mounting opposition to the passing of the Hindu Code Bill in the late 1940s and early 1950s.

AIWC circulars and correspondence with branches and amongst its own Executive Body in the late 1940s and 1950s reveal ongoing efforts by the organisation to encourage civic awareness and participation. 'Our association has long been trying to create in us a consciousness of our rights and has, at the present juncture, a special duty to see that now that independence is in sight and political rights are within grasp, our case may not go by default,'[31] wrote Mrs Asoka Gupta,[32] chairperson of the AIWC's newly established Civics Committee, in a circular to its branches in August 1948, outlining the purpose of the AIWC's civic education programme.

The AIWC's approach to voter education was two-pronged. Firstly, to educate its own members and encourage their participation in the upcoming General Elections, and secondly, to then get them to go out into their communities and do the same. This was done at the branch level through running adult literacy and basic education classes. And nationally, by sharing accurate information and encouragement of discussion facilitated by the distribution of circulars from the AIWC Central Office to branches, and through organising meetings across branches and organisations. It was also done through encouraging women to participate in other capacities in these General Elections, not just as voters, but also as enumerators and supervisors in the drafting of the electoral roll and as electoral candidates. '[T]his conference appeals to all women's organisations to mobilise their strength to encourage women to seek representation in local bodies' to 'enable them to participate in the management and direction of local affairs', the Association resolved at its Annual Conference in January 1949.[33] Two

---

[31] Asoka Gupta, Civics Committee Circular, August 1948, File 116, AIWC Papers, NMML.

[32] Gupta was an AIWC leader based in Calcutta. She was a Gandhian who accompanied the Mahatma on his peace missions through violence-ravaged Noakhali in 1946.

[33] Resolutions Passed, 21st Session AIWC Conference Report, Gwalior, 26–29 January 1949, p. 26.

years later in January 1951, it urged 'its branches to encourage qualified women to stand for election and demand that political parties include a fair proportion of women as candidates in the list'.[34]

Activity reports from the AIWC Head Office and branches for the years 1949 – 51, give us a cross section of the different activities engaged in by the Conference to further this agenda. So, for example, the Civics Committee at Head Office had been in communication with authorities at All India Radio, and were, on the recommendations of its branches, forwarding 'a list of women speakers who could give talks' on women's franchise 'in different Indian languages…in simple and easy style', at the hour fixed for women listeners. Equally important was targeting refugee women and those displaced by Partition. The Committee reached out to such communities of women through 'organising talks in different refugee camps regarding their duties as citizens to their new neighbours and the new State', and by corresponding with the Central government for clarification regarding the 'citizenship rights of women migrated to India whose husbands are still in Pakistan, and the citizenship rights of abandoned wives whose husbands cannot be traced'.[35]

Working together with the National Council of Women in India (NCWI), the AIWC Calcutta branch had 'helped to hold a largely attended meeting at the Y.M.C.A. Hall, Calcutta' on women's franchise.[36] The Patna branch in Bihar had been 'devising methods of educating the masses by holding public meetings in mohallas as well as by instructing the constituent branches to make similar efforts in their own area'. The Dhanbad branch, also in Bihar, reported that they had 'organised the women of Dhanbad and held public meetings to arouse civic consciousness of women'.[37]

---

34 Resolutions Passed, 22nd Session AIWC Conference Report, Bangalore, 28–31 January 1951, p. 22.

35 Report of the Civics Section by Mrs Ashoka Gupta in 21st Session AIWC Conference Report, Gwalior, 26–29 January 1949, pp. 34–35.

36 Report of the Civics Department by Smt Ashoka Gupta, Member-in-Charge, 22nd Session AIWC Conference Report, Bangalore, 28–31 January 1951, pp. 50–51.

37 Reports of Work Done by the Branches 1949–51, Bihar, Patna, Dhanbad Branch, in 22nd Session AIWC Conference Report, Bangalore, 28–31 January 1951, pp. 62–63.

One of the new activities introduced by the East Punjab branch included 'Help given in preparing voters list'.[38] The Agra branches in the United Provinces informed the Conference that they had been conducting work 'so that the A.I.W.C. members may contest the forthcoming Municipal elections'.[39] Meanwhile, the Rajasthan branch was tackling another challenge. In this state, women had been enrolled 'as wives, sisters and mothers of some man' and were being refused the right of the franchise in this capacity. The Rajasthan branch was fighting against this restriction.[40]

Although the Rajasthan branch reports that 'they had fought and agitated a great deal' and 'in the end forced the government to recognise women as women and give them the right to vote'.[41] It is unclear whether these women were able to participate at the time of the elections. As Ramachandra Guha explains, conservative social practices in northern India meant that women like these did not want to be registered on the electoral roll under their own names. India's first Chief Election Commissioner Sukumar Sen would not permit this practice, even though it had been allowed in earlier elections.[42] Government officials were instructed to correct the rolls by inserting the names of these women rather than having them registered on the electoral roll under the name of a male relative. This message was conveyed widely through the press, and the government also encouraged local bureaucrats to enlist women workers and enumerators to support such efforts. Nevertheless, 2.8 million eligible women voters did not cooperate, or their husbands did not allow them to, and were struck off the rolls.[43]

---

38 Reports of Work Done by the Branches 1949–51, East Punjab Branch, in 22nd Session AIWC Conference Report, Bangalore, 28–31 January 1951, p. 81.

39 Reports of Work Done by the Branches 1949–51, U.P. Agra Branch, in 22nd Session AIWC Conference Report, Bangalore, 28–31 January 1951, p. 85.

40 Reports of Work Done by the Branches 1949–51, Rajasthan Branch, in 22nd Session AIWC Conference Report, Bangalore, 28–31 January 1951, p. 82.

41 Reports of Work Done by the Branches 1949–51, Rajasthan Branch, in 22nd Session AIWC Conference Report, Bangalore, 28–31 January 1951, p. 82.

42 R. Guha, 'Democracy's Biggest Gamble: India's First Democratic Elections in 1952'. *World Policy Journal* 19: 1 (2002), p. 96; Shani, *How India Became Democratic*, p. 46.

43 Guha, 'Democracy's Biggest Gamble', p. 96.

Getting women correctly registered on the electoral roll was, therefore, an important part of the Civics Committee's work and a prerequisite in enabling women to exercise the right to vote judiciously. 'Special stress was given to get women enrolled for the coming elections,' notes the Civics Committee yearly report presented to members at the AIWC's Annual Conference in January 1949. In addition to its general voter education, the Committee also sought to bring women on board as active participants in the election process by encouraging them to assist as enumerators and supervisors in the formidable task of preparing the electoral roll. The committee reported that since its establishment, it had sought to sign up women volunteers to act as supervisors during the enumeration of voters, while the member-in-charge of the Civics Committee had made contact with 'the officers of government charged with the duty of preparing voters' lists and induced them to employ women enumerators and supervisors so that no eligible woman voter was excluded'. Some progress had been made. By the end of 1948, 'Twelve active women were enrolled as volunteers and appointed on our recommendations as government supervisors for supervising enumeration' in the Calcutta area. They had since 'submitted a report of their work to us and have seen to it that no women's name is omitted in the Calcutta area'. These volunteers had attended 'three group classes' 'by the member-in-charge' of the Civics Committee, before joining government classes to learn about the enrolment process.[44]

Purdah or seclusion as practised by certain Muslim and Hindu communities posed a particular challenge for registering women voters. The AIWC's emphasis on recruiting women enumerators and supervisors reflects an awareness that a female electorate would be more comfortable engaging and talking to other women, especially if this involved contact with a stranger and the disclosure of personal information. It was also grounded on the notion of female solidarity; that women had a duty and a responsibility to other women to ensure that they were registered correctly and could exercise their right to vote.

---

[44] Report of the Civics Section by Mrs Ashoka Gupta, 21st Session AIWC Conference Report, Gwalior, 26–29 January 1949, pp. 34–35.

Ornit Shani argues that the participation of ordinary citizens as village-level enumerators, and the agitation of citizens associations to secure the registration of refugees and displaced persons on the electoral roll, played an important role in turning 'the idea of democratic citizenship into a living practice'. Equally importantly, these acts of engagement and participation helped counter some of the exclusionary forces that the bureaucratisation of the electoral process tended to foster,[45] which, for example, had contributed to the exclusion of the 2.8 million women registered in the name of a male relative rather than in their own names. The AIWC's efforts to educate women about the importance of voting, how to register successfully, their encouragement of women enumerators, their support for the voting rights of women registered under a husband or father in the electoral roll, and their targeting of refugee women and those displaced by Partition in their campaigns, were likewise intended to act as inclusionary forces. The AIWC's Civics Campaign aimed to reach out to communities of women on the margins and bring them into the processes of democracy.

Another aspect of the AIWC Civics Committee's work was to encourage women voters to use their vote strategically, by voting for candidates with progressive views who supported the government's commitment to equality between men and women. 'It is of the utmost importance for women voters to understand for whom she exercises her vote,' an AIWC circular from the period tells us.[46] Branches were asked to contact women voters in their areas and advise them to back candidates 'who accept the principles for which the AIWC has always stood', 'irrespective of their party affiliations'.[47]

In addition to educating women in tactical voting, the AIWC promoted their agenda by reminding political parties of the power women could wield if they withheld their vote. The AIWC lobbied the various political parties in existence to select only men and women candidates:

---

[45] Shani, *How India became Democratic: Citizenship and the Making of the Universal Franchise* (Cambridge University Press, Cambridge, 2017), pp. 16–17, 41.

[46] Presidential Circular (draft version), undated, File 159, AIWC Papers, NMML.

[47] H. Sen, President's Circular Letter No. 6 to the Standing Committee, 22 September 1951, File 159, AIWC Papers, NMML.

> who possess [...] integrity as candidates to the various state legislatures and the House of the People, and who are of progressive views and will support those measures which are in conformity with the fundamental rights as defined in our new Constitution, (such as the Hindu Code Bill) and such other laws.[48]

'The vote of women is a big factor in this election, and I hope you all select such candidates as can inspire voters to exercise their vote in favour of these candidates,' reminded the AIWC acting President in a letter dated 1 November 1951, addressed to the leaders of the Congress party, Socialist party, Communist party, Bhartiya Tara Sangh, Mazdur Kisan Party, Scheduled Caste Federation, Workers and Peasants Party and the Hindu Mahasabha Party. 'Your party should promise to plan out such a sound social structure, where the individual is the unit and is assured of his or her fundamental rights.' In this letter, a copy of the 'demands which women voters will expect the candidates to support' was also included.[49] An additional prong of this programme was to motivate women themselves to get involved in politics by standing as candidates in local, provincial and national elections, and encourage AIWC members to support other women in their campaigns. This position was endorsed in 1951 at an AIWC Standing Committee meeting, where the Conference's President, Hannah Sen, announced that any suitable woman candidate who wished to stand in the elections would receive AIWC support.[50]

---

48 Standing Committee Circular (handwritten), undated, File 159, AIWC Papers, NMML.

49 Hannah Sen to leaders of the Indian political parties, 1 November 1951, File 159, AIWC Papers, NMML. Also see the resolution passed at Sholapur, June 1957, File 322, AIWC Papers, NMML. This resolution, while congratulating women who had been appointed Ministers and Deputy Ministers in the Union and State Ministries, commented on the continued under-representation of women as legislators and the tendency for women in the Union Cabinet and State Cabinets to be restricted to specific portfolios, such as education and health, 'thus denying their talents full opportunity'. The resolution concludes that 'ongoing public opinion is yet to be educated to think that, women should be treated as citizens cable of holding positions of responsibility'.

50 Mukerjee to Sen, 22 October 1951; Sen to Chairman of the Central Parliamentary Election Board, 1 November 1951; Action Committee of the Hindu Code Bill (meeting report), 4 October 1951; 'Vote of Women is a big factor in your Election' (handwritten memorandum), undated, all documents located in File 159, AIWC Papers, NMML.

In rejecting special reservations for women, the AIWC and its leadership had in effect rejected the notion of women as a special constituency. However, the organisation's attempts to rally women together as a voting bloc, to push through legislation such as the Hindu Code Bill, and their encouragement of women to enter electoral politics as candidates, could be interpreted as inconsistent with this initial rejection. This tension can perhaps be explained by the fact that the franchise, while providing a platform for mobilising women, was not seen by the AIWC as an end in itself, but rather a means to another end: a transformed and inclusive society, such as that envisioned in the *Charter of Woman's Rights and Duties*, 'where freedom and equality are essential to human developments' and where 'woman is as much a human being as man'.[51]

Mobilising women voters, with the objective of working towards such a transformed society, where women were part of an inclusive and integrated whole, was an expression of active citizenship. It indicated that AIWC leaders were no longer prepared to view themselves simply as subjects of the State, that they now considered themselves participants in its creation. According to Maxine Molyneux, active citizenship refers to not only the conferral of formal rights on passive subjects but the existence of a relationship that promotes participation and agency.[52] Active citizenship could take different forms, from social activism to party politics and social service, but it was characterised by the conscious engagement of the individual with the State to shape the nature of government and society.

For much of the nineteenth and into the twentieth century, a protectionist discourse dominated the relationship between the Indian woman and the colonial State. This discourse is epitomised in a diagram that Muthulakshmi Reddi used as part of her 1933 Presidential address at the Seventh annual provincial conference of the Andhra AIWC. Her topic was the importance of government intervention in implementing social reform legislation to uplift and protect the populace of India, in

---

51 'Draft of the Indian Women's Charter of Rights and Duties', *Roshni*, pp. 12–13.

52 M. Mukhopadhyay, 'Introduction' in M. Mukhopadhyay and N. Singh (eds.), *Gender Justice, Citizenship and Development* (Zubaan Books, New Delhi, 2007), p. 6.

particular, its women. Set against the *Mother India* controversy, where Indian nationalists and feminists had turned the critical gaze back on the colonial government,[53] Reddi argued that the colonial government had an important responsibility to protect and uplift the Indian populace, which it had wilfully neglected. To illustrate her talk, she used a diagram of 'the functions of the government and how the governmental policy affects the mother in her home and through her, the home, the society and the nation', originally published as a chart in the *Labour Women's Magazine* in England. At the centre of this diagram, in a small circle, is the 'mother in the home'. Radiating outwards from the mother, like spokes of a wheel, are various pieces of legislation, covering the areas of education, employment, civil rights, health and housing. These provide a protective moat separating the 'mother in the home' from the harmful and destructive social, economic and environmental forces of 'Disorder, Disease, Ignorance and Starvation'. This diagram is illustrative of the nineteenth and early twentieth century perspective of legal reform, where legislation operated upon and shielded the vulnerable and passive subject.[54] As voters, and later as social workers administering service, and as protestors demanding services and rehabilitation, the articulation of rights and duties was intended to enable the 'mother in the home' to engage and interact with the State as well as civil society. The emergence of the Indian woman as a political citizen and the close

[53] In 1927, an American journalist called Katherine Mayo drew international attention when she published a book, entitled *Mother India,* on the social conditions of India's women. Evoking dramatic images of widow immolation and trembling child brides, she pointed a finger at 'Hindu culture' as the key perpetrator. *Mother India* created a dilemma for Indian women activists who were both nationalists and feminists because it tore their loyalty between support for the cause of women's upliftment, which led them to agree with a number of criticisms of Indian society made by the book—although not necessarily the way these were presented—and their loyalty to the nationalist movement, which required the complete rejection of the text as illegitimate. One of the ways in which this generation of women activists sought to negotiate this dilemma, as Mrinalini Sinha argues, was to turn the critical gaze back on the colonial government, arguing that the injustices women faced were as much due to the ineptitude of Britain as colonial government, as being due to Indian society itself. See M. Sinha, *Specters of Mother India: The Global Restructuring of an Empire* (Duke University Press, Durham, 2006).

[54] M. Reddi, Presidential address, 4–5 November 1933, File 4, AIWC Papers, NMML.

association between citizenship and rights, as well as citizenship and duty, provided the individual with legislation as a tool to engage with these outer spheres rather than to be acted upon by them.

The Shifting Terminology of Backwardness: An Intersection between Gender and Caste?

The CA debates are striking because of the marked absence of the 'women's question' within them. At a rhetorical level, this absence could be explained by the fact that equality between the sexes, and the persona of the Indian woman as political citizen, had already been accepted as an abstract principle and was, therefore, taken as a given. The dismissal of separate electorates or reservations for women as a political constituency further contributed to this invisibility.

Although the women's question remained largely absent in the CA, this did not mean that women as symbolic markers of identity were invisible. India's relationship with Pakistan, dominated by the narrative of Partition violence, the rape and abduction of Hindu, Muslim and Sikh women, and the urgency of their recovery through the Abducted Persons (Recovery and Restoration) Bill was one of the areas where women became visible in CA debates, but where they were spoken for as victims. They assumed a long established identity as the markers of communal identity and symbols of family honour. In these discussions, paternal citizenship dominated conceptualisations of gender relationships within the community, and between the individual and the State. The visibility of women in this context, therefore, did not guarantee them an independent voice or sense of agency. The Abducted Persons (Recovery and Restoration) Bill was a subject of debate wherein Indian women were highly visible, but their ability to communicate their needs and lived experience remained muted. This was merely a symbolic visibility, which could be counterproductive, or even destructive, to the agenda of securing substantive equality. It could reinforce paternal citizenship for Indian women, void of any emancipatory objective. From this angle, it is possible to understand the logic underpinning identification as the 'sexless citizen'.

The invisibility of the women's question in the CA debates both reflected and facilitated a shift away from the Indian woman and towards caste as a site of State paternalism and for the construction of the progressive and democratic Indian nation-state. It is possible to trace how the terminology of backwardness and disability came to be applied to the position of untouchables, and backward and scheduled castes in these debates. The fact that the label 'backward castes' became a term in its own right, used to define one of the 'legitimate' categories of minorities, is itself significant. This language is evident in the presentation of, and consequent justification for, the Report on Minority Rights and its set of recommendations. This report envisioned the 'creation of a Statutory Commission...to investigate and see what are the real things that are keeping these people 'backward' in all the social, economic and educational spheres...It is up to the majority community to see that justice is done so that these minorities may rise....'[55]

The terminology of backwardness brought with itself a set of metaphors about depression and elevation, unconsciousness and awakening that were evoked in these debates to describe the position of untouchables and other socio-economically backward castes. For example, V.I. Muniswami Pillai, speaking on the occasion of the presentation of the Report on Minority Rights, offered a history of untouchability in India, where he described how:

> ...it was given to Mahatma Gandhi as great Avathar to find the disabilities of a section of the Hindus, namely, depressed classes known by various names, to come to their rescue...It was that Poona Pact to which you yourself have been signatory along with me and Dr Ambedkar, that produced a great awakening in this country.[56]

Backwardness was a term that had its origins in the nineteenth century, and had been claimed and used by Indian nationalists and British colonialists, as well as Indian women reformers and rights campaigners,

---

[55] CA Debates (Legislative), Report on Minority Rights, Vol. V, No. 8, 27 August 1947, p. 218.

[56] Ibid., p. 217.

and their British, European and American sisters in the name of maternal imperialism.[57] In the 1920s and 1930s, the terminology of disability and backwardness was commonly evoked to describe the position of Indian women in society. For example, Mrs P.K. Ray, speaking during the Presidential Address of the Sixth AIWC annual conference in 1931, made regular references to both the 'social disabilities' and the 'legal disabilities' that Indian women faced, and the importance of the 'uplift work' that the AIWC was called to undertake. She commented that the Conference was 'more or less in agreement on the point that we women suffer from many social disabilities and these have to be changed and reformed if we wish to maintain our proper position in the world as Indian women'. By this stage, the language of social disability and backwardness sat side by side with the newer lexicon of rights and citizenship that was becoming increasingly prominent in the discourse of the AIWC. So, while Mrs P. K. Ray emphasised the social and political disabilities of Indian women in this speech, she also spoke about Indian women as future citizens and the preparation that would be required in order to enable them to be proactive. She reminded her audience that besides education, 'There are great many other points we have to think of. There is "the rights and duties of citizenship" of which our boys and girls have no idea, the franchise side of the question from the educational point of view, the political side.'[58]

Discussion around the reform of personal laws especially made reference to the language of disability and backwardness. In the late 1930s, a number of bills concerned with the reform of women's legal status in the family were introduced in the Central Legislative Assembly (which was later dissolved upon independence and taken over by the Constituent Assembly), while in the provincial parliaments anti-dowry bills, marriage laws and legislation to enable women to inherit property were introduced. When G.V. Deshmukh introduced the Hindu Women's Right to Property Bill in the Central Assembly, he advocated for the Bill on the basis that it would remove 'the existing

---

[57] See Mayo, *Mother India* (1927).

[58] See Presidential Address of Mrs P. K Ray, AIWC, 6th Annual Conference Report, 28 December 1931 to 1 January 1932, Madras, pp. 20, 29.

disabilities from which Hindu women suffer'. In fact, the very name of the committee established as a result of this flurry of bills, the 'Committee on the Legal Disabilities of Women',[59] included the term. A decade later, in a renewed debate on the necessity of such a committee, reference to this language was once again invoked by Begum Hamid Ali in AIWC, emphasising that women were 'asking for nothing more than just and humane treatment and to be liberated from their disabilities'.[60]

Although the Indian woman as an economic citizen had emerged clearly by the time of the publication of the *Women's Role in Planned Economy* report, this report, too, makes references to women's 'social backwardness' which continued to keep them enslaved through the 'ignorance and superstition' of 'evil customs'. In this report, the terminology of 'citizenship' and 'equal rights' sits alongside that of social 'backwardness' and 'evil customs' as parallel discourses for envisioning the cause of, and escape from, women's state of oppression.[61]

In contrast, there is surprisingly little evocation in the CA debates of the term 'backwardness' or the conceptualisation of women's status in the home and society as a state of 'disability', as there had been in these other contemporary documents. We see disability being replaced with the term 'discrimination' and consequently, inequality is increasingly framed in terms of rights rather than in terms of disabilities.[62] This shift from disability to discrimination is highly significant. It reveals the emergence of a more active concept of citizenship defined by a rejection of paternal notions of belonging within the civic community.

---

59 'The Hindu Women's Right to Property Act, 1937', File.28/25/38, Judicial 1938, Home Department, quoted in Forbes, *Women in Modern India,* pp. 113–115.

60 AIWC, 14th Annual Conference Report, 26–29 January 1949, Gwalior, quoted in Forbes, *Women in Modern India,* p.116.

61 Shah (ed.), *Women's Role in Planned Economy*', pp. 20, 110.

62 This does not lead to the end of the use of the term 'backwardness' in the discussion on the position of women. Women's welfare and rights organisations and activists, in fact, reclaim the concept of backwardness in the post-independence era, precisely because, as an expression of caste inequality, it gave added weight and leverage to the injustice of gender inequality. 'Backwardness', legal and social disability continued to be used to describe the position of Indian women and to advocate for reform in these spheres. The point that I wish to make in the above observation is that within CA debates, this terminology is largely absent in relation to women's position.

The AIWC laid claim to the franchise to create a role and purpose for its members, both individually and collectively, not just as voters, but also as lobbyists, voter and literacy educators, enumerators and electoral candidates. This was a participatory notion of citizenship, which created a platform for the organisation's members and leadership to begin owning 'the principle of adult franchise, and conceiving of themselves as the protagonists of the story'.[63] Likewise, mobilising women voters to use their vote strategically for the benefit of themselves as a political community in the case of the Hindu Code Bill was an expression of active citizenship. It indicated that AIWC leaders were no longer prepared to view themselves simply as subjects of the State but that they actively sought to engage as participants and builders in its creation.[64]

However, mobilising around the exercise of the franchise exposed tensions and contradictions in the AIWC's conceptualisation of women as electoral citizens. In the AIWC's rejection of special electorates and reservations for women, the abstract sexless citizen divorced from social context and belonging, prominent at Karachi, dominates. This alienated Muslim women within the organisation and those from scheduled castes and scheduled tribes for whom identity politics was a source of strength and assertion.

The priority of crafting a constitution that embodied an egalitarian relationship between the sexes was partly eclipsed in the CA debates by a range of other national concerns. In particular, the need to reconcile minority and majority communities in a cohesive unity was deemed pressing. Identity and the claim to citizenship that was seen to arise from it were approached largely in a siloed and segmented way in the drafting of the Indian Constitution. This inhibited the development of a notion of citizenship able to accommodate a layered and complex identity. This was a blindness that Kaur, Mehta and their AIWC colleagues were susceptible to, in their contribution to these debates. Although they collaborated and worked hard to ensure that

---

[63] Shani, *How India became Democratic*, p. 86.

[64] M. Mukhopadhyay, 'Introduction' in M. Mukhopadhyay and N. Singh (eds.), *Gender Justice, Citizenship and Development* (Kali for Women, New Delhi, 2007), p. 6.

they represented and voiced the needs, struggles and ambitions of all Indian women, they overlooked a potential opportunity to give voice to neglected communities through an acknowledgement of the value of difference.

In their insistence on claiming a liberal notion of the abstract, universal 'sexless' citizen as a way of belonging politically and electorally to the new nation-state, Chattopadhyay's generation equated 'equity and fair play' with indistinguishability. This position stemmed from anxieties about national unity, as well as the past experiences of this generation where their symbolic visibility as women had often reinforced paternal notions of citizenship.

Chapter 3

Citizenship through Service

> The service of India means the service of the millions who suffer. It means the ending of poverty and ignorance and disease and inequality of opportunity. The ambition of the greatest man of our generation has been to wipe every tear from every eye. That may be beyond us, but as long as there are tears and suffering, so long our work will not be over and so we have to labour and to work, and work hard, to give reality to our dreams...[1]

Nehru's midnight hour speech on the eve of independence captured the imagination of Indians across the subcontinent. For AIWC members, it held particular significance. To 'labour' meant to serve in the making of the new nation. While there was little space for a gendered notion of citizenship based on social feminism within the electoral or constitutional sphere, this was not the case when it came to welfare and social development in the new Republic. The provision of welfare and social development through service was a labour of love and an act of sacrifice, but it was equally an expression of citizenship. 'Labouring' through the act of social service was an important mandate for the AIWC in Nehruvian India, providing a way of mobilising the human capital of Indian women as citizens through voluntary action and enabling the organisation to fashion a specific role for itself in the development of a welfare infrastructure and ethos.

Drawing from the Gandhian legacy of constructive work and the rich history of social reform in India, the act of social service offered a way of fulfilling the responsibilities and duties ascribed to the Indian

[1] Excerpt from Jawaharlal Nehru's Speech on the Granting of Independence, 14 August 1947 in B. McArthur (ed.), *Penguin Book of Twentieth Century Speeches* (Penguin, London, 1992), pp. 234–237. Quoted in *Modern History Sourcebook*. Accessed 23 February 2014 at http://www.fordham.edu/halsall/mod/1947nehru1.html [ebook]

woman in AIWC's *Indian Woman's Charter of Rights and Duties.* Furthermore, the organisation was able to use a claim to the labour and expertise of service, to expand and engender the meaning of citizenship in various ways. Its leadership actively embarked on remoulding service through welfare. They aimed to construct a certain identity and role for middle-class Indian women as citizens, and their rural sisters, as well as a specific institutional role for women's organisations as the providers of welfare services, and knowledge and expertise in this field.

A History of Service in India

What exactly did it mean to serve? And what did such service entail? The roots of service can be traced back to the social reform movements of the nineteenth century that created a demand for the provision of welfare institutions, and for social reform activists and workers to administer these services. Social reform was the product of the complex engagement between an emerging Indian nationalism and the British colonial authority. The colonial economy facilitated new agrarian and industrial relations, together with a growing bureaucratic structure. This brought dominant groups together and they eventually emerged as an Indian bourgeois class. Developing under Western control, the new Indian bourgeoisie sought to reform itself through initiating campaigns against caste inequality, untouchability, polytheism, idolatry, animism, as well as purdah, child marriage and sati.[2] The first Indian Social Reform movement was pioneered by the emergence of new societies, such as the Brahmo Samaj initiated by Ram Mohan Roy in Bengal.[3] Central to the movement was also the promotion of education for girls and women.

There were many facets to the Social Reform movement in India. This chapter briefly emphasises two aspects that are relevant to the

---

[2] R. Kumar, *The History of Doing: The Women's Movement in India* (Verso, London, 1994) pp. 7–8.

[3] C. Watt, *Serving the Nation: Cultures of Service, Association and Citizenship* (Oxford University Press, New Delhi, 2005), p. 4. Accessed 18 July 2014, at http://ezproxy.ouls.ox.ac.uk:2058/view/10.1093/acprof:oso/9780195668025.001.0001/acprof-9780195668025 [ebook]

development of service as it came to be practised by later generations of Gandhian nationalists and social workers. The first is that such work brought social reformers out into communities to conduct activities that today would be classified as grassroots welfare. These included the rescue of potential victims of sati, child brides and widows; the establishment of homes for widows, efforts to facilitate their remarriage; propaganda and education programmes with families and local communities against the practices of purdah and child marriage; and the creation and maintenance of schools for girls. In so doing, they began to establish an indigenous welfare infrastructure in India, and imbue the practice of service through welfare activities with particular kinds of meaning and value. This, in turn, facilitated a reconstitution of people's political and cultural identity.

Secondly, the discourse of social reform, like the civilising mission of colonial authority, targeted certain categories of women as sites for intervention and reform. Drawing on Lata Mani's analysis of the debate around sati in nineteenth-century colonial India,[4] we can see how colonial discourse functioned to construct an archetype of the 'Indian woman' and the 'Indian man'. It then defined the dynamics of the relationship between the two in order to claim legitimacy for colonial rule through its moral civilising agenda.[5] The emerging Indian bourgeois class, in turn, challenged this authority through their own reworking of gender identities and relationships. They articulated an alternative, and affirmative, identity for themselves within the context of the Indian Social Reform movement. Colonial discourse was inverted through the argument that their progressive treatment of women reflected their capacity for self-governance. Feminist scholars like Tanika Sarkar and Lata Mani contend that women were positioned

---

[4] See, for example, Mani, *Contentious Traditions*, (University of California Press, Los Angeles, 1998) pp. 88–126.

[5] The British justified colonial rule by arguing that the 'barbaric' treatment of women in India, expressed in practices such as sati and child marriage, was evidence of the 'uncivilised' nature of this society and, therefore, legitimised the civilising mission of colonial rule. Using this discourse, Britain was able to claim a 'moral responsibility' as the 'protector' of Indian women. Gayatri Spivak refers to this as 'white men saving brown women from brown men'. See Spivak, 'Can the Subaltern Speak?', pp. 66–111.

as objects, rather than subjects within this discourse.[6] As Uma Chakravarti argues in 'Whatever Happened to the Vedic Dasi?', this reflected a new kind of restructured patriarchy, one which responded to the changing context, agendas and objectives of nineteenth-century nationalism. This patriarchy could represent themselves as progressive, but they did this by continuing to anchor women firmly within the space of the home and the domestic context.

Social reform might not have had women's empowerment as its primary objective, but this did not inhibit the possibility of women taking advantage of the new opportunities opened to them. Although the movement was initiated by male reformers, by the second half of the century, pioneering women, such as Pandita Ramabai, Anandibai Karve and Parvatibai Athavale, had taken up this cause, thereby becoming outspoken advocates for women's education and social reform. These women introduced social service as a new profession for middle-class and elite women, and played a vital role in shaping social service as a voluntary vocation based on the idea of selfless service and imbued with a particular set of values. They consequently became role models for the later generation of AIWC women who claimed a new mandate of service in the nation-building project.

The close interlinking of the Social Reform movement in India with nineteenth-century nationalism meant that the practice and discourse of social service and welfare became highly political in many ways and could become a powerful expression of political resistance. This interlinking of nationalist and welfare agendas continued to evolve with the proliferation of a range of service and self-help associations in the first two decades of the twentieth century. These were dedicated to education, social service and self-help, and included the Servants of India, founded by Gopal Krishna Gokhale, and the Theosophical

---

6 See, for example, Mani, *Contentious Traditions*; U. Chakravarti, 'Whatever Happened to the Vedic *Dasi*? Orientalism, Nationalism, and a Script for the Past', in K. Sangari and S. Vaid (eds.), *Recasting Women: Essays in Colonial History* (Rutgers University Press, New Jersey, 1999); P. Chatterjee, 'The Nationalist Resolution of the Women's Question', in G. Castle (ed.), *Postcolonial Discourses: An Anthology* (Blackwell, Oxford, 2001), pp. 151–166; T. Sarkar, *Hindu Wife, Hindu Nation: Community, Religion and Cultural Nationalism* (Indiana University Press, Bloomington, 2001)

Society. They enabled a rich associational culture to develop along with the growth of various caste associations. The emergence of Gandhian nationalism in the 1920s built on this existing culture.[7]

At the core of Gandhi's political philosophy of *Hind Swaraj* was the belief that political independence would be meaningless without the social, economic and moral transformation of society. There were two prongs to Gandhi's campaign for *Hind Swaraj*. The first was the strategic use of the technique of Satyagraha. The second was the implementation of his constructive programme, which sought to improve the living standards of India's rural population and enable them to become economically self-sufficient. This called for social upliftment through the integration of Dalits in village communities, improved sanitation, preventative healthcare, as well as education and village economic development through activities, such as spinning cloth, the manufacture of khadi and local craft production. He called nationalist workers to be constructive workers too, by initiating and participating in such rural development programmes.

Constructive work was reliant on outreach into Indian villages and urban slums. For this generation of AIWC activists, it allowed for interaction across class and caste lines, and gave them valuable exposure to contexts of poverty and inequality that were to shape their developmental praxis later on. Furthermore, the delivery of such constructive work, through the act of service, was to continue to command respect. Delivery of social upliftment, like Satyagraha, was an act of service. It was something that one offered, rather than an action performed, making its voluntary nature essential. As an action, it was as much about the transformation of the self as it was about the reform of society. 'Woman is the embodiment of sacrifice and suffering, and her advent to public life should, therefore, result in purifying it,'[8] Gandhi believed. It was these qualities that made Indian women ideal nationalists and constructive workers in his

---

[7] Watt provides further details of the development of this associational culture in the chapter entitled 'Nation-building' in his book *Serving the Nation: Cultures of Service, Association and Citizenship* (Oxford University Press, London, 2005)

[8] 'Position of Women', from Young India, 17 October 1929, in M. Gandhi, *The Collected Works of Mahatma Gandhi*, Vol. XLII (October 1929–February 1930), p. 5.

world view. Social service was essential in facilitating the entry of Indian women into nationalist politics and gave them new roles and opportunities. Yet, it simultaneously reinforced a restrictive, highly gendered and class-based understanding of their role as wives and mothers.[9]

When the AIWC engineered its social service programmes and ethos in the post-independence era, it drew on the rich tradition of service to claim a unique role for itself in the nation-building project. Channelling the impact of service through social work had helped win political freedom. Now, its potential could be tapped in pursuit of a second freedom, that of social and economic emancipation. At the time of independence, the majority of India's population still resided in villages, with rural women constituting over 50 per cent of India's 5,00,000 villages in 1955.[10] This was the 'real' India, according to Mahatma Gandhi; 'Where better can you find yourselves than by being true to the highest traditions of Indian women, by serving your unhappy sisters today,'[11] argued Gandhi when he instructed women to work for rural reconstruction and development within the nationalist struggle. Now that India had won independence, this remained an urgent and valid calling. It was through supplying welfare, health and educational facilities that the AIWC saw itself being able to reach and uplift the rural Indian woman.

This concern with reaching and uplifting the rural Indian woman through service is exemplified by the AIWC's Skippo project. Working to deliver primary healthcare facilities to remote villages in the form of a mobile van, which was equipped with medicines and staffed with a nurse or doctor. The initiative was started in 1946 by Lady Rama Rau of the Bombay AIWC, after Mrs Hilda Seligman of England, a supporter of the Conference, offered 'to present a

---

9 See, for example, Forbes, *Women in Modern* India (Cambridge University Press, Cambridge, 1996); J. Kumari, *Feminism and Nationalism in the Third World* (Verso, London, 1994) and G. Minault (ed.), *The Extended Family: Women and Political Participation in India* (Chanakya Publications, Delhi, 1981)

10 K. Nimbkar, 'Rural Women & Development Work in the Second Plan', 18 July 1955, File 218, AIWC Papers, NMML.

11 M. Kishwar, *Gandhi and Women* (Sage, Delhi, 1986), p. 34.

mobile health van if the AIWC would undertake the responsibility of maintaining and operating it'. The project was officially launched as the 'Asoka Akbar Van' but it quickly became known by the name of its mascot, Skippo, a 'frisky mountain goat', who was a character in Mrs Seligman's children's book of the same name. The profits from the book sales had been used for the purchase of the aforementioned van.[12] As a mountain goat, Skippo was able to climb rugged and inaccessible mountain landscapes, and this was exactly what the Bombay branch of the AIWC hoped to achieve through running this new project, as its motto suggests:

> Social service aiming to spread
> Knowledge of hygiene, children welfare, animal husbandry & rural economy amongst the
> Isolated villages in many lands and with the
> Password:
> Prevention rather than cure, help to
> Overcome the evils arising.
> From
> Under-
> Nourishment, ignorance and
> Dearth[13]

The motto shows the twofold nature of the project. It incorporated a more old-fashioned and paternalistic conception of welfare, as an act of charity and kindness, targeted at vulnerable groups in society for the alleviation of suffering 'from undernourishment, ignorance and dearth', but it was also open to the more progressive possibility of transforming the lives of beneficiaries through knowledge, skills and awareness.

The Bombay branch of the Skippo project chose the village of Talasari, a jungle area inhabited by Adivasi people along the Gujarat coast, 120 kilometres from Bombay, as its base. The van completed a circuit twice weekly around surrounding villages, delivering health services

---

12 Skippo Van Committee, 'Some details of the working of the Mobile Health Vans', undated, File 167, AIWC Papers, NMML.

13 AIWC Skippo Van Committee to H. Seligman (see in particular the Skippo Fund letterhead), 15 September 1951, File 182, AIWC Papers, NMML.

and education. Malaria, eye and skin diseases, and illnesses caused by malnutrition and poor hygiene were treated, and minor operations were performed on the spot. 'On average 5,000 to 6,000 patients' were treated on an annual basis over the first three years, records the 1959 Project Annual Report. The success of the project led to the construction of a small hospital in Talasari village to expand health facilities, then the introduction of a second van in Gujarat, followed by one each in Delhi, Maharashtra and Phaltan in the Deccan.[14] By 1955, eight centres with Skippo vans had been established across Bombay, Delhi, Gujarat, Phaltan, Kodaikanal, Malabar, Karnataka and Hyderabad.[15] These centres expanded their activities to include sanitation and hygiene education, the management of epidemics, and referral in the case of diagnosis of more serious conditions, such as tuberculosis and cancer. By the end of the decade, Skippo operations in Bombay reached 14,366 patients per annum.[16]

Community Development and the Central Social Welfare Board

Constructive engagement with the populace of India's villages was a concern that the AIWC shared with the new Indian government. In fact, reaching and transforming the lives of the villagers was positioned as the ultimate success of the modernising vision of the Nehruvian State. For example, the Bhore Report, commissioned in 1946 to provide a blueprint for healthcare policy after independence, directs the creation of health services 'designed to reach the rural areas specially' with the 'villager' as the 'chief beneficiary'.[17] Winning the support of 'the villager'

[14] 'Some details of the working of the Mobile Health Vans', File 167, AIWC Papers, NMML.

[15] Honorary General Secretary, 'Six-monthly Report January to July 1955', undated, File 206, AIWC Papers, NMML.

[16] 14,366 patients were treated between December 1958 and November 1959. See Central Skippo Committee, 'Annual Report, December 1958 to November 1959', 22 January 1960, File 402, AIWC Papers, NMML.

[17] These statistics were quoted in an AIWC summary of the Bhore report. See Reports in A Nutshell No. 3, 'Report of the Health Survey and Development Committee', 1946, File 56, AIWC Papers, NMML.

for agricultural development is also a recurring theme in India's first Five-Year Plan.[18]

A commitment to social transformation was built into India's new Constitution (1950), which promised poverty elimination, the removal of various forms of social inequality and the raising of living standards.[19] For Nehru, social inequality and the various forms of oppression that it facilitated was rooted in material and economic conditions. Economic empowerment was positioned as the route towards freedom. Poverty, unequal distribution of resources and unemployment had to be tackled through employment generation and income expansion.[20] Democratic governance together with Nehruvian socialism, defined by a mixed economy and a system of centralised development planning, was the model embarked upon for achieving this ambitious agenda.

In order to transform the social and economic life of villagers, the Nehruvian government adopted community development as a 'focal point' for the first Five-Year Plan. An Indo-US Technical Cooperation agreement, together with assistance from the Ford Foundation,[21] enabled the Indian government to embark on this 'rural extension', or 'rural community projects' work as it was known.[22]

The primary aim of this programme was economic and technical advancement; to increase production through improving land use and agricultural practices, and to raise the standard of living. It functioned by grouping villages within a particular geographical area in a cluster, known as a National Extension Service (NES) Block, which then became the gateway for the government's technical interventions and primary

---

18 'Chapter 15: Community Development and Rural Extension', First Five-Year Plan 1951–56, Government of India, p. 15. Accessed 15 July 2012, at http://planningcommission.nic.in/plans/planrel/fiveyr/welcome.html

19 Kasturi, 'Development, Patriarchy, and Politics', p. 6.

20 A. Sengupta, 'Fifty Years of Development Policy in India', in H. Karlekar (ed.), *Independent India the First Fifty Years*, (Oxford University Press, Delhi, 1998), p. 134.

21 C. Watt, 'Philanthropy and Civilising Missions in India 1836–1960: States, NGOs and Development' in Watt, C., and Mann, (eds.), *Civilising Missions in Colonial and Postcolonial Asia: From Improvement to Development*, (Anthem Press, London, 2011). Accessed 28 June 2014, at http://site.ebrary.com/lib/bodleian/docDetail.action?docID=10523546, p. 299.

22 President's Circular Letter No. 11, 2 May 1952, File 159, AIWC Papers, NMML.

services such as health.[23] The Community Development Programme was initiated in October 1952 and underwent rapid expansion.[24] During the period of the first Five-Year Plan (1951 – 56), the foundations of 500 National Extension Blocks and 622 Community Development Blocks, covering a population of 80 million people, were established.[25]

Although the Community Development Programme crafted by the Planning Committee included a social welfare component, the draft of the first Five-Year Plan made no concrete budgetary provision for supporting or developing social welfare activities for vulnerable groups in Indian society.[26] This was despite its 'grand ideology about the protection of the weaker sections, equal opportunities, equality before the law'. A clear gap between the priorities of developmental rhetoric and those of tangible economics is apparent. One of the members of the PC, Durgabai Deshmukh, was outspoken in her criticism of this oversight.

A lawyer in the High Court of Madras with a long-standing career in social welfare and women's literacy, and a member of the small but vocal group of women in India's CA, Deshmukh joined the PC in June 1952, on the invitation of Nehru, as the member in charge of Social Service.[27] Durgabai had played a leading role in the establishment of the Andhra Mahila Sabha, a social welfare organisation which she had helped to found in Madras in 1937. It provided welfare services to women and children, promoted adult education, offered training for auxiliary nurses and midwives and arranged for free legal aid. She was, therefore, well attuned to the difficulties facing many voluntary

---

23 'Annual Report of the Directorate General of Health Services 1958', Department of Health, Government of India (New Delhi, 1959), pp. 70–72.

24 'A Brief Review of the Working of the Community Projects and National Extension Service' (Seminar on Voluntary Agencies and Rural Development), 20–22 April 1956, File 246, AIWC Papers, NMML.

25 Ibid.

26 Durgabai Deshmukh, Interview Transcript 16 (Session I), 5 January 1967, pp. 15–18. In her interview, Deshmukh explains that by 'vulnerable groups' she was not referring to those identifiable as particular pressure groups such as Backward Classes and Tribes who had constitutional safeguards, but she was referring to the disabled, the old and infirm, children, destitute and the delinquent.

27 Social service was a broad category, including housing, labour, education, health and public cooperation and social welfare.

organisations trying to fundraise to maintain their outreach activities, at the time of independence.

India has a history of established voluntary organisations playing a leading role in the delivery of welfare services. The British colonial government claimed the right to rule based on their welfare responsibilities, but these generally did not find expression beyond the limited public utility charity work of the Company State and crown,[28] and the introduction of various pieces of legislative reform, such as the Sati Prevention Act of 1829 and the Child Marriage Restraint Act (Sarda Act) of 1929. The colonial government left welfare work to Christian missionary societies, Indian social reform organisations, such as the Arya Samaj and the Brahmo Samaj, elite Indian women's organisations, and philanthropic societies run by the wives of colonial officials such as the Countess Dufferin Fund.[29] The focus of these organisations tended to be on education, the establishment of the first schools for girls, the provision of primary healthcare, maternity hospitals, the training of lady doctors and the launching of hospices and sanatoriums. Christian missionaries played a crucial role in expanding such facilities to rural areas.[30] The promotion of welfare in colonial India was consequently shaped and driven by the emergence of citizens' institutions, resulting in the implementation of The Societies Registration Act of 1860 to regulate NGO activity.[31]

Political freedom for India, however, brought with it a new ethos and set of values. There was a clear commitment to social transformation that was put into action by the cultivation of a welfare State. The first Five-Year Plan specified that the main objective of such a welfare State was to bring about a 'socialist pattern of society' in which all citizens would have the fullest opportunity for a rich and diverse life for the development of their

---

[28] Watt, 'Philanthropy and Civilising Missions in India', pp. 276–278.

[29] The Countess Dufferin Fund was established by Lady Dufferin to supply medical aid to Indian women. See S. Hodges, 'Towards a History of Reproduction in Modern India' in S. Hodges (ed.), *Reproductive Health in India: History, Politics, Controversies* (Orient Longman, Hyderabad, 2006), p. 6.

[30] See A. Chatterjee, 'NGOs: an Alternative Democracy', in H. Karlekar (ed.), *Independent India: The First Fifty Years* (Oxford University Press, Delhi, 1998), p. 282.

[31] Ibid. This trend continues in the early twentieth century.

full potentialities.'[32] In chapter 36 on Welfare of the first Five-Year Plan, the influence of the Gandhian principle of self-help was evident in the way in which welfare, as the basis of social justice, was framed in the plan as the joint responsibility of communities and the government. This was expressed in terms of devolution of power and the promotion of the idea of people's participation in the development process.[33] Nehru envisioned a central role for volunteerism and service. In practice, however, he wanted this volunteerism to be State-directed and was reluctant to accept existing Indian philanthropic and social organisations for this task, marginalising them in terms of funding and representation on planning initiatives.[34] Durgabai challenged this position, arguing with Nehru and the Finance Minister that the rhetoric of partnership in the Plan would carry little weight if they were left to struggle on their own to fulfil what was, in fact, a constitutional commitment.

To rectify this planning failure, she suggested that the government, instead of struggling to build State welfare institutions from scratch, channel State resources into the voluntary sector for this purpose. This would help fulfil the commitment to a welfare State in a context of limited infrastructure and human capital, and provide such voluntary organisations with much-needed financial support. Projects could be screened and assessed first to ensure their suitability and impact. As the system grew, State grants could then be used to regulate and improve quality welfare services and to professionalise and expand them. Durgabai brought her case before the Finance Minister. At that stage, the financial allocation had already been 'all fixed up', but she argued determinedly and was able to secure Rs 4 crore for the remainder of the first Five-Year Plan.[35]

Durgabai recommended an autonomous and non-statutory board, which came to be known as the Central Social Welfare Board (CSWB), as the mechanism for channelling the funding from the State to voluntary bodies. She insisted that the body be made up of non-officials, individuals

---

[32] Sengupta, 'Fifty Years of Development Policy in India', p. 134.

[33] Buch, 'State Welfare Policy and Women', p. WS-18.

[34] See Watt, 'Philanthropy and Civilising Missions in India', pp. 293–296.

[35] Deshmukh, Interview Transcript 16 (Session I), 5 January 1967, pp. 17–18.

with experience in the voluntary sector, who would be chosen on the basis of merit and past experience. This would ensure efficient delivery, unencumbered by the red tape of bureaucratic procedures and politics.[36] The CSWB began functioning on 13 August 1953 'with a view to directing and promoting welfare programmes throughout the country on a sound and scientific basis, specifically for aiding voluntary welfare organisations to improve, expand their activities and for starting new organisations in places where there are none.'[37] Deshmukh resigned from her position on the PC to take up the Board's Chairpersonship. State-wide boards were also established to assist the Board with its work.

The CSWB demarcated areas known as Welfare Extension Projects within some of the National Extension Blocks of the government's Community Development Programme. It then encouraged voluntary organisations to set up new projects or to expand existing projects within these demarcated areas.[38] The Board also designated areas for urban Welfare Extension Projects, encouraging voluntary organisations to follow suit.

Upon its formation, 'wide publicity' was given through the press, inviting social welfare organisations to send in applications for assistance from the Board.[39] Over the course of the first Five-Year Plan, AIWC branches from across the country applied for and received grants from the CSWB to assist them with their initiatives. 'The branches have started taking keen interest in the activities of the Social Welfare Projects undertaken by the government,'[40] states the AIWC Annual Conference Report in February 1955. By July 1955, the bi-annual Report of the Honorary General Secretary of the AIWC records that a number of branches were receiving aid from the CSWB for the running of various projects, including youth camps within the National

36 Ibid., pp. 19–20.

37 'Item 3 Consideration of the report of the work done by the Board since the last meeting', undated, Account no. 87 (Correspondence), Durgabai Deshmukh papers, NMML.

38 'Central Social Welfare Board Progress Report 1955–1956', Department of Education, Government of India (New Delhi, 1957), p. 10.

39 'Item 3 Consideration of the report of the work done by the Board since the last meeting', undated, Account no. 87, Deshmukh papers, NMML.

40 AIWC, 24th Annual Conference Report, 2–4 February 1955, Phaltan, p. 54.

Extension Blocks and reception homes for vulnerable women.[41] In fact, in an attempt to minimise the administrative work of the various state Welfare Boards, the CSWB tried unsuccessfully to persuade the AIWC Central Office to take on part of the initial screening of projects of local AIWC branches for suitability for welfare grants.[42]

During the course of the second Five-Year plan (1956 – 61), the amount of funding available expanded to Rs 15 crore, followed later by Rs 28 crore, and an additional Rs 3 crore specifically dedicated to child welfare.[43] The AIWC's Annual Conference Report of 1960 gives an indication of the types of projects receiving grants from the CSWB by the end of the decade. An Urban Welfare Extension Project was being run by the branches in Gujarat on CSWB funding, as were sewing classes, a cooperative store, play centre, dispensary and a family planning centre. The Calcutta branch received a small grant to assist with their Skippo van, a primary school and with sewing classes. In West Bengal and Maharashtra, the AIWC branches were also running Urban Welfare Projects with CSWB grants; in Uttar Pradesh, projects dealing with adult education, family planning and women and children's health, and a children's home were supported by the CSWB.[44]

The AIWC in the Implementation of Community Development Initiatives

In the early 1950s, the AIWC aspired to expand its membership base and sustain its public profile in a rapidly changing environment. Although the organisation had maintained a non-partisan stance in politics, many of

---

41 K.C. Shah to President of the Bombay State Social Welfare Board, 8 August 1957, File 318, AIWC Papers, NMML; Honorary General Secretary, 'Six Monthly Report of Activities, January–July 1955', File 206, AIWC Papers, NMML.

42 CSWB to AIWC head office, undated, File 206, AIWC Papers, NMML.

43 The source in which these figures are quoted does not specify when the Rs 28 crore and additional Rs 3 crore for child welfare were given to the Board for distribution. However, it is most likely that these were provided during the course of the third Five-Year Plan (1961 – 66) as this would fit the time period being discussed in the source. See Deshmukh, Interview Transcript 16: Session I, 5 January 1967, p. 22.

44 AIWC, 13th Annual Conference Report, December 1960, Surat, pp. 57–69.

its activities had revolved around nationalist activities in the late colonial era. Now with the nation-building project underway, a reorientation of its programme of work and objectives was called for. Its leadership was eager to bring new communities of women into its fold, but did not have a concrete strategy towards achieving this. Furthermore, older sources of funding that had helped it to launch and build its pre-independence projects were drying up.[45] In this context, working in partnership with the government offered an alternative revenue stream for growth. The CSWB was not an exclusive source of funding for the AIWC, but it was one of a number of streams that bound the organisation and the government together in a cooperative and symbiotic relationship. AIWC branches also received grants from the Department of Health for initiatives, such as the Skippo vans; the Department of Education for literary and education project; and the Ministry of Welfare and the Department of Relief and Rehabilitation for their projects with Partition refugees.

The extent of government dependency on voluntary organisations, such as the AIWC's Skippo vans project, for the implementation of its mandate of social justice, is evident when we look at the budgets of the Department of Health. For the years 1956 – 57 and 1957 – 58, as Table 3.1 below shows, the Union Health Department sanctioned more funding for voluntary organisations, as compared to the state governments, from its departmental budget. Although this table gives only a partial picture, with a number of figures missing, if we take the two states of Bombay and Madras, we can see that in both cases, and over both fiscal years, the amounts sanctioned to voluntary organisations and local bodies came to more than that budgeted amount for state spending on health. Furthermore, in seven out of the 11 states where there are complete figures for the fiscal year 1957 – 58, the amount budgeted for voluntary

45 There is considerable correspondence between AIWC branches and leadership during the 1950s, discussing the importance of expanding and diversifying the membership of the organisation as a means for revitalising the Conference and securing its mandate as a voice for women's interests. See, for example, Assamese Provincial Mahila Samiti Resolutions to the AIWC, which call for the Conference to be revised on a more 'broad-based and democratic basis' and for local Mahila Samitis to become the primary units of the organisation, 1951, File 47, AIWC Papers, NMML.

organisations together with local bodies exceeded the amount given to states like West Bengal, Uttar Pradesh and Andhra Pradesh.

Table 3.1				
	Amount sanctioned during 1956 – 57		Amount sanctioned during 1957 – 58	
States/Union Territories	State Govt	Local Bodies & Voluntary Organisations	State Govt	Local Bodies and Voluntary Organisations
Andhra Pradesh		8,761	90,621	11,630
Assam			91,500	25,696
Bihar			38,442	9,760
Bombay	11,500	5,11,186	71,240	8,39,963
Jammu & Kashmir				
Kerala		3,000		46,386
Madhya Pradesh			7,000	17,000
Madras	14,363	15,713	36,840	38,613
Mysore		22,000	52,908	25,228
Orissa	17,000			
Punjab		15,000	71,367	87,513
Rajasthan			1,55,180	13,089
Uttar Pradesh		9,515	600	1,48,127
West Bengal		19,484	70,597	1,98,119
Delhi	15,000	2,000		1,40,892
Himachal Pradesh				
Manipur				7,750
Tripura				
Total	**57,863**	**6,06,659**	**6,86,295**	**16,09,766**

Table 3.1: Indian National Health Department budget allocation comparing amounts given to state governments versus local bodies and voluntary organisations for the years 1956 – 57 and 1957 – 58. Taken from the *Annual Report of the Directorate General of Health Services* 1957 (New Delhi), p. 224.

The Welfare Extension Projects, therefore, became sites of interaction between the State and voluntary organisations, such as the AIWC. This fostered a collaborative relationship between the AIWC and the Indian government, managed via the CSWB. One of the consequences of this was the blurring of boundaries between civil society and the State. Over the course of 1955 and 1956, the AIWC Delhi branch began 'supervising the work of the Delhi state Welfare Board's Welfare Extension Project work' in 20 villages in the Shahdara district,[46] while in 1959, 300 Welfare Extension Projects that had been run under the auspices of the CSWB were taken over by the AIWC.[47]

Such a dynamic initiative could also work in the opposite direction. The AIWC could provide innovative and best practice models, which the State was prepared to assume responsibility for, expand and replicate elsewhere, once they had been piloted by local AIWC branches. Mrs Dhage, a member of the Hyderabad branch of the AIWC, explained in an informal meeting between her branch and the Standing Committee of the AIWC in 1952: she talks about how 'she had started a small clinic for polio-stricken patients, and that the government, having been suitably impressed by the need of proper treatment of these patients, had agreed to take over the clinic and run it on a larger scale. It was now running satisfactorily.'[48]

In return for their support in the providing of welfare services, the CSWB provided an opportunity for women's organisations, such as the AIWC, to enter the structures and institutions of the State at a local level, as agents of development. The CSWB gave only partial grants for new or expanded projects, which had to be matched by the fundraising efforts of local voluntary organisations. There were complaints about the limited size of these grants and their administration, from local and regional AIWC offices. Never the less, this partnership gave the organisation prestige and visibility, and consequently a degree of leverage and influence within the government. The AIWC used

[46] AIWC, 26th Annual Conference Report, 24–28 December 1956, Indore, p. 29.

[47] 'Annual Report of the Directorate General of Health Services 1958', p. 236.

[48] 'Report of the Informal Discussion Held on the 7 February 1952', Hyderabad, File 159, AIWC Papers, NMML.

its status in the Welfare Extension Projects and its relationship with the CSWB to push for more formal recognition and influence in the planning process. After the launch of the first Five-Year Plan, the President of the AIWC wrote to the Chairperson of the PC requesting that, as 'the premier women's organisation in India, with some 300 branches and sub-branches scattered throughout the country', the organisation be given the opportunity to collaborate with the PC 'in framing and implementing schemes for the welfare of women and children.'[49] Although the AIWC did have some level of influence on the PC's Panel on Social Welfare, there was a general consensus that women's organisations and representatives had not been adequately consulted in the preparation of first Five-Year Plan.[50] Three years later, with a number of Welfare Extension Projects underway, the AIWC was able to approach the government once more with greater confidence on this matter:

> The women's organisations in India now feel that the time has come for a more accurate assessment of women's participation and cooperation in such national activities as are intended to be developed through the various extension services and community projects. Moreover, there is a definite feeling that the participation of women's organisations would endow these policies with a realistic approach as they are constantly engaged in fieldwork.[51]

In this memorandum, the AIWC requested the formation of, and representation on, a government-appointed consultative panel of women who would advise on 'the formulation of policy with regard to the problems of training of workers, coordination of various women's activities and allied matters.'[52] They asked, in addition, that the second Five-Year Plan 'lay greater emphasis on the representatives of women,

---

49 Ibid.

50 Nimbkar, 'Rural Women & Development Work in the Second Plan', 18 July 1955, File 159, AIWC Papers, NMML.

51 AIWC to the Chairman of the Planning Commission, 'Memorandum on ways to secure full and effective cooperation with the Planning Commission', 7 March 1955, File 215, AIWC Papers, NMML.

52 'Welfare Extension Projects under Second Five-Year Plan', undated, File 215, AIWC Papers, NMML.

and allocation of responsibilities to them in all villages, panchayats and other local developmental agencies.'[53] By the time of the drafting of the third Five-Year Plan at the close of the 1950s, the AIWC was demanding not only a greater role in shaping welfare policy but greater authority in terms of implementation. 'For voluntary workers, public work is no longer a hobby. They are no longer content with a merely advisory function. They want to share in the responsibility for planning as also for execution of a plan.'[54] In its correspondence with the government and the PC, the AIWC drew on its expertise and contribution in the field to request State recognition as an official provider of training to those conducting social welfare activities.[55] This included fellow social workers and village-level workers. The AIWC were laying claim to an institutional role as producers and guardians of knowledge and expertise.[56]

Welfare created an important sense of agency for middle-class women, endowing them with a purpose and unique role. Service through social work, or social welfare, accommodated the gendered citizen in a capacity that the formal political sphere did not. In the latter, the emphasis was on achieving equality through equal treatment and opportunity, signalling the rise of the Indian woman as the 'sexless citizen'. In the area of social service, however, duty accommodated and celebrated gendered

---

53 Ibid.

54 'Draft third Year Plan for Social Welfare', 24 March 1955, File 192, AIWC Papers, NMML.

55 D. Deshmukh to V.T. Krishnamachari (Deputy Chairman, PC), 'Welfare Extension Projects under Second Five-Year Plan', AIWC Papers, File 215. In this memorandum, the AIWC requests that the government 'recognise the AIWC as being accredited to provide training in social service'. See also 'Draft third Year Plan for Social Welfare', File 192, AIWC Papers, NMML.

56 The AIWC also sought to use the networks of the Central Social Welfare Board, its State Boards and Welfare Extension Projects to expand its own membership. See, for example, correspondence between R. Saran (AIWC President) and AIWC Standing Committee Members, in which she suggests that the organisation 'establish branches 'where our welfare extension projects are already functioning', 10 March 1959, File 192, AIWC Papers, NMML; correspondence between R. Kaur, A. Chand (Chairman of the State Social Advisory Board in Himachal Pradesh) and I. Maydeo (Hon. General Secretary of the AIWC) discussing the AIWC Executive Committee's request to establish a branch in Himachal Pradesh, 9 January 1955 and 20 January 1955, File 323, AIWC Papers, NMML.

difference.[57] Social service allowed AIWC activists to exercise a new kind of citizenship for themselves, while reaching, and remaking the identity of, the 'rural Indian woman.' 'Social education' formed a key component within these welfare projects. The CSWB progress report for the years 1955 – 57 lay down a pilot model for carrying out such education through teaching and demonstration centres, where village women would be educated in domestic science, basic child development and nutrition. These were to draw inspiration from traditional Gram Sevika structures and be staffed by 'voluntary women' of the 'highest standards of public service and public morality'. A lower rung of paid women workers would be employed in addition, but only 'under the guidance and supervision' of these 'honorary non-official women'.

This system of 'social education' was dependent on reproducing traditional gender and class roles, which defined women primarily as mothers, wives, carers and homemakers, and rural and working class Indian women as the beneficiaries of various services. It also suggested an element of class bias through its moral or social policing.[58] Evident in this particular model is the way in which the provision of welfare services became a means of grooming and teaching Indian women how to be good citizens through the pursuit of certain kinds of domesticity and consumerism.

The practice and philosophy of social work promoted by the AIWC had an inherent class and caste element. It was dependant on the availability of a vast network of middle-class Indian women able to volunteer to serve poor and lower middle-class women and their families. Such an approach excluded and ignored the potential contribution of women who worked full time outside of the home, whether they were professional or working class. It also reinforced the undervaluing of 'caring', traditionally female labour, through its assumption that women should be willing to contribute this labour on a voluntary basis, without compensation, to the nation-building project. In this respect, this was a policy that went against the recommendations of the *Report on Women's Role in Planned Economy*.

---

[57] Kishwar, *Gandhi and Women*, p. 34.

[58] 'Central Social Welfare Board Progress Report 1955–56', pp. 10–14.

As Carey Watt's work has emphasised, social service was not inherently progressive or liberating for the beneficiaries or the parties involved, despite its close associations with Indian nationalism. Educated elite and middle-class social service associations could reinforce Brahminical values and hierarchies through their practices. Their focus on the upliftment of the 'depressed classes' could also impose upper-caste notions of civility, propriety and hierarchy on these classes while trying to 'uplift' them.[59] Was agency for this class of women, therefore, being created by the denial of agency for various categories of peasant and working-class women? Was it reproducing, on a national scale, the earlier dynamics of maternal imperialism? This was the criticism expressed by the Communist party against the Community Development Programme and the AIWC's collaboration in its welfare component. The Communist Party of India (CPI), equally eager to reach the 'toiling masses', argued that the American development aid being used to implement the Community Development Programme was driving its real agenda. This was, they suggested, not rural development but the placation of the peasantry without real agrarian transformation, particularly in the wake of the Tebhaga and Telengana struggles and contemporary worker unrest.[60] According to CPI documents, community projects focused on technology, improved seeds, fertilisers, irrigation and roads, as well as community 'welfare', but did not include any agrarian land reforms to rectify the existing inequalities that were the root cause of poverty and social backwardness.[61] Welfare was viewed as a means to appease and maintain the status quo rather than to empower. The true beneficiaries of such rural agricultural development, the Party claimed, were the landowners and not the landless tenants or small shopkeepers.[62] For communist women, therefore, the AIWC's partnership with the government in the implementation of the welfare

---

59 Watt, *Serving the Nation*, p. 10, 14.

60 'Our Tasks among the Peasant Masses', April 1954, File 1954/23, Communist Party of India Papers (hereafter CPI), Joshi Archives.

61 'The Problem and The Plan–On Paper', undated, File 1953/ 47, CPI Papers, Joshi Archives.

62 'A Strategic Project: Economic disruption and Not Development', undated, File 1953/48, CPI Papers, Joshi Archives.

component of the Community Development Programme indicated a clear alignment with the Congress party government.

Interestingly enough, women's organisations such as the AIWC, drew on the mandate of social welfare precisely in order to claim the opposite; that service offered autonomy and space outside of the State and party politics, beyond the competitive and self-interested motives that this generation believed had come to dominate this sphere. Social welfare, as a concept, was utilised by the AIWC in the same way that 'development' and 'national planning' came to be used by the Nehruvian State. As Partha Chatterjee proposes, these terms were vested with a sense of neutrality and objectivity, and in so doing, provided a supposedly impartial platform for nation-building beyond the reach of vested interest groups.[63]

A recurring theme amongst this generation of women activists was the positioning of service in opposition to politics, each inhabiting its own sphere of interests and values. The government was perceived to have become corrupted by personal power struggles, political alliances and loyalties; these were dynamics that delayed and obstructed social progress. Social service, however, drawing on its Gandhian roots, was perceived to be able to distance itself from these kinds of agendas. 'There is no competition in doing service,' stressed Dr Sarojini Varadappan, a veteran member of the AIWC, while discussing the merits of social work as a career. These sentiments were articulated in similar terms by Mrs Ranade, another AIWC veteran based in Pune, 'There are people who are naturally attracted to politics and here [in the AIWC] we want people who are ready to sacrifice that honour and whatever you get by entering politics.'[64]

Framing their agenda in terms of social welfare enabled the AIWC to claim a space beyond the reach of religious differences and electoral politics, and to maintain their official position of political and religious neutrality. But what about gendered and class biases? Did service become its own brand of politics, an internalised form of maternal

---

[63] See P. Chatterjee, 'Development Planning and the Indian State' in Z. Hasan (ed.), *Politics and the State in India* (Sage India, New Delhi, 2000)

[64] Interview with S. Ranade, AIWC veteran and member, 6 January 2012, Kolkata.

imperialism? And did the AIWC's collaboration with the CSWB lead to its co option into the State and the embracing of patriarchal values, which framed women as passive beneficiaries and dependants in need of State protection?

Social service through welfare did indeed become its own brand of politics through its use as a means to access State resources, influence and power. However, to define it merely as a remoulded form of maternal imperialism is far too simplistic an understanding of the way in which it created new civic identities for Indian women. The Welfare Extension Projects were one of many different expressions of citizenship through service. In particular contexts, they took on a more conservative dimension or interpretation, but there were other expressions of service through social welfare with radical potential. These had a developmental agenda, concerned with bringing into being the constitutional vision of social justice and inclusion. They revealed the potential to evolve and, through their services, aimed to transform not only their voluntary members but also their beneficiaries, and to reconfigure a more active and engaged role for civil society within the new Indian government. The final section of this chapter introduces two other examples of philanthropic institution-building by AIWC branches and leaders. These exemplify the complex ways in which citizenship through service enabled this generation to create a unique sense of 'belonging' in the nation-building project, while maintaining a distinctive identity as a conduit between the State and civil society, between the Indian traditions of service and self-help, and between those of science, technology and international human rights.

The Madras Cancer Institute and the National Council of Child Welfare

In India, the inheritance of an untransformed civil service, ill-equipped for democratic and developmental governance, is recognised as one of the factors that have inhibited the complete transition from colonial Raj to social democracy. Its institutions continued to function as a means for reinforcing inequalities, rather than as mechanisms for the implementation of radical social and political change.[65] There is however a counter-narrative to the one of staid colonial institutional inheritance. The late 1940s and 1950s saw a proliferation of new institutions founded and developed by social workers and nationalists that continue to remain present in the landscape of community development today. Many of the founders and board members of such voluntary organisations also held formal positions within the government bureaucracy. For example, Rajkumari Amrit Kaur, the Minister of Health and Executive member of the AIWC, sat on and chaired the committees of the TB Association of India, the Indian Red Cross and the St. John's Ambulance, while Rameshwari Nehru, Honorary Director of the Women's Section of the Relief and Rehabilitation Ministry, was also a committee member of the Association for Moral and Social Hygiene. As the midwives of independence, Deshmukh and her contemporaries had the unprecedented opportunity to put their ideas and visions into practice. They were able to experiment and test new models of welfare work when they took up various leadership positions within the government and private sector. These institutions were built on existing associational cultures and older traditions of service, while through their focus on local community and rural development and their 'claimed' quasi-autonomous positioning, they continued to bear the mark of a Gandhian nationalist project. In so doing, they presented a picture of a Nehruvian India that departed from the established narrative of the centralised, modernising State. Many of these institutions also represented something innovative in their capacity to bridge the traditions of Gandhian nationalism with the priorities of a scientific and rational system of economic planning. As the driving force and energy behind the CSWB, Deshmukh exemplified the way in which personality and personal vision often shaped such institutions and the policies they advocated.

The Cancer Institute of Madras provides an example of another institution that continues to bear the imprint of its advocate and founder, Dr Muthulakshmi Reddi. As a doctor, cancer treatment and prevention

---

[65] P. Chatterjee, *Wages of Freedom: Fifty Years of the Indian Nation-State* (Oxford University Press, Delhi, 1998), p. 194.

was a professional area of interest for Reddi, but she had a personal connection with the disease too. In 1923, her younger sister tragically died of misdiagnosed and mistreated cancer. This became an important cause for Reddi, which she took up together with her AIWC colleagues in Madras after independence in 1947.[66] Although a doctor by training, Reddi was also a social reformer and grassroots community worker and, like Durgabai Deshmukh, was orientated towards practical action. The Madras Cancer Institute reflected this pragmatism by creating an environment for the application of healthcare for the benefit of ordinary Indians. Initially, the focus of the Institute was on treatment and public education to encourage early diagnosis. However, as Reddi continued to fundraise and build the Institute, it was able to develop into both a treatment centre and a leading cancer research institute.

The National Council of Child Welfare (NCCW) provides an interesting case study of how localised, shorter-term, more traditional relief efforts initiated by AIWC members could provide a starting point for the growth of a national organisation with a much longer-term vision and agenda. The All India Save the Children Committee and the Indian National Committee of the United Nations Appeal for Children two of the NCCW's parent organisations,[67] were both born out of emergency. The former was set up in 1943 by Vijayalakshmi Pandit to raise funds for the establishment of children's homes after the Bengal Famine.[68] The Indian National Committee of the United Nations Appeal for Children was established in 1948, with Rajkumari Amrit Kaur as its President and Hannah Sen as its Honorary Secretary, to provide 'relief from distress' for children affected by the upheaval of Partition.[69]

---

[66] V. Shanta, 'A Good Samaritan' in A. Basu (ed.), *The Pathfinder: Dr. Muthulakshmi Reddi* (Pune, AIWC, 1986), p. 57.

[67] The third parent organisation was the Indian Council of Child Welfare (ICCW). See P. Guha, 'An Outstanding Personality – Rajkumari Amrit Kaur' in *Rajkumari Amrit Kaur*, Eminent parliamentarians monograph series:15, p.70.

[68] Ibid., p. 69; Lady Rama Rau was the President of this Committee, while other AIWC members involved included Rameshwari Nehru, Shyam Kumari Khan, Maitrayee Bose, Urmila Mehta, Hansa Mehta, Avabai Wadia and Kamaladevi Chattopadhyay.

[69] Hannah Sen (Honorary Secretary of the United Nations Appeal for Children, Indian National Committee), 6 October 1948, File 114, AIWC Papers, NMML.

At the time of the establishment of the Indian National Committee of the United Nations Appeal for Children in the late 1940s, the language of rights was encouraging a new methodology of child welfare amongst some AIWC members and leaders. These rights were not only those regarding the material necessities of life, but also rights to physical and psychological safety and well-being, and the right 'to develop their full personality...,'[70] as emphasised in the AIWC's *Indian Woman's Charter of Rights and Duties*. In December 1952, the AIWC hosted the International Study Conference on Child Welfare in Bombay.[71] This was also the year the Women's Conference printed its reformulated Constitution, including in its aims and objectives a commitment 'to work actively for the general progress and welfare of women and children and to help utilise to the fullest the fundamental rights conferred on them by the Constitution of the Indian Union.'[72] The founding of the NCCW in 1952, with the objective of facilitating 'the total well-being of the child' by 'providing adequate opportunities for growth, development and social participation, and protection against neglect, exploitation and the consequences of poverty and social injustice'[73] was another expression of this shift in thinking.[74]

The NCCW was established by the AIWC, in cooperation with other voluntary organisations, as a national coordinating body. Its creation was intended to encourage collaboration between government and civil society in the advancement of policy on child development and infrastructure. It was equally an attempt to respond to 'lack of proper direction, trained personnel and adequate financial resources' faced by the Union and state governments in their efforts to address child welfare needs.[75] Rajkumari Amrit Kaur was elected the first Honorary General President of the NCCW and was succeeded by Tara Ali Baig,

---

70 'Indian Women's Charter of Rights and Duties', *Roshni*, p. 12.

71 See AIWC correspondence in File 159, AIWC Papers, NMML.

72 'All India Women's Conference' (promotional brochure), undated, File 259, AIWC Papers, NMML.

73 Ibid.

74 'Plan for a National Child Welfare Centre', undated, Rameshwari Nehru Papers (hereafter R/N), Subject File 5, Rameshwari Nehru Papers (hereafter R/N), NMML.

75 'Indian Council for Child Welfare Memorandum: Presented to the Planning Commission', 9 July 1952, Subject File 5, R/N Papers, NMML.

another AIWC Committee member. The NCCW played a key role in pioneering innovative and progressive models of child development. This was especially apparent in their work on the education of tribal children and the reform of children's institutions in the capital city of Delhi.[76] Through its efforts to foster research and data collection on child welfare issues, and its piloting of new models of childcare, it assisted in the passage of the 1961 Model Children's Bill.[77]

Organisations, such as the NCCW and the Cancer Institute of Madras, straddled an unclear space between State and civil society. They were often dependent on networks of voluntary workers but simultaneously linked to the State through streams of funding, the private sector through philanthropic fundraising and support, and the sphere of international development. This is illustrated by the early financial history of the Madras Cancer Institute. When it was initially launched in 1951 as the WIA's Cancer Relief fund,[78] the Institute drew on both private philanthropy, including the voluntary efforts of bands of AIWC social workers, and municipal support in the form of a land grant and finances. From these efforts 'a small charity hospital of nine beds', was opened on 1 June 1954.[79] From its inception, the Institute was woven into the historical fabric of the AIWC itself. Therefore, when the foundation stone for the new hospital was laid in June 1952 after the government of Madras donated a piece of land for a building, the AIWC chose to celebrate this event as part of its own Silver Jubilee Anniversary celebrations.[80]

The project was at first dismissed by government officials as prohibitive in terms of cost, particularly in the context of India's limited resources, technology and medical skills.[81] However, one of the characteristics of this generation of women activists was that they were incredibly well connected with each other, and to various networks within the civil society and the new government. They could,

---

76 'Indian Council for Child Welfare Report', 1961, File 148, AIWC Papers, NMML.

77 'Indian Council for Child Welfare Memorandum', Subject File 5, R/N Papers, NMML.

78 AIWC, 22nd Annual Conference Report, p. 75.

79 AIWC, 24th Annual Conference Report, p. 73; Shanta, 'A Good Samaritan', p. 57.

80 AIWC, 22nd Annual Conference Report, p. 75.

81 Shanta, 'A Good Samaritan', p. 57.

therefore, use their extensive social networks and personal influence to raise the necessary funding and other resources to get such institutions off the ground. Sarojini Varadappan, a colleague of Reddi's in the Madras WIA,[82] recalled her remarkable perseverance in this regard, '[t]he way she collected funds was an art in itself. She never hesitated to approach anyone for the good cause.'[83] Consequently, Reddi managed to get most of the major pieces of equipment needed by the Institute donated through gifts of international philanthropy.[84] A complex web of connections then, at the centre of which were AIWC leaders, such as Reddi, Tara Ali Baig, Hannah Sen and Rajkumari Amrit Kaur, linked these institutions to both State and international networks of development funding. In the 1950s and 1960s, the NCCW benefitted from a number of UNICEF and WHO[85] grants, which it used to develop its maternal and child welfare programmes and services. Such connections facilitated not only the exchange of resources but also skills and ideas, giving these institutions respectable standing among the Indian government and the public.

The 'welfare model' promoted by the Madras Cancer Institute, the Skippo van project and the NCCW also challenged the accepted picture of the Nehruvian State as the key provider of services. These institutions demonstrate how the private sector, in fact, was taking the lead in fulfilling the State's constitutional mandate of socio-economic justice. When the Cancer Institute of Madras opened in 1954, the hospital responded to an immediate need. 'Within days of opening, we were flooded with patients. All of them poor,' recalled the hospital's first medical officer.[86] The Institute began as a small project, with only nine beds but there was scope for some of these other institutions to develop

---

82 The Madras WIA was also a branch of the AIWC.

83 S.Varadappan, 'Lamp of Dedication' in Basu (ed.), *The Pathfinder: Dr Muthulakshmi Reddi*, p. 30.

84 Shanta, 'A Good Samaritan', p. 58.

85 Rajkumari Amrit Kaur was well-recognised and respected in the international health community, having been elected President of the WHO in 1950. Her connections to the AIWC, NCCW and WHO are likely to have helped facilitate the funding relationship that developed between the WHO and Indian government in the 1950s and 1960s.

86 Shanta, 'A Good Samaritan', p. 56.

significant reach. By the end of the decade, the Skippo van project in Bombay alone was reaching 14,366 patients per annum.[87] With vans operating in eight different locations by this stage, the project had the potential to reach more than 1,00,000 patients per annum.

Shifting from political to social citizenship, this chapter analyses the collaborative relationship that develops between the AIWC and the Indian government's CSWB in the delivery of social services within India's Community Development Programme in the 1950s and 1960s. It argues that this collaborative relationship was something new; illustrative of the adaptive capacity of this pre-independence women's organisation to combine the Gandhian traditions of self-help, voluntarism and village-centred development with rational economic planning, and in so doing to remould nationalist notions of service through the framework of Nehruvian development. The result was to expand and engender the meaning of citizenship for middle-class Indian women in particular ways and to carve out a unique role for women's organisations as the gatekeepers of welfare services and as producers of expertise in this field in independent India. It argues furthermore, that this relationship was one of the numerous kinds of public-private partnerships, institutions and policy-making bodies, often pioneered by women's organisations, such as the Cancer Institute of Madras, the National Council of Child Welfare and the Family Planning Association of India, which encourage a re-orientation of the State-centric historiography of nation-building. These shift the focus onto civil society as the agent of change and social justice, and present an alternate picture of Nehruvian India as far more open and fluid to both civil society and the influence of international development.

---

[87] See Central Skippo Committee, 'Annual Report, December 1958 to November 1959', 22 January 1960, File 402, AIWC Papers, NMML.

Chapter 4

The Reluctant Citizen: India's 'Doubtful and Resisting' Women

'I definitely know of a girl from Lahore who wishes to remain permanently in the home of her abducting husband and who has found happiness with him,' wrote AIWC member Shyam Kumari Khan to AIWC President Hannah Sen in September 1951.[1] Khan was critiquing the Indian government's recovery of Hindu, Sikh and Muslim women abducted by the 'other' community during the violence and upheaval that accompanied the India-Pakistan Partition on 15 August 1947. Both countries agreed that the State had an obligation to rescue abducted women and restore them to their families and that the mass conversions and forced unions that frequently accompanied such abduction would not be recognised. To facilitate this objective, several bilateral agreements were signed between the two powers, including the Liaquat-Nehru Pact of 8 April 1950 to which Khan's letter refers to. Although primarily concerned with guaranteeing the citizenship rights of minorities, the safe passage of refugees and the protection of refugee property, the Pact included a clause on abducted women, which reinforced the link between abduction and forced conversion and union across religious lines.[2] Appraising both the substance and spirit of this clause, Khan illustrated in her letter how its blanket application could result in further personal hardship for the very women it sought to protect, violating basic principles of individual

[1] Khan to H. Sen (AIWC President), 26 September 1951, File no 147, AIWC Papers, NMML.

[2] Clause C4 of the Liaquat-Nehru Pact stated that forced conversions and unions across religious lines would not be recognised. Any conversion effected during a period of communal disturbance was to be deemed a forced conversion, and those found guilty of forcible conversion were to face punishment.

freedom and self-expression. This girl, Khan tells us, chose to remain behind in Lahore 'with a Pakistani doctor and has borne a son to him.'

> [A]fter being forcibly brought to India by the Police and Recovery officers...[she] has made it clear to me that someday—whenever she is free to go back she will go to Lahore and allow her baby to go back to his natural father...I have been informed by various officers of the Law that in case she makes any attempt at the moment to go back she will be arrested...I am now helping her to find an independent career for herself as she refuses blankly to get married here... This case has brought to my mind the question of a woman's inherent right to decide her own future. This right should definitely be considered.[3]

Creating 'Order Out of That Chaos of Human Sorrow'

The forging of a political identity for the Indian nation-state and the shift from colonial subject to citizen emerges out of a cauldron of energy that is both creative and destructive. While Khan's colleagues in the CA negotiated the making of the Indian woman as an autonomous political citizen, the social upheaval created by the geopolitical restructuring of Partition constrained such citizens from coming into being. Partition ignited wide-scale communal violence along the fault lines of Bengal, the Punjab and the Sindh, resulting in death and severe physical and psychological trauma. 'Millions were thrown out of their homes and all standards of civilised life were violated,' a 1952 Ministry of Rehabilitation report, detailing the State's relief efforts, tells us in its opening sentences, 'Children were torn away from their parents and thousands of women lost the security of their home and hearth.'[4]

The official government report into these events, *Stern Reckoning: A Survey of Events Leading Up To and Following Partition of India*

[3] Khan to H. Sen (AIWC President), 26 September 1951, File no 147, AIWC Papers, NMML.

[4] 'A Report on the Care and Maintenance of Unattached Women and Children, the Aged and the Infirm', (Ministry of Rehabilitation), 1952, Report 1, R/N Papers, NMML.

by G.D. Khosla, placed the loss of life to both warring communities at between 2,00,000 and 2,50,000 people.[5] Other estimates, such as those quoted by Menon and Bhasin, double this figure, estimating a death toll of between 5,00,000 and 10,00,000.[6] The nature of the violence was heavily gendered; rape and abduction were employed to mark women as the sites of community identity and honour. Public debate and State responses to the plight of women who were victims of communal violence, abduction or displacement reveals the ongoing tension over female identity. The tension between the autonomous women as political citizens versus the Indian woman as a social being under communal and patriarchal influence is clear.

Driven by fear and uncertainty, waves of migrants and refugees crossed the borders into the newly created countries of India and Pakistan like a 'sea of Humanity',[7] dramatically altering the demographic profile of the Punjab and Bengal regions. With the Punjab now divided, an estimated four-and-a-half million Hindus and Sikhs moved from West Punjab and Sindh into the eastern areas that became a part of India and an estimated five-and-a-half million Muslims moved in the opposite direction to their new homeland of Pakistan. In East Bengal, Hindus who found themselves on the wrong side of the border began migrating into West Bengal, Assam and Tripura. By the end of 1956, a total of 3.33 million refugees had moved from East Pakistan into these regions of India.[8] Often traumatised and terror-stricken, 'they arrived, half-dead, weary, and footsore and as a result of their experience, needed psychological treatment'.[9]

---

5 G.D. Khosla, *Stern Reckoning: A Survey of Events Leading Upto and Following Partition of India* (Oxford University Press, Delhi, 1989), pp. 298–299.

6 R. Menon and K. Bhasin, *Borders and Boundaries: Women in India's Partition* (Rutgers University Press, New Jersey, 2007), p. 35.

7 'A Report on the Care and Maintenance of Unattached Women and Children', Report 1, R/N Papers, NMML

8 For a comprehensive account of pre- and post-Partition politics in West Bengal, and the rehabilitation of Bengali refugees, see J. Chatterjee, *The Spoils of Partition: Bengal and India: 1947-1967* (Cambridge University Press, Cambridge, 2007). See also Chapter 9, 'And still they come' in Ray, *My Reminiscences* (Stree, 2005) pp. 152–170.

9 Ray, *My Reminiscences*, p. 152.

Responding to this crisis, the Congress appointed a Central Relief Committee with Sucheta Kripalani as its Secretary. Meanwhile, a United Council for Relief and Welfare was established under the chairmanship of Lady Mountbatten.[10] At a national level, the government formed a Ministry of Relief and Rehabilitation under the ministership of Gopalaswami Ayyangar. State-level ministries were also installed in affected areas, such as West Bengal and East Punjab. Working together with voluntary associations, women's organisations and student groups, these government departments launched wide-scale relief efforts. Large refugee camps, such as Dhubulia and Chandmari in West Bengal, and Kingsway and Purana Qila in New Delhi, were set up to house those displaced. These coordinating bodies worked together to provide shelter, food, clothing and blankets, manage issues of sanitation, prevent the outbreak of diseases and ensure the maintenance of law and order.[11] In addition, provision of schooling for refugee children had to be organised.

Longer-term rehabilitation required the resettlement of refugees through the building of new urban settlements, such as Chandigarh in West Punjab and Faridabad in Haryana, and relocation onto agricultural land, which was most successful in the Punjab.[12] Loans had to be provided so that refugees could start new businesses or purchase land and property. In addition, the States of India and Pakistan were tasked with managing the compensation of property for those who had fled their homes and businesses, often with the intention of returning later.

Rehabilitation of the displaced was essential to the nation-building project, presenting an image of a 'civilised state' with the authority and power to restore both legal and moral order:

---

[10] 'A Report on the Care and Maintenance of Unattached Women and Children', Report 1, R/N Papers, NMML.

[11] Cholera, in particular, was a concern frequently accompanying the development of refugee settlements.

[12] Ray emphasised that the context of refugees differed considerably between Punjab and West Bengal. See Ray, *My Reminiscences*, pp. 152–170.

> When the first onrush of lone women and children came, there was no agency in the country which could meet the menacing situation. But the country and people soon rose to the occasion. The government went all out to meet the demands of food, clothing and shelter; whereas voluntary workers all over the country organised themselves to supplement the efforts of official machinery. The[y] assisted in the reception and care of the people in the relief and transit camps and helped to create order out of that chaos of human sorrow and suffering.[13]

Relief and rehabilitation become an expression of State duty and responsibility towards its citizens. In addition, it was necessary for the construction of the productive citizen, who was independent and able to contribute economically to the nation-building project.

The Rescue and Recovery of Abducted Women

An important component of the Indian government's relief and rehabilitation programme included the identification and location of women who had been, or were feared to have been, abducted during the upheaval of Partition, and their restoration to their natal or conjugal families. During the course of the violence proceeding 15 August 1947, 'tens of thousands of women were kept in the "other" country, as permanent hostages, captives or forced wives', while their families migrated.[14] In the aftermath, the governments of both India and Pakistan were inundated with complaints by relatives of missing women, attempting to locate them through government, military or voluntary effort.[15] Abducted and dislocated women also wrote to the Indian government themselves requesting assistance.[16]

The divided Punjab was the main site of such abductions. The Sindh, Delhi Province, Bahawalpur state, the Indian states and

---

13 'A Report on the Care and Maintenance of Unattached Women and Children', Report 1, R/N Papers, NMML.

14 Y. Khan, *The Great Partition: The Making of India and Pakistan* (Yale University Press, New Haven, 2007), p. 135.

15 Menon and Bhasin, *Borders and Boundaries*, p. 67.

16 See S. Purushotham, 'Sovereignty, Violence, and the Making of the Postcolonial State in India 1946–1952', PhD Book, Faculty of History, Cambridge University, 2013.

Jammu and Kashmir also witnessed incidents.[17] Abductions and forced conversions formed part of a broader spectrum of violence that included acts of rape, murder and mutilation. When the matter was discussed in the CA on 15 December 1949, it was stated that 33,000 Hindu and Sikh women had been abducted by Muslims, and 50,000 Muslim women were abducted by Hindu and Sikh men'.[18] 'The important question of recovery of abducted girls from both the dominions of India and Pakistan was agitating the public mind from the very beginning after Partition,' records a Ministry of Relief and Rehabilitation Report from 1949.[19] In fact, the provisional Indian government had begun to put measures in place to deal with such activities prior to Partition when violence flared in the Punjab in March 1947.

After Partition, a series of meetings and bilateral agreements[20] between the governments of India and Pakistan culminated in the passing of an ordinance in November 1948 between Pakistan and India, laying out terms for rescue and recovery, and a year later the Abducted Persons (Recovery and Restoration) Act (1949) was passed in India.[21] The government of Pakistan passed a similar piece of legislation to guide recovery work in its own country. No official agreement was reached between India and Pakistan regarding the management of abducted women in East Bengal. Here, recovery work was managed

[17] R. Nehru, 'Recovery of Abducted Women Up to 15th July 1948', (Women's Section, Ministry of Relief and Rehabilitation) undated, Report 3, R/N Papers, NMML.

[18] V. Das, 'National Honour and Practical Kinship: Of Unwanted Women and Children' in *Critical Events: An Anthropological Perspective on Contemporary India* (Oxford University Press, Delhi, 1996), p. 59.

[19] 'Recovery of Abducted Women Up to 15th July 1948', Report 3, R/N Papers, NMML.

[20] According to the first inter-dominion agreement of 3 September 1947, and the 6 December 1947 agreement, forced conversions were not to be recognised. This position was also taken in the November 1948 ordinances, issues by both countries, the 1949 Abducted Persons (Recovery and Restoration) Act and the Liaquat-Nehru Pact of the 8 April 1950. See R. Menon and K. Bhasin, 'Recovery Rupture, Resistance: Indian State and Abduction of Women during Partition', *EPW*, 28:17 (1993), p. WS4.

[21] This Act was extended up until 1955 when the Abducted Persons (Recovery and Restoration) Continuance Bill (1955) was passed.

in an informal capacity by Mridula Sarabhai, head of the Indian government's rescue operations.[22]

A whole apparatus of institutions developed to implement this rescue and recovery work. This included search bureaus managed by the Search Services Organisation, local police and government officials, teams of social workers, transit and reception camps for recovered women and an Indo-Pakistan tribunal to adjudicate disputed cases.[23] These various processes were overseen by the Central Recovery Organisation (CRO), headed by Mridula Sarabhai. Operations were complicated and of a delicate nature, dependant on co-operation between the two dominions in an atmosphere of mutual tension and mistrust. Initial recovery was carried out by joint teams of police, social workers and rescue officials. However, both countries agreed by the end of December 1947 that 'recovery would now rest on the country where the abductions had taken place'.[24] This meant that each dominion was responsible for the recovery of the 'others'' women and children. In Pakistan, local police and social workers tracked down Hindu and Sikh women and children who they suspected had been abducted, and then handed them over to Indian officials stationed in the country, while in India local police and social workers were responsible for tracking down and recovering Muslim women and children who were suspected victims of abduction.

On the Indian side, rescue and recovery operations were coordinated through the 'Women's Section' of the Ministry of Relief and Rehabilitation, with Sarabhai appointed as the Chief India Organiser, and Rameshwari Nehru, as its Honorary Director. The Women's Section was responsible for the management and rehabilitation of a number of categories of vulnerable women and children, including those who had been separated from their families, and women and children left

---

[22] 'Arrangements for Care of Recovered Persons in Camps and Homes', 29 September 1953, File no R/Govt/4–1953, Mridula Sarabhai Papers (hereafter M/S Papers) available on microfilm, NMML.

[23] In the early stages of the operations, the Military Evacuation Organisation (MEO), the Office of the Deputy High Commissioner, the Chief Liaison officer and the Organisation for the Recovery of Abducted women were responsible for managing rescue and recovery in the Punjab.

[24] K. Patel, *Torn from the Roots: A Partition Memoir*. Translated by Uma Randeria. (Women Unlimited, New Delhi, 2006), p. xxi.

without guardians, and widows. The Section worked to locate families and relatives, coordinated vocational training and managed long-term institutional care. In 1950, the Central Recovery Organisation was established under the directorship of Mridula Sarabhai to coordinate all recovery activities. This structure was moved from the Ministry of Relief and Rehabilitation and placed under the charge of Ministry of External Affairs.

Local search service bureaus under the Search Services Organisation were set up in affected areas like East Punjab, especially near refugee camps, to liaise with communities and facilitate the reporting of missing persons.[25] Through this liaison process, lists of missing Hindu and Sikh women were compiled and then handed over to the Pakistani government for further investigation. Once a woman had been recovered, she would be placed in a transit camp, normally in the country in which she had been found, and then transported across the border to a reception camp where she would be reunited with her relatives, or await her future fate. Between December 1947 and August 1955, as a result of such rescue and recovery efforts, 9,032 Hindu and Sikh women and children were recovered from the Pakistani regions of Punjab, North Eastern Frontier, Baluchistan and Jammu and Kashmir, while 20,728 Muslim women were recovered from the Indian regions of the Punjab, Patiala, East Punjab, Rajasthan and Jammu and Kashmir.[26]

Fear or Rebellion? The 'Doubtful and Resisting' of India's Abducted Women

Those involved in the rescue and recovery operations found themselves in particular difficulty when the supposed victims they had sought to rescue and restore to their families resisted their attempts. Women countered State-sanctioned narratives of kidnapping, violence and coercion with alternative narratives of choice, freedom or resignation.

---

[25] Das, 'National Honour and Practical Kinship', p. 67.

[26] See Appendix II: Number of women and children recovered from Pakistan and India (December 1947–August 1955) in Menon and Bhasin, *Borders and Boundaries*, pp. 264–267.

Such individuals were referred to in official reports as 'doubtful and resisting' women. Their resistance took a number of forms and was motivated by a range of factors. Some women refused to change out of the clothes they were wearing when they were recovered. Others tried to escape from the camps or threatened suicide.[27] Both Rameshwari Nehru and Mridula Sarabhai mention reports of Muslim women in Ambala going on a hunger strike to resist being forcibly returned to Pakistan, in their correspondence.[28] Rescue officials were quick to dismiss this resistance as illegitimate. A Ministry brief from 1948, with the sub-heading 'Problem of Doubtful and Resisting Women', reports incidents of rescued women who 'resent being taken out of their present surroundings and stage violent demonstrations when they are brought to the transit camps'. But it goes on to conclude that 'experience has shown that the resentment and stubbornness on the part of these women' is due to fear of their future and of public opinion, doubts concerning how they will be received by their original families and a 'sense of shame on having lost their honour'.[29]

The tension between the Indian woman as the autonomous political citizen versus her as a social being and site for the reworking of communal and patriarchal identities was brought to the fore in cases of these 'doubtful and resisting' women. This chapter focuses on the case study of Kumari Khan's girl from Lahore, a Hindu or Sikh woman who chose to remain in Pakistan and marry a Muslim husband, and her counterpart Nissa, also known by her Indian alias of Shanti of Alwar, a resisting Muslim woman recovered in Rajasthan and claimed by Pakistan, who appears in Mridula Sarabhai's correspondence. These examples highlight the tension between the two versions of the Indian woman and expose the ambiguous and unsettled relationship between women and the new Indian nation-state. The stories of these two women go against the grain of the metanarrative of victimisation, coercion and violation, underpinning the Indian State's legitimacy as

---

27 Ibid., p.97.

28 R. Nehru, 'Memorandum on Recovery of Women: Review of the position since October 1948–June 1949', Report no 1, R/N Papers, NMML.

29 'Memorandum on Recovery of Abducted Women Up to 15th July 1948', Report 3, R/N Papers, NMML.

protector and guardian. This chapter traces the impact of the Abducted Persons (Recovery and Restoration) Act of 1949, and the surrounding institutions and culture of recovery work, on the life trajectory of these two women. It explores the complex ways in which law and ideas of justice were co-opted in the remaking of postcolonial patriarchy and demonstrates the limitations of the principles of law, and the 'liberal citizen' for a politics of substantive equality. The differing responses of Mridula Sarabhai and Rameshwari Nehru, who both played leading roles in recovery operations, as they attempted to reconcile their roles as State bureaucrats with their feminist principles, will also prove revealing.

The Indian State would have taken an interest in Nissa and Khan's girl from Lahore for different reasons. In the case of the latter, because the girl's relatives were Hindu or Sikh and because they had settled in India after Partition, this young woman would have been classified as a citizen of India, belonging within the fold of the Indian nation-state. On these grounds, she would have been claimed by India, as one of the thousands of 'Sitas' in need of rescue and recovery to restore 'dignity' to both the Hindu family and the nation-state. According to the bilateral agreement signed between India and Pakistan on 6 December 1947, and Clause C4 of the Nehru-Liaquat Pact, her marriage and status as wife a to a Muslim man in Pakistan would have held no legal weight, and her child would have also been considered illegitimate. On this basis, she would have been recovered from Lahore by Pakistani rescue officials under the Pakistani side of the bilateral agreement. After this, she would have been handed into the custody of Indian social workers and officials in Lahore, who would have brought her and her son to Allahabad in the United Provinces. Assuming her family and relatives were located, she appears to have made the decision not to return to them. She did not want to remarry but sought independence, and this is most probably how she came into contact with Khan, who was the General Secretary of the Allahabad branch of the All India Save the Children Committee.

Given that Nissa had grown up in a Muslim family, who had relocated to Pakistan, the Indian government's interest in her case stemmed from a concern with policing the 'purity' of the 'Hindu' nation by restoring her to her 'authentic' Muslim family in Pakistan. Nissa's identification as a Muslim and the settlement of her family in Pakistan, together with the fact she was living as a Hindu woman in India, would have defined her, according to the Abducted Persons (Recovery and Restoration) Act of India, as an abducted person:

> … 'abducted person' means a male child under the age of sixteen years or a female of whatever age who is, or immediately before the first day of March, 1947, was a Muslim and who, on or after that day and before the first day of January 1949, has become separated from his or her family and is found to be living with or under the control of any other individual or family, and in the latter case includes a child born to any such female after said date.[30]

Under the terms of this Act, Nissa would have been recovered, forcibly if necessary, and placed in a transit camp in India with other recovered Muslim women, under the control of Pakistani social workers, while she awaited the necessary arrangements to be made for her transportation across the border and reunification with her family.

Although the Abducted Persons (Recovery and Restoration) Act of India referred to Muslim women abducted by Hindus and Sikhs in India,[31] Menon and Bhasin argue that in the public and parliamentary discourse that accompanied the recovery operations in India, Hindu and Sikh women in Pakistan were the 'real subjects' of the Act. Only 'token concessions' were made 'regarding moral lapses on the part of the Indian people'. In these narratives, the violation of Hindu and Sikh women is by default always committed by the 'other', or the 'other community', with Muslim men as the perpetrators and the Hindu husband, father or son as the legitimate guardian and protector. 'The terms within which the debates were conducted reveal individual as

---

[30] Appendix I Abducted Persons (Recovery and Restoration) Act 1949 (Act No. LXV of 1949) in Menon and Bhasin, *Borders and Boundaries*, p. 261.

[31] The rescue of Hindu and Sikh women in Pakistan was beyond the jurisdiction of the Indian state and, therefore, had to be facilitated through the Pakistani side of bilateral agreements and its own national legislation. The Abducted Persons (Recovery and Restoration) Act of 1949 did, however, provide for the placement of Hindu and Sikh women in Indian-run camps in Pakistan and their restoration and rehabilitation from this point onwards.

well as commonly-held biases that make it clear that the communal dimension was never lost sight of.'[32]

As Khan's letter referred to at the beginning of this chapter implies, the young woman she befriended in Allahabad who had been rescued from Lahore had been recovered against her will, as were many other recorded cases of Hindu and Sikh women in Pakistan. Her resistance had not been acknowledged by the mechanics of rescue and recovery. Perhaps at the time of these events, she did not speak out, and her resistance was only registered after these events, once she found herself in India. Even if she had spoken out at the time, it is unlikely that her objections would have been regarded. According to the bilateral agreement of 6 December 1947, abducted women were to be recovered regardless of their will.

The 1949 Abducted Persons (Recovery and Restoration) Act of India attempted to make provision in cases of resistance by constituting an Indo-Pakistani tribunal to adjudicate on such cases. It was under these terms of the Act that Nissa's story came to be registered. According to a CRO circular, from the start of recovery work up until 30 November 1949, 1,464 disputed cases were registered out of a total of 18,729 cases of recovered women from India and Pakistan.[33] They were only a minority of the total number of rescued and recovered women, but at 7.8 per cent they were not an insignificant minority, both numerically and symbolically sounding a 'discordant note' in the official narrative of successful rehabilitation and the subsequent nation-building story.

The resistance of Khan's girl from Lahore and Nissa or Shanti of Alwar endowed their narratives with specific identities that

[32] Menon and Bhasin, *Borders and Boundaries*, p. 92–93.

[33] The total number of persons recovered in India up to 30 November 1949 was recorded as 12,478, while those recovered from Pakistan came to 6,251, making a total of 18,729. Of this number, 252 cases were disputed in Pakistan and 1,212 in India, making a total of 1,464 disputed cases. These figures were taken from 'Recovery of Abducted Persons Tribunal and its Problems', (Central Recovery Office), 5 December 1949, R/Govt 15 1948-54, R/M Papers (on microfilm), NMML. Not all disputed cases would have involved resisting women. Cases could also have been disputed if there were different family members and relatives vying for guardianship of the woman or if the abductor filed a case against the rescue and recovery operations.

distinguished them from the thousands of faceless and nameless statistics of rescue and recovery, bringing their personalities and their stories into the archives.[34] But these were also conflictual identities, exposing the latent contradictions inherent in the Indian State's categorisation of 'legitimate' and 'illegitimate' citizens. The dual identity of Nissa or Shanti of Alwar illustrates this contradiction. For both India and Pakistan, it was ideologically necessary for her to be Nissa. But through her resistance to recovery, and her wish to remain with her current family in the city of Alwar in India, she claimed Shanti as her authentic identity. Shanti means peace in Hindi. Had her new name and identity possibly been part of a conscious choice to remake a fresh life, rather than being imposed through an act of coercion and violation? Grounded in the absoluteness and righteousness of recovery as an act of restoring the Hindu nation, the 1949 Act, despite the introduction of special measures such as the Indo-Pakistani tribunal, could not conceive of such a possibility.

The Abducted Persons (Recovery and Restoration) Act (1949)

When the Abducted Persons (Recovery and Restoration) Bill was introduced into the Indian Lok Sabha in December 1949, it was met with significant opposition. Opponents criticised the indiscriminate powers given to local police and rescue officials, which were easily open to abuse, and highlighted the loopholes in the Bill's definition of an abducted person, condemning the Bill for its failure to take into consideration the will of the woman involved. Gopalaswami Ayyangar, Minister of Relief and Rehabilitation, who introduced the Bill, was

[34] Here I wish to clarify that I am not necessarily defining resistance as a conscious act of agency on the part of these women, however, I am using a broader interpretation of the act of resistance as a means of imagining subjectivity for them as historical characters. Agency can take many forms, from consent, to transgression and subversion. I agree with Janaki Nair that there is a need to redefine agency in feminist historiography, to acknowledge the complexity and particular historical situated-ness of its construction. See J. Nair, 'On the Question of Agency in Indian Feminist Historiography', *Gender and History*, 6:1 (April 1994), pp. 83, 87.

cautious in his response to this last point of criticism. He was not prepared to include in the Bill a mechanism to ensure that 'no unwilling woman was forced to return to her country.' 'Despite the urging of some members', he 'simply gave a verbal assurance that no compulsion or coercion would be used', claiming that 'he had never come across such a case of women being pushed to go back against her will'. This cleverly allowed the Minister to counter this criticism and claim adherence to liberal democratic practices, without having these securely inscribed into the law. The Act was passed ultimately with no amendments.[35]

The particular definition of an abducted person according to the Act, and the policy of enforced rescue and recovery for those fitting the category, regardless of the will of the individual involved, meant that Act and the rescue and recovery operation facilitating its implementation could misidentify cases of abduction. They could even coerce those who fitted the definition, regardless of their actual circumstances and background, into recovery. Both Nissa and Khan's girl from Lahore appear to have become victims of such coercion.

Khan's girl from Lahore would have grown up in a Hindu or Sikh family in the cosmopolitan city of Lahore. Her family and relatives are likely to have been one of the many groups of refugees who fled the city when communal riots and violence broke out in March, April and July of 1947 or during the 'August Anarchy.' Alternatively, they might have been part of a smaller number of migrants who chose to leave their homes and businesses, either on a temporary or permanent basis, to resettle in India. The circumstances under which this particular young woman got left behind, or chose to stay in Lahore, remain unknown, as do the exact circumstances of her marriage to the Pakistani doctor. Hers might have been a genuine case of abduction, but even if this was so, the circumstances of abduction could vary widely.[36] *Stern Reckoning* records many incidents of women being kidnapped while hiding or trying to escape their homes during communal riots and violence. The arduous forced migrations that were central to the experience of Partition for so many families were also often

[35] Menon and Bhasin, *Borders and Boundaries*, pp. 105–106.

[36] Ibid., p. 90.

accompanied by large-scale abduction and conversion of women and children.[37] In other instances, women found themselves abandoned or given away by their families to barter their own safe passage. There were cases of fathers who decided to marry their daughters to the sons of neighbouring Muslims or Hindus in order to protect them from the danger of violation. Family narratives collected by Veena Das reveal evidence that 'sometimes, Muslim men married Hindu girls and Hindu or Sikh men married Muslim girls, especially if they were from the same village, to save them from the dishonour of being abducted by unknown men'.[38]

Many women who were located did have brutal stories to tell and were happy to be reunited with their families or relatives. Not all abducted women were converted and married off, some found themselves in situations open to exploitation and human trafficking, forced to become domestic workers or sex workers, or subject to other forms of bonded labour. For such individuals, recovery offered an escape, a welcome reunion with family, or simply a new chance at life. But reunion and reintegration, too, could be a painful and difficult process. Rejection and shunning by family, heightened in the case of returning with children from a 'wrongful' union, were real concerns. The Indian government and Gandhi himself appealed to the Indian public to accept these women back with open arms.

While '[s]ome women never recovered from Partition, others saw in this rupture a moment of unexpected liberation for themselves as women'.[39] In such cases, women might have taken advantage of the dispersal and disruption of authority to marry partners of their choice, rather than those designated and approved by parents and elders. Others might have been taken in situations of force, but then found themselves integrated into contexts where they had greater freedom. The Lahore girl Khan speaks of might have been one such case. Alternatively, she might have been one of a spectrum of cases, which started in an incident

---

37 Ibid., pp. 20.

38 Das, 'National Honour and Practical Kinship', p. 75.

39 Menon and Bhasin, *Borders and Boundaries*, p. 19. This argument is also made by Anjali Bhardwaj Datta in her article 'Gendering Oral History of Partition: Interrogating Patriarchy' in *EPW*, 41:22 (3–9 June), p. 229.

of abduction, but, under a range of circumstances, transformed into a situation wherein she was integrated into the family of her abductor.

Discussing the correct procedures to be followed in rescue and recovery operations, Mridula Sarabhai wrote to Raja Rana of Jubbal, the Under Secretary to the Government of India, saying:

> 'We have been entrusted with not only a humanitarian problem, but our activities lead to the "making and unmaking" of lives, and therefore I have always pleaded with my colleagues that we should be extremely careful in dealing with cases, give individual attention to it and not fall into the tendency of [a] mass approach to the problem in a routine way.'[40]

Despite Sarabhai's plea, the rigid ideological underpinnings of the Act and the nature of the institutional and bureaucratic mechanisms put in place to facilitate its implementation worked against the possibility of assessing cases individually. The Abducted Persons (Recovery and Restoration) Act was, in fact, dependent upon the tyranny of such a mechanised and bureaucratic approach. For Khan's girl, the mechanisms of the Act were indeed to result in the 'unmaking' of the life that she had begun to build with her Pakistani husband in Lahore.

There were two ways in which an individual could be identified as a potential case of abduction. She could either be suspected of being someone on a list of missing persons or rescue and recovery officials operating in the area could identify her as a suspected case, perhaps someone from a different background who had recently come to live with the household. A proof was not required. Suspicion on part of local police and social workers was sufficient to allow women to be taken into custody while further investigation was carried out.

Because the Act designated responsibility for recovery to the country in which the individual was located, Pakistani officials, local police and social workers would have been responsible for tracking down Khan's girl in her home in Lahore. She would have then been taken to the transit camp in Sir Ganga Ram Hospital in Lahore, especially

---

[40] Sarabhai to Raja Rana of Jubbal (Under-Secretary to the Government of India), 7 February 1953, File no R/Govt/4 -1953, M/S Papers (on microfilm), NMML.

designated for recovered Hindu and Sikh women and children, where she would have been handed over to Indian authorities. The Sir Ganga Ram Hospital was one of a number of India-run transit camps set up to house rescued Hindu and Sikh women while their circumstances were further investigated, and preparations were made to transport them across the border. Other camps were located in the districts of Sheikhupura, Multan, Montgomery, Lyallpur and Sargodha.[41] From here, Khan's girl would have been taken across the border into India and placed in the Gandhi Vanita Ashram in Jalandhar, following which she would have been moved to a camp or home in Allahabad.

If she had been recovered on suspicion, but without being reported missing by family or relatives in India, social workers would have followed a similar procedure and attempted to locate relatives or family once she arrived in India. Being unsuccessful in these efforts, an arranged marriage seems to have been suggested as an alternative. Arranged marriages were regularly employed as a rehabilitation strategy for various categories of displaced women who were not self-supporting and lacked families or guardians to maintain them. State marriage bureaus were established to facilitate these unions, and social workers played an active role in sourcing suitable bridegrooms at a local level, raising donations for dowry and arranging wedding ceremonies. The State and its institutions of welfare and rehabilitation took on the mantle of the 'Indian family' in these circumstances, assuming responsibility for the care and maintenance of displaced women. But as Khan reports in her letter, 'She refuses blankly to get married here.' She would have then been exposed to a course of 'occupational therapy' to equip her with a skill, often seamstressing or tailoring, to enable her to earn an independent living. Alternatively, she would have been placed in a liability camp, an institution of care run by the State or by a voluntary organisation. Khan is most likely to have come into contact with this young woman during this process of rehabilitation through her work in the All India Save the Children Committee, the Allahabad AIWC, or another local civic organisation,

[41] A. Basu, *Mridula Sarabhai: Rebel with a Cause* (Oxford University Press, New Delhi, 1996), p. 129.

such as the YMCA, which were all involved in relief and rehabilitation efforts.

Nissa's journey would have been the counter version of the Lahore girl's narrative. Nissa was tracked down by the CRO in the town of Alwar in Rajasthan. She had grown up as a Muslim, but at the time of her recovery, she was living as a Hindu in India, married to a Hindu husband, while her Muslim relatives had relocated to Western Punjab in Pakistan. After her recovery, Nissa would have been placed at a base camp in Delhi which had been specifically set up in 1948 to accommodate 'resisting' Muslim women who had been recovered from Alwar, Bharatpur and Delhi provinces.[42] Because Nissa resisted recovery and because her 'husband', or according to the Indian State, her 'abductor', then filed a suit in the Punjab High court against her detention, hers became a disputed case and her journey across the border was delayed.[43]

Recent feminist scholarship offers a critical analysis of how such rescue and recovery operations revealed the '[m]ultiple patriarchies of community, family and State as experienced by women in their transition to freedom' and the complicities between them.[44] In giving the government extended powers to take action in the name of the sanctity of the Hindu family, and the restoration of abducted women to their 'legitimate' place within the home, the Act reinforced a bureaucratic and policy understanding of women as legal minors. Furthermore, because an abducted women's identity, indeed her claim to citizenship, came to be inextricably linked to her designated religious community, religious identity was reworked as the basis for citizenship and belonging. This undermined the secular, democratic and neutral claims of the new nation-state.

The Abducted Persons (Recovery and Restoration) Act was an extraordinary piece of legislation in certain respects, chafing against many other constitutional and legislative trends and developments in India at the time. The excessive powers required to implement rescue and recovery

---

[42] 'Recovery of Abducted Women Upto 15th July 1948', Report 3, R/N Papers, NMML.

[43] Basu, *Mridula Sarabhai: Rebel with a Cause*, p. 142.

[44] Menon and Bhasin, *Borders and Boundaries*, p. 20.

operations necessitated new legislation. In the initial stages of rescue and recovery, prior to the introduction of the Ordinance in November 1948, certain actions, such as trespassing on private property without a search warrant and detaining persons against their will, left the Indian State open to challenge on the grounds of law. In April 1948, such a challenge was brought against the Indian State in its claimed role of protector and custodian of abducted Hindu and Sikh women. Kamla Patel, a social worker and associate of Mridula Sarabhai, working in West Pakistan recalled this event in her memoirs. As part of the Indian team of rescue and recovery officials, she received summons one day to appear before the Lahore High Court. The case involved seven women and children classified as Hindu or Sikh and hence 'belonging' to India, who had been recovered by Pakistani police in Western Punjab and then handed over to Indian rescue officials. They were then interred at the Ganga Ram Hospital camp in Lahore, from where they were to be sent across the border.

The supposed abductors of these women and children in Pakistan had brought a writ of habeas corpus against Indian rescue workers operating on behalf of the Indian state. Their lawyers argued that these women and children were being detained against their will in the hospital camp, and Indian social workers and rescue officials had no authority to detain them if they wished to leave. The Court found in favour of the complainant and ordered all seven women and children to be released immediately, arguing that without legal sanction the bilateral agreement between India and Pakistan could not be used to enforce or justify such detention, 'as long as this understanding between India and Pakistan did not take the shape of law, its value in court was that of a blank piece of paper'.[45]

The governmental and public rhetoric around rescue and recovery in India suggests that even without legal sanction, the Indian state had always considered its recovery actions to be moral and justifiable. Recovery officials, such as Patel, saw the court order as an act of sabotage on the part of the Pakistani bureaucracy and government, intended to derail rescue and recovery efforts in West Punjab, rather than a matter of respect for the principles of law.

---

[45] Patel, *Torn from the Roots*, p. 105; Menon and Bhasin, *Borders and Boundaries*, p. 112.

The Indian Ordinance of 1948 and the Abducted Persons (Recovery and Restoration) Act of 1949 were, therefore, both premised on the necessity for legal structures and authority to enable rescue and recovery institutions, and mechanisms to carry out their work undeterred. However, in so doing, they took the problematic practices of rescue and recovery, together with the moral worldview and gender relations they were grounded on, and built them into the structure of the State by inscribing them into law. The Act was intended to prevent individuals from questioning and suing the government for actions undertaken as part of the rescue and recovery process. For this, it was necessary to grant the police, tribunal and various other government officials, the power to define and control 'abducted' women. For example, Section 8 of the Act stated that detention in a camp could not be questioned by a court, while Section 9 'Protection of action taken under Act' proclaimed that no suit or prosecution would be able to be brought against the national government for their pursuance of this Act.[46]

Caught between the Nation and the Law

The introduction of the new Act, however, created another set of problems for the Indian State. It operated in tension with some of the basic legal principles and ethos of the new Indian Constitution. The Act was passed in December 1949 and in January 1950, India's new Constitution came into effect. Whereas before individuals had been able to challenge the rescue and recovery operations on the grounds that they were not sanctioned by law, now rescue and recovery operations could be challenged on the basis of the unconstitutionality of the legislation authorising them. The coexistence of these two legal documents, the Constitution and the 1949 Act, actually enabled 'abductors' and those with a vested interest in a particular case, to take the Indian government to court on this basis. Since the introduction of the Act, abductors had tried to 'drag us into the Court and this has increased

[46] See Clauses 8 and 9 of the Abducted Persons (Recovery and Restoration) Act, 1949 (Act No. LXV of 1949) in Appendix I, Menon and Bhasin, *Borders and Boundaries*, p. 263.

with the introduction of the Constitution', bemoaned Sarabhai.[47] Here, she was referring to a number of cases involving the writ of habeas corpus that had been brought against the Indian state in the High Court of East Punjab regarding the detention of Muslim women in transit camps. These cases resulted in the East Punjab High Court declaring a judgement that stated that the Act was ultra vires by virtue of Article 22 of the Indian Constitution. The Court ordered the release of all persons in all camps and gave a judgement that no recovered woman could be repatriated to Pakistan as they were henceforth citizens of India.[48] Consequently, after June 1952, recovery work was halted, and it was only once the Supreme Court of India overruled the judgement of the East Punjab High Court that it could recommence.[49] As a result of this judgement, the v decided to only investigate and recover 'such new cases in which there were guides or definite information from the relatives or according to the list supplied to us'.[50]

In both the 1948 Lahore case in Pakistan and the East Punjab High Court decision in India, the abductors claimed the writ of habeas corpus, the very language of citizenship, to challenge rescue and recovery. One of the intended functions of the Act was to prevent this type of abuse, but in so doing, it was itself implicated in undermining these principles, by denying recovered women the chance to have a voice in their own future.

Since the Act classified certain situations as forced conversions and refused to recognise them as legitimate, the possibility of the exercise of choice was denied in the operation of rescue and recovery. This undermined one of the foundational principles of liberal democratic citizenship, that of free will. Khan's critique of these operations used this liberal understanding of citizenship to make her case, 'This case has brought to my mind the question of a women's inherent right to decide

---

[47] 'The Abducted Persons (Recovery and Restoration Act)', 20 June 1952, R/Govt/14-1949–55, M/S Papers (on microfilm), NMML.

[48] 'Report on the Recovery of Abducted Persons for the period June 52 to October 52', File R/MS/20, M/S Papers (on microfilm), NMML.

[49] Basu, *Mridula Sarabhai: Rebel with a Cause*, pp. 139–140.

[50] 'The Abducted Persons Recovery and Restoration Act' (Draft), 20 June 1952, File no: R/Govt/14-1949-55, M/S Papers (on microfilm), NMML.

her own future. This right should definitely be considered.'[51] At the time of the girl's recovery, however, no mechanism was in place to prevent such misuse. It was only in 1954, more than three years later, that an Indo-Pakistani government decision ensured that women would not be rescued and recovered against their wishes.

Khan's letter of complaint at the beginning of this chapter illustrates how the liberal concept of citizenship and India's commitment to it, was used to challenge the application of the Abducted Persons (Recovery and Restoration) Act. Yet, beyond this, the Indian woman as an individual with the 'right' of choice was also incorporated into the justificatory discourse of rescue and recovery itself. Even though the Act, with its communal underpinnings and patriarchal ethos, dismissed the individual in favour of Hindu and male group interests, it actually did lay claim to the language of choice.[52] Consider, for example, the Congress's resolution in November 1946[53] on abducted women, which states, 'Women who have been abducted and forcibly married must be restored to their houses; mass conversions have no significance or validity, and people must be given every opportunity to return to the life of their choice.'[54]

---

[51] Khan to H. Sen, 26 September 1951, File 147, AIWC Papers, NMML.

[52] Tanika Sarkar illustrates how problematic the concept of consent can be as an indicator of women's emancipation in her analysis of the discourse and debate around the Age of Consent Bill in colonial Bengal in the 1890s. During the course of this debate, the woman as a 'rights-bearing' citizen became visible for the first time, providing a new conceptual framework for thinking about women as individuals and legal beings. However, the right to consent in this context did not necessarily free women from their social and scriptural confines, in fact, particular interpretations of consent, as Sarkar argues, became a way to tie women back into these confines in new ways. For example, by linking consent to medical opinion on the physical capacities of women's bodies. See T. Sarkar, 'A Prehistory of Rights: The Age of Consent Debate in Colonial Bengal' in *Feminist Studies*, 26:3 (Fall 2000), pp. 614–617.

[53] The Congress's Resolution of November 1946 was the first conscious state policy on abducted women and children. It acknowledged the obligation of the Congress towards the recovery and restoration of abducted women and agreed that forced conversions would not be recognised. It set the terms of the 6 December 1947 bilateral agreement, the 1948 Ordinances and the 1949 Abducted Persons (Recovery and Restoration) Act. See Das, 'National Honour and Practical Kinship', pp. 60–61.

[54] Indian National Congress, Resolution 6 November 1946, quoted in Menon and Bhasin, *Borders and Boundaries*, p. 69.

Mridula Sarabhai and Rameshwari Nehru: Reconciling Fear and Choice

Sarabhai framed the necessity of rescue and recovery in terms of the duty of the State to its citizens, but she justified it in relation to the abducted woman's right to a life of her choice. The seeming contradiction between forced recovery and protecting the possibility of choice was resolved by evoking the idea of a false consciousness. Sarabhai had a strong opinion on the motives behind 'doubtful and resisting' women. This was shaped by her own convictions concerning the social, political and moral importance of rescue and recovery for India as both a humane and democratic state. She believed that all 'doubtful and resisting' women, such as Nissa, were victims driven by fear; they resisted because they were afraid of defying their abductors and experiencing rejection and shame at the hands of their original families. Sarabhai believed, like many of the Indian social workers implementing India's recovery operations, that this 'fear complex' encouraged rescued women to protect their abductors by lying about their circumstances. This same line of reasoning was reflected in the official government position on the issue, as articulated in the 1948 Ministry of Rehabilitation Report: 'Experience has shown that the resentment and stubbornness on the part of these women' is due to fear of their future and of public opinion, doubts concerning how they will be received by their original families and a 'sense of shame on having lost their honour'.[55]

These fears were, in some circumstances, completely valid. Forced conversions and marriage targeted the sexuality of women, just as the Indian State's interest in the rescue and recovery of women was premised not 'upon their definition as citizens, but as sexual and reproductive beings'. 'The honour of the nation was at stake because women as sexual and reproductive beings were forcibly held by the other side.'[56] As both the physical and cultural bearers of the nation, a woman's sexuality was invested with the identity and honour of the community. It was, therefore,

[55] 'Recovery of Abducted Women Upto 15th July 1948', Report 3, R/N Papers, NMML.

[56] Das, 'National Honour and Practical Kinship', p. 68.

especially vulnerable. To counteract this, a campaign was launched by the Indian government to encourage families and communities to accept rescued women back with 'open arms'. However, this could not necessarily account for all cases of resistance.

The 'fear complex', which Sarabhai believed acted as a false consciousness driving the behaviour of abducted women, made it imperative for her and her team of social workers to represent the best interests of such women. It was only in restoring them to their kin and to an environment of safety, familiarity and belonging that access to choice, and with it the authentic voice of these women, could be 'recovered'. To do this, Sarabhai insisted that rescued women be made to feel at home and comfortable in the transit camps:

> In camps, not only physical needs of recovered persons have to be catered for, but special effort has to be made to create an atmosphere of confidence and retaliation from fear. So efforts are made that these camps and homes do not become "*dharm salas* or detention camps", but a "home" atmosphere is created...On arrival, a recovered person is a bundle of nerves, full of tensions and moods. On one side she is a victim of fear complex of the future—a nervous wreck—on the other hand, she is furious. Is she a prisoner, a criminal that police should bring her in camps? So to all such new arrivals friendly and homely approach has to be made...The camps in-charge and other members staying in the camp need to create a feeling that the static guard posted outside is not there to safeguard against escapes from camps, against recovered persons, but to save and protect them from attacks of dacoits.[57]

But her instructions in themselves reveal the instability and ambiguity of the Indian State's claim as the paternal protector. What makes these camps 'homes' as opposed to 'detention camps'? Are these women being protected from their own fear and from the outside world of their abductors, or are they being imprisoned? Are they being protected until they resist? The very language of these rescue and recovery institutions and their mechanisms speaks to their coercive nature. Documents dealing with the administration of internment and transit camps often

[57] 'Arrangements for Care of Recovered Persons in camps and homes', 29 September 1953, R/Govt/4 -1953, M/S Papers (on microfilm), NMML.

refer to residents as inmates, while the workings of the tribunal use terms associated with trial and judgement, such as evidence and truth.

Sarabhai agreed that the consent of the victim had to be taken into consideration, but she argued that the conditions under which this consent was granted should determine its validity. In the case of Nissa, a disagreement arose between Sarabhai and A.L. Fletcher, the high-powered officer in charge of administering disputed cases in India, precisely around this issue of obtaining consent. That is how a part of Nissa's story, or rather an interpretation of her story, appeared in the archival records. Fletcher interviewed Nissa while she was interned in India. He decided that because she was over 21 her wish to remain with her adopted family in Alwar should be respected, and she should be returned to them. Sarabhai disagreed with his assessment. She advocated that rescued women needed to have a chance to meet their family and relatives and return to their 'correct' homeland prior to consent being obtained. She argued that Nissa should not have been asked her opinion until she had been sent back to live with her relatives in Pakistan. She should have been allowed a couple of months to adjust to her new life and to gain assurance that she would be accepted and protected by her original family.[58]

Mridula Sarabhai is a perplexing case study in many respects. Her conviction of the moral necessity of rescue and recovery, and her passion in implementing it, initially seem to place her firmly within a patriarchal and paternal framework. As the architect of the Abducted Persons (Recovery and Restoration) Act, her actions ally her with the conservative wing of the Congress, who opposed the reform of the Hindu Code Bill, and the Hindu Mahasabha that tries to articulate a notion of the Indian citizen grounded on Hindu-ness, and to incite communal discord. On closer analysis, however, it becomes evident that her personal and political support for rescue and recovery was far more complex.

Sarabhai's career in the nationalist movement, her lifestyle and her politics do not sit easily with this initial positioning. Her personal contacts

[58] See correspondence between Sarabhai and Fletcher in File no: R/Govt/13-1949-55, M/S Papers (on microfilm), NMML.

and good relations with Pakistan, including those with Prime Minister Jinnah (which assisted her in getting the bilateral cooperation necessary for the workings of the Ordinances and the Act) and her support for Sheikh Abdullah, Prime Minister of Jammu and Kashmir, against the wishes of Jawaharlal Nehru,[59] discredit a communal bias towards India.

Sarabhai was an outspoken advocate for women's equality in society, but did not espouse the social feminism of many of her generation. She saw liberation in the ability of women to be able to 'claim' and own for themselves the attributes of masculinity. With her bobbed hair and her salwar kameez, she did not fit neatly into the image of the traditional Indian social worker. In her own social persona, Sarabhai rejected feminine qualities, such as 'shyness, softness, helplessness, dependency, lady-like manners', which she regarded as hindering women's progress:

> I don't want to be a doll for show either for men or society. I don't want to be artificial, unnatural...I have tried to keep away from the so-called womanly qualities and tried to cultivate certain manly qualities which I consider essential for a woman—desire for adventure, daringness, self-confidence, discipline, ability to do one's work, control one's mind and emotions; one's physique and way of walking should be like that of a soldier.[60]

She also had a strong sense of justice. 'Any form of injustice aroused her passion.'[61] She was outraged at the way in which women had been used in the conflict between communities during Partition. 'To all these women, Mridula's advice always was that they should not suffer such humiliation; they should learn to be independent and self-reliant and then men would respect them.'[62] Strongly influenced by Gandhian thinking, she resented the way in which women were treated as 'dolls and objects of indulgence' and sought instead an identity for women as 'crusaders in common service'.[63] In Sarabhai's worldview, abduction,

---

[59] See Basu, *Mridula Sarabhai: Rebel with a Cause*, p. 144.

[60] Ibid, p. 68.

[61] Ibid., p. 68..

[62] Ibid., p. 75.

[63] Ibid., pp. 232.

rape and gendered violence showed the ultimate lack of respect for women in a society. She saw this as an injustice that had to be corrected and this could only be done through the rescue and recovery of 'abducted' women. It was an idealised vision and it was ideological. For her, as Aparna Basu stresses, 'Social work was the other face of politics.'[64] She was passionate in her beliefs and actions, rather than self-reflective, and often aggressive in her approach.

Mridula Sarabhai was driven by a particular kind of gender politics, which had an emancipatory objective. However, the methods that she came to employ, namely in relation to the Rescue and Recovery Act and its implementation, aligned with other interest groups driven by very different agendas. Sarabhai and her team of social workers show how communities of women could become complicit in the structures of a reworked national patriarchy, even with the best intentions.

The Indian state's rescue and recovery operations attracted many women activists, eager to participate in rebuilding the nation. These ranged from the social workers in the transit and holding camps to bureaucrats, such as Renuka Ray and Rameshwari Nehru in the Ministry of Relief and Rehabilitation. Even AIWC branches became involved, running a propaganda campaign to encourage families to embrace their recovered women with open arms. Did all of these women, like Sarabhai, become complicit in the mechanics of recovery, which left their sisters, such as Nissa and Khan's girl from Lahore, in a state of perpetual exile?

The final section of this chapter looks at the response developed by Rameshwari Nehru to the rescue and recovery operations. As Honorary Director of the Women's Section of the Relief and Rehabilitation Ministry, Nehru had initially supported the rescue and recovery operations. However, her experience of working within the field soon led her to change her mind. After about a year into her post, she concluded that operations were not achieving their intended purpose and that the removal of women who had settled with their new families and made peace with their new situation would only cause further harm to those it was intended to help. Nehru developed a maternal,

---

64 Menon and Bhasin , *Borders and Boundaries*, p. 191.

protective version of citizenship, which provided a way of negotiating between the absolute certainties of paternal protective citizenship and the abstract idealism of liberal citizenship.

Maternal citizenship acknowledged the importance of government protection for women and recognised the importance of the family and 'moral' society, but was also far more self-reflexive in its recognition of the limitations of the State to fulfil such obligations. '[W]e must admit that we have sent away these unwilling and helpless women to a future that they can neither control nor choose,' stressed Nehru in a Rehabilitation Report from June 1949, in which she argued against continuing with recovery work. Furthermore, maternal citizenship was able to recognise the way in which mechanisms of recovery objectified women as their intended beneficiaries; 'The women's will is not taken into consideration at all,' Nehru went on to stress in the same report, 'She is once again reduced to the goods and chattel status without having the right to decide her own future or mould her own life.'[65]

Nehru had a very different understanding of the goal of rescue and recovery operations compared to Mridula Sarabhai. For her, their primary function was to alleviate hardship, suffering and insecurity:

> We must assure ourselves that in recovering women, we have in some way, advanced their happiness. This is the human angle of approach. Viewed from this angle, I am convinced that we have not achieved our purpose and that it is inadvisable to continue the work of recovery any longer.
>
> Two years have elapsed since the original crimes were committed, and though there may still be a considerable number of unrecovered women, to remove them at this stage from their homes, in which they have settled, would result in untold misery and suffering.[66]

It was an approach driven by pragmatic concerns rather than constitutional ideals. Whereas the idealism and absolutism of the Abducted Persons (Recovery and Restoration) Act sought to create the appearance of 'choice' and freedom where there was none, maternal

---

[65] 'Memorandum on Recovery of Women: Review of the position since October 1948,' June 1949, Report 1, R/N Papers, NMML.

[66] Ibid.

citizenship exposed this as an illusion. It responded to the reality of the lack of choice in the lives of abducted women, and the consequent powerlessness of the State to alter this position, and in so doing exposed the double bind that abducted women so often found themselves in; whether to remain with their abductors or to return to their original families, both held equal amounts of uncertainty.

The dislocation of Partition created a crisis of authority in the structure of the family, community and state. Discourses and institutions of refugee relief and rehabilitation, together with those of development, democracy and welfare, attempted to reconfigure this authority by delineating the boundaries of legitimate citizenship. By restoring the 'dignity' of the community and the authority of the Hindu family, the rescue and recovery of abducted women became a fundamental component of this project of rehabilitation. The resistance of recovered women, however, disrupted the official narrative of nation-building. By their refusal 'to conform to the demands of either their own families or their government, and fall in line with their notions of what was legitimate and acceptable',[67] such cases exposed the collusion between family, community and State in the remaking of postcolonial citizenship. Meanwhile, the engagement of these women with the bilateral agreements of rescue and recovery, and the 1949 Act, co-opted the 'liberal citizen', the rule of law and the idea of justice in this coercive agenda. Resisting women, such as Khan's girl from Lahore and Nissa, consequently found themselves in a state of perpetual exile. In their refusal to conform, they were caught between two nations, and two different family contexts, revealing the fluidity and complexity of identity that has become part of the experience of postcolonial nation-making.

---

[67] Menon and Bhasin, *Borders and Boundaries*, p. 97.

Chapter 5

Citizenship through Struggle: The National Federation of Indian Women

The participation of Indian women in a range of struggles provided the basis for new forms of collective organisation and identity. This chapter documents and analyses some of the developments that led to the formation of the NFIW in 1954. The first section traces the roots of this new body back to the beginning of the 1940s, looking at the growth of communism in India, the impact of organising relief work during the Bengal Famine of 1943 and the influence of women's participation in the Telengana and Tebhaga peasant struggles of the late 1940s and early 1950s. The second section outlines two parallel processes—the growth of refugee women's *samitis* in Calcutta and the formal establishment of the NFIW—in order to show how a shared agenda of relief work and rehabilitation brought these two processes together. This, in turn, facilitated the intersection of two very different kinds of struggles, one for socio-economic rights and services at a municipal level, and the other for legislative equality at a national level. The NFIW's campaign for the Hindu Code Bill provided the grounds for this intersection. The campaign brought communities of refugee women into the Federation and also enabled their expression of an active notion of citizenship based on the claim to socio-economic rights.

Woven into the account of these public and collective struggles is a reflection on personal struggle in the lives of NFIW founding members where participation in the sphere of agitational politics could create tension and conflict between familial responsibilities and commitment as an activist. The act and symbol of struggle occur throughout this chapter in many different guises. The meaning of struggle as process, experience and motif is explored, as is the question of how it facilitated new ways of collective belonging for various communities of women in the sphere of both government and agitational politics, and new kinds of 'being' for NFIW members and leaders, through enabling subjectivities that could be both individual and collective.

The Growth of Communism in India, and the Bengal Famine of 1943

For the millions of Indian civilians in wartime Bengal, whose rice and grain supplies were cut off by the dynamics of World War II in Asia and the government's wartime policy, the Bengal Famine was a struggle for survival. It was the story of desperate migration from rural areas to big cities in search of sustenance. For women activists who responded to the crisis, the famine represented both a logistical battle to coordinate relief work and supplies, and a search for justice in the face of corrupt and apathetic state and central governments.

The famine was important for women involved in relief efforts across the ideological and organisational spectrum. It sharpened their political consciousness and their sense of resistance to injustice, and fostered an awareness of the politics of the body, teaching them how regional, national and international political forces can play themselves out on the bodies and lives of local communities. The Bengal Famine and the wartime context were particularly significant for communist women, encouraging the growth of local women's organisations in West Bengal, which were later to become one of the nuclei of the NFIW.

Although Bengal was a region particularly prone to famine due to its demographic and agricultural context, the famine of 1943 was caused by a combination of wartime government policy, adverse weather conditions and corruption.[1] The Japanese invasion of South East Asia in the spring of 1942 led to the drying up of Burmese rice supplies, which were a staple food in the region. This was followed by a cyclone hitting the Indian east coast in October, destroying the rice crop and

---

[1] B.R. Tomlinson, *The Economy of Modern India 1860–1970* (Cambridge University Press, Cambridge, 1993), p. 72; S. Sarkar, *Modern India: 1885–1947* (Pearson, Delhi, 1983), p. 406.

necessitating all the surplus rice in the region being consumed by the following spring. 'This situation worsened in May and June 1943, reaching its nadir in the autumn.'[2] After the fall of Burma, fears of an invasion into eastern Bengal through Assam, together with the Japanese bombing of India's Eastern borders, led the colonial government to pursue a scorched earth policy. This resulted in the destruction of vital food transportation networks in the region and prevented much-needed supplies from reaching the interior.[3]

The Bengal Famine is approached from two perspectives in this section. Firstly, it is analysed as an important precursor to the formation of the NFIW, politicising women around the issues of self-defence and food security. Secondly, it is approached as a lens through which we reflect on the relationship between citizenship and access to basic socio-economic resources necessary for life and survival. This relationship is later significantly reworked with the articulation of active citizenship and the claim to socio-economic rights amongst the NFIW in West Bengal.

The famine was man-made, caused not so much by a complete absence of foodstuffs, but rather by what historians have identified as skewed patterns of food distribution and distorted pricing, which encouraged a general climate of food insecurity in the region.[4] Starvation was the devastating consequence of an unequal distribution of food. Grain produced in Bengal and Bihar was primarily reserved for Allied troops stationed in the Middle East, while grain from the delta region was directed to troops and war workers based in Calcutta.[5] Food

---

[2] M. Misra, *Vishnu's Crowded Temple: India Since the Great Rebellion* (Yale University Press, London, 2008), p. 214.

[3] Sarkar, *Modern India*, p. 406. For a more detailed account of the broader context of Bengal leading up to the famine, see A.K. Sen, 'Famine Mortality: A Study of the Bengal Famine of 1943' in E. Hobsbawm (ed.), *Peasants in History: Essays in Honour of Daniel Thorner* (Oxford University Press, Calcutta, 1980) and P.R. Greenough, *Prosperity and Misery in Modern Bengal: The Famine of 1943–1944* (Oxford University Press, New York, 1982). The colonial government also produced an official report by a Famine Inquiry Commission, entitled *India: Famine Inquiry Commission (Final Report)* (New Delhi, 1945).

[4] Tomlinson, *The Economy of Modern India*, p. 72; Sarkar, *Modern India*, p. 406; Pandit, *The Scope of Happiness*, p. 172.

[5] Misra, *Vishnu's Crowded Temple*, p. 215.

shortage led to inflation, which, in turn, resulted in hoarding and the development of a black market,[6] increasing the price of available grain beyond the reach of not only working-class and peasant families but also the middle classes.

The rural poor of Bengal were most affected. With no food, desperate villagers began to migrate to Calcutta in search of sustenance, bringing cholera in their wake.[7] Vijayalakshmi Pandit, Renuka Ray and Kamaladevi Chattopadhyay toured the famine-affected areas of Bengal in 1943, as official representatives of the AIWC, setting up relief efforts and lobbying the provincial and central governments for speedy intervention. Shocking scenes 'of horror, extreme suffering and despair' met them in Calcutta. As Pandit describes in her autobiography, 'Streams of peasants from villages, in varying degrees of illness and incapacity, most of whom had walked miles to escape starvation in their areas' flooded the city.[8] Such images are also evoked in Renuka Ray's account of her travels through the famine-affected regions. 'On our way to Midnapore from Howrah,' she recalls, 'at every station at which the train stopped, we were greeted with plaintive wails: "Give us something to eat, give us something to eat." Mothers with babies and men and women who looked like skeletons were there all along the line...It was a nightmare.'[9]

The response of both the central and provincial governments was delayed and inadequate. The central government was preoccupied with suppressing Indian nationalism.[10] Apathy, corruption and denial defined the provincial government's response, with local politicians participating in and profiteering from speculation and the growth of a black market.[11] For Vijayalakshmi Pandit, who led AIWC relief efforts in the state, the most shocking aspect of the famine was the fact that 'starvation existed side by side with plenty'. In Calcutta, wealthy Indians and foreigners 'continued to live in a state of affluence surrounded

---

6 Sarkar, *Modern India*, p. 406.

7 Ibid.

8 Pandit, *The Scope of Happiness*, p. 172.

9 Ray, *My Reminiscences*, p. 109.

10 Pandit, *The Scope of Happiness*, p. 172.

11 Sarkar, *Modern India*, p. 406.

by every conceivable luxury, while people outside their gates died of hunger and despair'.[12] The famine was devastating, with an estimated death rate of three million Indians.[13]

The Bengal Famine, and the context of WWII, provide the background for two distinct but interconnected developments within the broader framework of the Indian women's movement in the 1940s. The first is the growing presence and influence of communist women within existing women's organisations, such as the AIWC. The second is the formation of new organisations of communist women, such as the Mahila Atma Raksha Samiti (MARS) in Bengal, the Lok Stree Sabha in Punjab, the Golden Rocks Mattar Sangham in Madras and the Mahila Sangha in Andhra Pradesh.[14]

These developments must be contextualised within the broader history of communism in India, and its growth and influence in the twentieth century. Many future NFIW leaders, like Renu Chakravartty, Sarla Sharma, Vimla Dang and Vidya Munshi, cut their political teeth through a growing student movement in the late 1930s and early 1940s that was particularly receptive to Marxist ideas and closely aligned with the CPI. Sarla Sharma was one of the first to join the All India Students Conference in 1936, after reading some Marxist literature she had been given for safekeeping. 'I hid it away for a few days but then my inquisitiveness got the better of me and I decided that I should read it. And that was the start.' It was after this that she began attending CPI meetings and was soon actively involved in initiating and leading agitations, as well as visiting girls' colleges to mobilise students for national action. Sarla's student activism, in turn, encouraged her to join the CPI in 1939, where she was one of the earliest members of the Party's organising committee.[15]

In 1942, the banning of the CPI was revoked with the entry of the Soviet Union into the War on the side of the Allies. This enabled the Party to grow considerably during the early 1940s, especially in Bengal,

[12] Pandit, *The Scope of Happiness*, p. 173.

[13] Tomlinson, *The Economy of Modern India*, p. 72.

[14] Interview with S. Sharma, NFIW veteran, 19 December 2011, New Delhi; Interview with G. Chakravartty, NFIW member and academic, 4 November 2011, New Delhi.

[15] Interview with Sharma, 19 December 2011.

mobilising and organising peasants, establishing contacts in urban industrial areas and conducting constructive and relief work.[16] This coincided with the establishment of specific female student movements, records Renu Chakravartty in her account of women in the communist movement.[17]

A generation of young Indians, such as Vidya Munshi, were also being radicalised outside the country through contact with the India League and the British Left. Shortly before the outbreak of WWII, Munshi moved to Britain to study medicine at the age of 19:

> At that time there were many books that were not allowed to enter our country by the British. Like most Indian students going from a nationalist background, I too was interested in reading all that was not allowed in our country. So I became a member of the Left Wing club and started reading whatever I could get, including a number of books about the Soviet Union, about China and so on.[18]

This engagement exposed her to the poor socio-economic condition of Indians back home. In the eastern slum area of Bombay, in 1919, just two years after the Russian Revolution, she read how 'not even one child out of six lives up to the age of ten years and that made me feel that in that sort of country it is better to be a Communist than to be a doctor', Munshi reckoned that as a trained doctor she would never be able to reach the vast majority of poor Indians in the cities and towns, but as a communist, she would have greater power to uproot the whole corrupt system. This awareness encouraged her to continue reading more communist literature.[19]

Neither Munshi nor Sharma told their parents about their political activity. The demands of the family often ran counter to the ideals of political activities, exposing a different kind of struggle in the lives of these young activists: a struggle between loyalty to family and middle-class respectability, versus commitment to alternate social

---

[16] M. Sen, *In Search of Freedom* (Stree, Calcutta, 2001) p. 87.

[17] R. Chakravartty, *Communists in the Indian Women's Movement 1940–1950* (People's Publishing House, New Delhi, 1980), pp. 11–12.

[18] Interview with Munshi, 2 December 2011.

[19] Ibid.

ideals and political aspirations. 'In many families when children joined revolutionary movements they were kicked out,' recalled Sharma.[20] Vimla Dang, another founding member of the NFIW, involved in the student movement in Punjab, recalled coming across a fellow girl student being beaten by her father in public for refusing to quit her student activism, and other cases of girls whose studies were discontinued by their parents for fear they might join the communist movement.[21] This was a struggle that would require the sacrifice of family responsibilities and support at specific moments in their lives.

Sarla Sharma recalls a period in her early political life, where she encountered such a struggle and was forced to choose between her political commitment and her health and family. She was working underground for the CPI at the time, carrying information, when she was involved in an accident on her bicycle, and her leg was severely damaged. She had to be admitted to the hospital, but because she was working underground, the doctor had to hide her away in a storeroom rather than admit her officially, and she couldn't tell anyone where she was. It was here that she spent many lonely and painful months recovering. This was a time of great personal struggle for her, one filled with extreme pain as well as isolation and loneliness, as being in hiding meant that her friends and family couldn't visit her. After more than a year in the hospital, she was sent home with a diagnosis, that she would not be able to use the leg again.[22]

During this time, Sarla read the autobiography of a WWII Russian fighter pilot, Alexey Maresyev, who lost both his legs when his plane crashed. Refusing to give up, he embarked on a long process of rehabilitation and after much perseverance, he learned to fly with prosthetic legs and returned to action. It is not surprising that Sarla as a young communist would have turned to a Soviet hero at this moment. Encouraged by this story, Sarla decided to employ a practitioner of Ayurvedic massage to live in her household and to give her daily treatments. After several months, the circulation and

---

[20] Interview with Sharma, 19 December 2011.

[21] V. Dang, *Fragments of an Autobiography* (Asha Jyoti, Delhi, 2007), p. 31.

[22] Interview with Sharma, 19 December 2011.

feeling in her leg improved and she was able to use her leg again. Overcoming the physical impairment of her injury acts almost as a rite of passage in Sarla's account, shaping how she sees herself in the world; as a fighter, a survivor. Her personal struggle over pain, loneliness and disability become closely interwoven with her commitment to her political struggle for social justice and gender equality through Marxism.[23]

The early 1940s marked an era of growing militancy, with the rise of the Quit India Movement, together with various other emerging struggles, exposing a range of competing economic and political pathways towards emancipation. These activists were drawn towards Marxism as a vehicle for overturning the inequalities of colonial and capital domination. Their political activities were to bring them into contact with the devastating consequences of the Bengal Famine, and with the growing women's activism in this area.

Eager to harness the energy of new social justice and anti-colonial movements emerging at this time, the CPI encouraged the formation of MARS in 1943 and its sister organisations in the Punjab, Madras and Andhra Pradesh, to reach out to women within these communities, as well as to radicalise middle-class women in urban centres. '[W]e started with small meetings of women here and there in people's homes,' Sarla Sharma recalls. She adds:

> We had no public halls or microphones at that time. We communicated through speech but equally importantly, through culture using drama and song to get our messages across. These groups worked for Famine relief and lobbied the government to take steps against hoarding and [to] introduce a system of rationing—remember it was not just control over foodstuffs that was a problem but also distribution. It was small incidents like this that led to the development of a larger movement.[24]

The formation of MARS in 1943 and its sister organisations reflected the CPI's strategy of mass mobilisation. In the words of Sarla, the function of MARS was 'to make women aware and to arouse and mobilise them

[23] Interview with Sharma, 19 December 2011.

[24] Interview with Sharma, 19 December 2011.

for solidarity' in the name of supportive action. But these organisations equally reflected the response of communist women to the economic and political insecurity created by the forces of WWII. MARS was founded on the central concepts of self-defence and food security.[25] With the Japanese fighting on the side of the fascist Axis powers, MARS sought to teach women in Bengal self-defence in case of a Japanese invasion. The organisation participated in nationalist demonstrations, demanding the release of political prisoners and the establishment of a national government to fight the Japanese.

In addition, MARS was deeply involved in constructive work[26] and famine relief efforts.[27] Local and regional branches of the AIWC and MARS worked together to coordinate famine relief in affected areas and were both significantly involved in these efforts.[28] MARS and AIWC workers and branches took over the running of existing ineffective and limited government food kitchens, expanding these facilities, and setting up additional kitchens in some of the worst affected areas. They helped supply medical assistance, especially pertaining to the outbreaks of cholera in the countryside. They also set up receiving camps in the villages, where babies and small children whose parents were dead or missing, could be brought before being sent to the city.[29] They later established homes for children who had been orphaned.[30]

Although the legacy of mobilising women for relief work during the Bengal Famine is claimed by some of those who have written on the era, such as Renu Chakravartty, as a key period of political conscientisation

---

[25] Ibid.

[26] Such as milk distribution and the running of handicraft centres. See Sen, *In Search of Freedom*, p. 95.

[27] The CPI worked alongside these women's organisations undertaking relief activities as part of the political education and awareness raising campaign of the Party. See Sen, *In Search of Freedom*, pp. 87, 91, 95.

[28] Voluntary organisations worked together with the government on relief efforts as well. Other voluntary organisations such as the Ramakrishna Mission, the Marwari Relief Society and the Bharat Sevak Sangh (Bharat Sevasram) were also involved in famine relief efforts, in particular the running of food kitchens. See Sen, *In Search of Freedom*, pp. 89–92; Ray, *My Reminiscences*, p. 110.

[29] Pandit, *The Scope of Happiness*, p. 172.

[30] See P. Guha, 'Rajkumari Amrit Kaur: Her Life, Work and Ideology' in *Rajkumari Amrit Kaur*, p. 69.

for women on the radical Left,[31] the famine was influential in shaping the political consciousness of women across the ideological and organisational spectrum. The apathy and denial of provincial and colonial governments, the unfair prioritisation of food for troops and British civilians, and the hoarding and black-market profiteering that accompanied the famine aroused a powerful sense of injustice amongst women leaders who were involved in relief efforts. It spurred their inner voice of resistance and rebellion. 'The government could not tell the truth about the Famine as the actual things happening in the Famine areas were shocking,' Vijayalakshmi Pandit recalls, 'Those of us who were in contact with the suffering people realised that the truth had to be told, and we told it as loudly and clearly as we could.'[32]

For these activists, aware of the broader situation in India and larger Asia at the time, first-hand exposure to the devastating consequences of the famine on the body was crucial. The haunting images of hundreds of people emaciated 'like skeletons',[33] the exploitation of women who had turned to prostitution to survive and the loss of dignity and selfhood that such conditions perpetuated offered a powerful reminder of how political forces play themselves out on, and define the experience of, the individual. Anasuya Gyanchand stressed this connection, in her keynote address at the first NFIW Congress:

> We women may not understand the subtle difference in various 'isms' but we understand the difference between war and peace, between hunger and contentment, between insecurity and security, between the world where our children can be wiped out by the hydrogen bomb, and the world of peace and plenty.[34]

Hajrah Begum, too, made a similar connection in her speech representing the Indian delegation at the Women's International

[31] Chakravartty makes this particular argument in her memoirs. See, for example, Chakravartty, *Communists in the Indian Women's Movement*, pp. 11–28.

[32] Pandit, *The Scope of Happiness*, pp. 184–185.

[33] Ray, *My Reminiscences*, p. 109.

[34] S. Munsi, 'National Conference of Women in Calcutta', 13 June 1954, *New Age*, copy located in CPI Offices, Ajoy Bhavan.

Democratic Federation Conference (WIDF)[35] in Copenhagen in 1953, when she stated, 'We know that India will starve as long as there is war anywhere in Asia.' 'Our women realise more and more, if international trade barriers could be removed, there would be food in plenty for the people of the world. To fight famine, we must fight for peace, for friendship and cooperation between the people of the world,'[36] she continued. This condemnation of the geopolitics of the Bengal Famine, and the anger aroused in Indian women activists resonated with the experiences and beliefs of women in the emerging international women's movement. Attending the founding conference of the WIDF in Paris in 1945, Vidya Munshi remembers how 'women from so many European countries' wept when they heard a fellow Indian delegate, Ella Read, describe the conditions of the famine.[37]

For this generation of women activists, the Bengal Famine highlighted how local issues and those connected with the private sphere of the household, such as food and sexuality, could be determined by larger political forces. In so doing, it enabled them to see the relationship between territorial and diplomatic security, and the personal security and integrity of the body.[38] This, in turn, was to have an influence on their politics and advocacy. For Rameshwari Nehru, witnessing an increase in the trafficking and the prostitution of women who had sought refuge in the cities was one of the motivating factors behind her post-independence campaign to have anti-trafficking legislation implemented. She even sought regional and international cooperation and agreement on the issue.

---

[35] The Women's International Democratic Federation was the international women's body to which the NFIW affiliated once it was formed in 1954.

[36] Hajrah Begum's speech was given at the 1953 Women's International Democratic Federation Conference in Copenhagen, 5–10 June, and reprinted in 'Early Years of Women's International Democratic Federation and National Federation of Indian Women' (pamphlet) NFIW publication, July 2009, p.12.

[37] Interview with Munshi, 2 December 2011.

[38] This has been an association that later generations of activists have continued to develop; for example, in the case of abductions and violence against women in the disputed area of Kashmir. See S. Mulay and J. Kirk (eds.), *Women Building Peace between India and Pakistan* (Anthem Press, New Delhi, 2007) and A. Basu and S. Roy (eds.), *Violence and Democracy in India* (Seagull Books, Greenford, 2007.)

The Bengal Famine was an important period of consciousness building. This was the case not only for individuals working directly with famine relief and food security, such as Renu Chakravartty, Vijayalakshmi Pandit and Renuka Ray, but also for those who found themselves outside India, such as Vidya Munshi. A medical student studying in England at the time, Munshi organised a poster exhibition of the famine in Sheffield together with a fellow Tamil student. Using graphs and other materials from the magazine *India Today* and *The Problem of India,* the exhibition was intended to show 'how after the British came into India there had been seven famines one after the other in the years of British administration',[39] Munshi, like her fellow activists back home, was putting the famine within a broader political context and making important connections between this specific event and the dynamics of colonial domination on the Indian subcontinent.

The Telengana Struggle

As with relief efforts and political organising around the Bengal Famine, women's participation in the Telengana and Tebhaga peasant struggles of the late 1940s and early 1950s are claimed today as part of the prehistory of the NFIW. While the Bengal Famine represented a fight for survival for affected populations, and a struggle on behalf of women's organisations to coordinate relief and galvanise an apathetic wartime government into action, the Telengana and Tebhaga struggles were peasant struggles over access to land rights and control over local government. Emerging at the end of the turbulent decade of the 1940s, they reflected the growing influence of Marxism on Indian nationalism, as an alternative vision for a 'new social order' divergent from the Nehruvian and Gandhian models.

Commencing in September 1946, Tebhaga was a militant mass movement of sharecroppers fighting to keep a fairer share of the crop they produced from the usurping hands of the landowners of West Bengal. It was led by the CPI's Bengal Kisan Sabha, with

[39] Interview with Munshi, 2 December 2011.

urban student militants playing an important role in organising and mobilising sharecroppers.[40] Women were also recognised as significant participants, 'stimulating the moral strength for resistance'[41] through their presence in confrontations with the police, and their involvement in other activities, including the forced harvesting of crops, supplying food to rebels, maintaining communication networks and campaigning and organising of political activities.[42] Although Tebhaga was hugely significant for Indian Marxists, it was short-lived and was suppressed by March the following year.

Telengana was a violent peasant uprising against Muslim and high-caste Hindu revenue collectors and landlords in Telengana, one of the three linguistic regions of the princely state of Hyderabad.[43] Peasant farmers and labourers faced a number of exploitative practices in the state, including *vethi,* which enabled a landlord to claim a percentage of a peasant's crop or to extract forced labour from the peasant. Gendered violence formed a component of this exploitation. 'Rape was an everyday reality, the undenied right of the landlord or moneylender' while *Adi bapa,* a type of concubinage practised in the area, entitled a bridegroom to bring a female servant from the bride's household to his own upon marriage.[44]

Spanning the period from July 1946 to October 1951, the Telengana movement was organised and led by the CPI. However, it quickly became enmeshed in the larger struggle between the Muslim Nizam of Hyderabad, Asaf Jahi, and the Indian State around the question of whether Hyderabad was to accede to India or remain independent under the special provisions given to princely states. When the Nizam

---

[40] Tebhaga means two-thirds of the crop. The sharecroppers in this movement demanded the right to retain two-thirds of the crop they produced instead of being forced to hand over half, or even more than half, to the *jotedars* as payment for their rented land. See Sarkar, *Modern India*, pp. 439–440.

[41] D.K. Singha Roy, *Women in Peasant Movements: Tebhaga, Naxalite and After* (New Delhi, Manohar, 1992), p. 47.

[42] Ibid., p. 47.

[43] Sarkar, *Modern India*, p. 443.

[44] V. Kannabiran and K. Lalitha, 'That Magic Time: Women in the Telengana People's Struggle' in K. Sangari and S. Vaid (eds.), *Recasting Women: Essays in Indian Colonial History* (Rutgers University Press, New Brunswick, 1990), p. 182.

refused to accede and threatened to join Pakistan during negotiations, it pitted the Hyderabad Congress supporters in the state (who supported Indian accession) against the Razakars, the paramilitary body of the *Ittihad-ul-Muslimeen,* an organisation that supported the Nizam and wanted to safeguard the position of Muslims in the administration and politics of the state. Initially, the Telengana movement and Hyderabad Congress supporters found themselves on the same side, both resisting the Razakars in this standoff, and making CPI leaders and the Indian State covert allies. However, when the CPI changed its leadership and strategy in 1948, abandoning its commitment to 'loyal opposition', and embracing violent resistance to the Congress government instead, this situation changed. Under the CPI's new position, the Party hoped the success of Telengana could be the start of a countrywide communist rebellion.[45] The CPI had now become a direct and immediate threat to the Nehru government and was consequently banned in March 1948. Many of its leaders were imprisoned and a propaganda campaign against the Party was orchestrated by the government, reducing its support. When attempted negotiations with the Nizam failed in September of that year, the Indian army sent in troops to take control of the state and these troops were ordered to suppress the rebellion. As the movement went into retreat, its initial gains were relinquished. It was eventually brought to an end when the CPI reversed its hard-line stance in order to participate in the elections of 1952.

As both of these movements were led by the CPI, and as a number of the founding members and leaders of the NFIW were communists, there was a natural ideological affinity between them.[46] Former women Telengana and Tebhaga veterans in Andhra Pradesh and Bengal

---

[45] R. Guha, *India after Gandhi: The History of the World's Largest Democracy* (HarperCollins, London, 2007), pp. 52, 96–97.

[46] As a political organisation, the CPI was also significantly influenced by the stance taken by these peasant movements. In 1948, the Party decided to reject collaboration with the new government and instead adopt a position of revolutionary opposition, aligning its strategy with that of Telengana, by arguing that the freedom of independence was an unreal freedom and that 'the Telengana path is our path'. This resulted in the banning of the Party as well as the Women's Front in March 1948. Gargi Chakravartty emphasises that many communist women were unhappy about this new party line. Interview with Chakravartty, 4 November 2011.

became part of the local and regional women's organisations that were incorporated into the NFIW in the 1950s.[47] Prominent women figures associated with the uprisings were also incorporated into NFIW leadership positions in states like Kerala.[48]

The NFIW leadership and many communities of women who were early affiliates found inspiration in Telengana and Tebhaga women. They drew on women's participation in these movements to emphasise that having invested and sacrificed for the struggle, women had indeed 'earned' their revolutionary credentials. As participants and as leaders in such a radical process, they were entitled to be legitimate and equal members of any subsequent new social order to emerge from such a process.[49]

There is a tendency to romanticise and idealise the roles and experiences of women within these peasant uprisings and to present this as a movement defined by a radical reworking of gender relationships. This certainly comes across very clearly within the collective memory and history of the CPI and its allied organisations today. For the CPI, the narrative and identity of the women peasant revolutionary was part of the construction of that particular romanticised image. The participation of women reflected the democratic and broad-based nature of the movement and, therefore, gave it additional political clout and legitimacy. This organisational remembering offers a contributory history which 'writes in' and acknowledges the significant role of women within these historical events, but tends to be mythologising and uncritical. In claiming Telengana and Tebhaga women's involvement in this way, the NFIW has had to draw on the language and rhetoric of such a contributory history, where women are represented as 'glorified heroines', or as passive victims. There is little room for acknowledging the way in which feudal patriarchy was reinvented within structures of the movement itself.[50]

---

[47] Ibid.

[48] NFIW, *For Equality: For a Just Social Order* (NFIW, New Delhi, 1984), pp. 57–58.

[49] This is an affinity and claim that continues to be articulated by the contemporary NFIW leadership that I met during the course of my research and is very much part of the current institutional history of the Federation.

[50] Kannabiran and Lalitha, 'That Magic Time', pp. 31–32.

More recent oral histories, such as those by Kannabiran, Lalitha and others, have offered a more nuanced and critical reading of the role of women in the Telengana movement. These authors argue that Telengana did indeed open up new and previously unchartered and unimagined possibilities for women. It enabled them to move from the private to the public sphere and provided them with a new set of tools for analysing and articulating different forms of inequality in their society. Nevertheless, inequality in the form of middle-class gendered values and norms and a double moral standard were often reproduced in this movement. This is why these scholars identify a 'curious contradictoriness' that emerges in accounts of women for whom Telengana was a lived experience.[51]

It is possible, however, to acknowledge the significance of women's participation in these peasant struggles without reverting to the romantic and glorified representation of the peasant woman as a revolutionary fighter. The Indian woman as a political agent can be symbolically and practically reworked. The more recent critical history of women's participation in the Telengana movement is useful in this regard; it challenges the dichotomy between agent and passive spectator, or between agent and victim, encouraging us to think about agency in terms of a sliding scale, where degrees of agency can coexist with a context of restrictions.[52]

Telengana widened and expanded the possibilities and meanings of agency and subjectivity for women in the sphere of agitational politics. It did so through the motif of the woman guerrilla fighter, who represented the capacity to actively resist and challenge the status quo. A second point that should be stressed is the fact that the Telengana and Tebhaga struggles helped to bring two important gendered concerns

[51] Ibid., p. 181.

[52] The complexities of the experience of Telengana women and their subsequent significance for the newly formed NFIW calls for a rethinking of female agency in historiography, as, Janaki Nair argues, such agency can neither be 'wholly contained within a delineation of structures of oppression nor exhausted by accounts of female presence in history but must be posed within specific contexts'. See J, Nair, 'On the Question of Agency in Indian Feminist Historiography' in *Gender and History,* 6:1 (April 1994), p. 83.

more directly onto the agenda of the newly established NFIW. The first of these was that of violence against women, particularly sexual violence, through which the freedom and integrity of the body were discussed. The second was the demand for women's right to ownership and control over land, a demand that subsequently became incorporated into NFIW policy.

Domestic violence and rape are issues associated with the contemporary women's movement in India. The emergence of broad-based campaigns against such acts of violence are, in fact, recognised by scholars as marking a new stage in the development of contemporary feminism in India.[53] A 1984 brochure on the history of the NFIW, however, reminds the reader that 'work against social oppression and atrocities on women', including 'wife-beating, starvation, desertion, demands of more dowry, and even murders', as well as 'molestation and rape' have always been important activities of the Federation.[54] The early prioritisation of such concerns is reiterated by the organisational memory and perspective of contemporary NFIW leaders:

> It's always been addressed... If you go back further...the Telengana movement...the women were at the forefront for the land rights....Then we had the Tebhaga uprising, again the women were at the forefront... for the land struggle, addressing violence...All these struggles, which had taken place, left a footprint. Even today we go back and address those issues.[55]

The reports of CPI cadres touring Telengana-controlled villages and reporting back to the CPI regional command offer some examples of how the concerns of gendered violence came to be incorporated and addressed within this movement. In one report from 1948, the author and narrator of the trip describes 'Comrade G', a member of the local

---

[53] Domestic violence first became a subject of protest when it was taken up by the Shahada movement of tribal landless labourers in Maharashtra in the late 1960s. This movement was joined by the New Left in the early 1970s and focused on the physical violence associated with alcoholism. See R. Kumar, 'From Chipko to Sati: The Contemporary Indian Women's Movement' in N. Menon (ed.), *Gender and Politics in India* (Oxford University Press, New Delhi, 2001) pp. 343–344, 349, 353.

[54] NFIW, *For Equality: For a Just Social Order*, p. 63.

[55] Interview with A. Raja, NFIW President, 18 November 2013, New Delhi.

Sangham (the local village council established by the Dalams[56] to replace the authority of the landlord) addressing the village: 'Now you people will elect your village government. This government will have to see that no one starves in the village. It will open a school for the village children...Women will not be subject to any injustice. Men who beat women will be duly punished by this government.'[57]

In a different village, the narrator reports his conversation with another member of the Sangham who was an untouchable. He asks the man if anything has changed since the establishment of the *sangham*, and records the response of the man:

> How can things be as they were? ...the Harijans no longer work without payment.., six months back, we used to do forced labour. But as soon as the *sangham* arrived that practice was stopped. Similarly, earlier our men folk used to beat up the women; but now we have passed a law...[58]

On another occasion, the narrator reports the comments of a comrade from 'Village P', talking about the question of 'men beating up their women' in the village since the establishment of the Sangham: '[F] ormerly the woman quickly put up with it. But now they go at once and report it to the village government. The man is taken to task; he has to apologise to the woman and promise not to repeat such an act again.'[59]

Previous chapters of this book have shown how discourses of gendered violence in the context of Partition, and the rape and abduction of women, operated to reproduce the unequal power relationships of patriarchy by positioning women as sites of honour and communal identity. It is difficult to gauge the extent to which this change and reworking of gender relations operated at the level

---

[56] The CPI divided members up into working groups called Dalams with each Dalam responsible for a particular type of activity or task.

[57] District Council of the Communist Party (CP), discussing the lifting of the ban on the Andhra Mahasabha and the CP. The document also provides a description of the social and economic changes occurring in different villages in and around Warangal and other districts where the Sangham and Andhra Mahasabha had established village governments, 1948, Subject no: 359, Andhra Pradesh/ Telengana, CPI Papers, Ajoy Bhavan.

[58] Ibid.

[59] Ibid.

of rhetoric and political image, versus how widespread it was on the ground in Telengana villages. Certainly, discourses of rape and molestation provided a powerful justification for rebellion and delegitimised the actions and rights of landlords and rent collectors. But was the outrage against rape merely a way for men in the CPI to claim control of women for themselves, reinforcing a discourse which positioned women as property or a site of family and community honour? This discourse certainly does use the language of shame, honour and protection. For the CPI, gender equality, certainly at the level of rhetoric, functioned to articulate and reinforce the Party's broader ideological commitment to the destruction of social hierarchy and class privilege.

What is distinct about this discourse is the fact that rape and molestation of village women were not only seen to be perpetrated by the class enemy or the 'other', for example, by landlords, their 'goondas' and the police. Within this report, there is an acknowledgement of gendered violence being committed within the family—by one's own. By broaching domestic violence specifically, this report raises questions about power relationships in the family and calls for a reworking of such relationships, a challenge that holds revolutionary potential. Furthermore, even if this discourse operated merely at the level of rhetoric, rhetoric has the potential to take on a life of its own and be endowed with new kinds of power and meanings. In being taken up by the Party, this issue places domestic violence as a concern into the public space of Left-wing Indian politics. This is significant. The question that needs to be addressed in light of this is the extent to which the NFIW has been able to use this rhetoric for a genuine and transformative agenda.

The second important concern that Telengana and Tebhaga women helped to bring into the NFIW from the time of its formation was also fundamentally concerned with questions of power within the sphere of the household, but this time relating to economic power. The Telengana and Tebhaga movements are recognised as being progressive on gender issues for the time because they acknowledged and addressed the issue of women's right to own land.

One of the heroes of the Telengana Struggle is Chakali Ailamma, a peasant woman cultivator who stood up to the local zamindar by refusing to pay the heavy levy demanded for cultivation of his land. Her resistance was recounted by one of the Andhra Pradesh NFIW members who joined the Telengana struggle:

> She was cultivating four acres of land for the zamindar... And she had to pay some levy to the landlord. Whatever produce was on the land, they used to take away and leave very little. First she started saying, 'No I will not pay!' to the landlord. She was the first to raise her voice, to say that it was unjust for the zamindar to be taking all the produce. She was an inspiration for all the other people.[60]

The veneration of heroes of all revolutionary movements is based on fact but also embellished by propaganda, and it is always someone who represents the causes and ideals of the movement. This story was recounted specifically when the interviewee was asked how the Telengana struggle had started. Although the scholar cannot verify the facts of this account, the themes and concerns that it introduces are indeed relevant as a reflection of the major concerns of peasant fighters and communists involved. The story of Chakali Ailamma suggests that there was an awareness, amongst Telengana women veterans, of the importance of acquired land rights, and the insecurity that peasant women faced without these.

At the founding Conference of the NFIW in 1954, a resolution on peasant women, and their right to land was adopted:

> The foremost demand of the peasant women is the right to own land. Custom and tradition enforced by unjust laws have deprived a large section of our women of the right to own property. This Congress resolves to patiently and carefully explain to all sections of the people, both men and women, the justice of this right and win their support to it.[61]

---

[60] Interview with S. Suguna, NFIW member (Andhra Pradesh) and Telengana veteran, 31 December 2011, Hyderabad.

[61] 'Indian Women Meet in Conference', June 1954, pp. 5, 51. Land rights remained an ongoing concern with NFIW-affiliated organisations involved in various land rights struggles in the 1950s, 1960s and 1970s. See NFIW, *For Equality: For a Just Social Order*, p. 58.

This report reveals a concern not only with women's ownership of land as a means of livelihood, but also with the question of access to, and usage of, natural resources such as forests, grazing grounds, rivers and ponds. The Joint Secretaries of the NFIW's National Coordinating Committee reported that the work of affiliated organisations amongst peasants had:

> ...taken different forms in different areas. In some places, it is the question of grazing grounds, in another the right to bring wood from the forest, and yet in another the right to catch fish in the village pond, that becomes a burning question for peasant women. Often on a local scale and sometimes on a district or provincial basis, some of these struggles registered success.[62]

A peasant woman's right to own land offers scope for the renegotiation of power dynamics within the family, enabling a greater degree of economic independence. This has the potential to loosen her embeddedness in relationships of dominance and inequality in the family and the local community. Contemporary scholarship by Bina Agarwal and Pradeep Panda has confirmed this important connection.[63] Building on her groundbreaking study, *A Field of One's Own,* Agarwal and Panda have illustrated how owning a house or land for women in the southern state of Kerala reduces their chances of experiencing domestic violence. This research shows how lack of access and ownership over immovable property, in particular farmlands in South Asia, jeopardises women's welfare, agency and personal safety.[64]

Later in this chapter, it is shown how this connection between economic freedom and the freedom and integrity of the body, defined by a state of freedom from physical violence within the household, or

[62] Ibid., pp. 25–26.

[63] See, for example, B. Agarwal, *A Field of One's Own: Gender and Land Rights in South Asia* (Cambridge University Press, Cambridge, 1994.) and B. Agarwal, *Gender challenges: Property, Family and the State:* Volume 2, (Oxford University Press, New Delhi, 2016).

[64] S. Razavi, 'Gender Challenges, Volume 1: Agriculture, Technology, and Food Security/ Gender challenges Volume 2: Property, Family, and the State/Gender Challenges, Volume 3: Environmental Change and Collective Action' in *The Journal of Peasant Studies,* 45: 2 (2018), p. 475.

. the right to challenge and confront such violence, is reinforced through the NFIW's campaign in support of the Hindu Code Bill.

It was only much later in the 1990s, with the emergence of the conceptual framework of 'gender and development', that women's access to land and land rights came to be recognised as an important factor in the country's socio-economic development. The influence of Telengana and Tebhaga veterans in the NFIW meant that this issue was preempted in the agenda and concerns of the Federation decades before it gained official recognition in the international development community.

Refugee Women and the Claim to Socio-Economic Rights

Identity does not necessarily precede struggle. The dynamics of struggle, often around local and immediate needs, can also provide the context for the creation of new identities. The experience of refugee women in Calcutta illustrates this dynamic. Migrating across the border from East Pakistan into West Bengal, hundreds of thousands of refugees in Calcutta found themselves outside the official mechanisms of State relief and rehabilitation, and institutionally 'invisible'. In this context, refugees had to begin helping themselves. Women refugees took part in this process by forming local Samitis to coordinate the provision of relief activities and services. This work brought them into contact with established women's organisations that were also active amongst refugee communities and enabled the interaction of local grassroots struggles and their national counterparts, which eventually helped launch the National Federation of Indian Women in 1954. Relief and welfare activities and immediate socio-economic survival provided an entry point into both local political mobilisation and a national campaign for the Hindu Code Bill, ushering these communities of women into new forms of political citizenship.

The Partition of the subcontinent on 15 August 1947 unleashed one of the largest mass migrations in human history. An estimated eight to 10 million people moved across the borders of the newly created States of India and Pakistan. By the end of 1956, a total of 3.33 million

East Bengali Hindu refugees had moved from Pakistan into West Bengal, Assam and Tripura in India.[65] Although the government of West Bengal established a Ministry of Rehabilitation in 1947 to handle relief and rehabilitation efforts, the scale of the problem and a lack of understanding of the nature of migration meant that these efforts remained largely inadequate. Renuka Ray, who became West Bengal Minister for Relief and Rehabilitation after the 1952 elections, was highly critical of the Indian government's permanent resettlement programme for refugees in East India.[66] She explains in her autobiography that a large part of the problem stemmed from the fact that this response failed to recognise that the migration into West Bengal assumed a completely different dynamic compared to its counterpart in the Punjab. Punjab witnessed a mass exchange of populations over a more confined period, preceding and following Partition. In the east of the country, however, the first influx of refugees arrived in October 1946 after the retaliatory riots and violence of Noakhali and Tipperah. This continued with varying intensity, developing into a flow after the widespread communal violence of 1950, and then carrying on in dribs and drabs over the course of the following decade.[67]

The government tended to view the presence of migrants in Eastern India as a temporary problem rather than one of rehabilitation and resettlement. The state government lacked a coherent rehabilitation policy and any relief, when it was forthcoming, tended to be ad hoc. It was only in 1956 that a 'comprehensive policy of rehabilitation and economic reintegration was devised for East Bengali refugees'.[68] During the early years following the creation of Pakistan, 'there was considerable reluctance on the part of the central government to acknowledge that the displaced persons from East Pakistan were here

---

[65] Ray, *My Reminiscences,* pp. 152–153. Also see Chatterjee, *The Spoils of Partition* for an account of the influx and exodus of refugees and migrants from West Bengal.

[66] Ibid., p. 157.

[67] U. Sen, "Spinster, Prostitute, Pioneer?" Images of Refugee Women in Post-Partition Calcutta', European University Institute Working Papers 2011/32, p. 3. Also see U. Sen, 'Refugees and the Politics of Nation Building 1947–1971', PhD Book, Faculty of History, Cambridge University, 2009.

[68] Ibid., p. 7.

to stay,' Ray observed.[69] Furthermore, East Bengali refugees, unlike those from Punjab, 'had the onus of proving that they were the victims of coerced migration as opposed to being mere economic migrants'. It was only by being 'genuine' refugees that they could lay claim to relief and rehabilitation from the State.[70]

These rehabilitation efforts were further hampered by the fact that refugees who came into eastern India were adding to the second densest population in the country, and to an overcrowded West Bengal economy. In the west, there had been a roughly equal counter flow of Muslims from the Indian to the Pakistani region of the Punjab, creating space and infrastructure—in the form of vacant property and land—for the permanent resettlement of incoming migrants. But in eastern India, there was no vacant land or property where the newcomers could settle because, 'the Muslims leaving West Bengal were much fewer than those coming in from East Pakistan, and many who had fled later returned and got their lands back'. In some of the urban centres, such as Calcutta, this resulted in enormous overcrowding, with refugees spilling out onto the streets, and new needs in terms of sanitation, public health and law and order.[71] By March 1951, a total of 6,24,164 refugees were living in Calcutta and surrounding suburbs alone.[72]

However, only a small percentage of the total number of refugees in West Bengal, 70,000 in total, could be accommodated in government camps. These tended to be 'the poorer section of the displaced population who were totally dependent on State aid and had neither the resources nor energy to rehabilitate themselves'.[73] Refugees outside these camps were not given any rehabilitation assistance in terms of grants or alternative accommodation. Nor were any extra amenities provided in Calcutta or in the state of Tripura.[74] Urban

---

69 Ray, *My Reminiscences*, p. 153.

70 Sen, 'Spinster, Prostitute, Pioneer?', p. 4.

71 Ray, *My Reminiscences*, pp. 153–162.

72 Figures taken from the Census of India 1951, Volume VI Part 3, Calcutta City, quoted in Sen, 'Spinster, Prostitute, Pioneer?', pp. 3–4.

73 H. Bandyopadhyay, *Udbastu* (Sahitya Samsad, Calcutta, 1970) quoted in Sen, 'Spinster, Prostitute, Pioneer?', p. 9.

74 Ray, *My Reminiscences*, pp. 152–161.

and rural middle-class East Bengali families, who had lost all their assets, and who did not have family or friends in West Bengal to help, therefore, found themselves out on the streets, largely invisible and ignored in terms of relief and rehabilitation efforts. This lack of recognition in effect denied these refugees a civic identity as city dwellers entitled to local municipal services, living space and economic opportunities, and relegated them to political and social margins. In and around Calcutta, non-camp refugees had no choice but to settle on whatever land was available and to occupy this land illegally.[75] At first, they squatted and later, they began establishing more formalised refugee colonies.[76]

The early years of independence consequently saw the rapid growth of innumerable refugee colonies in Calcutta, extending in a line from Dumdum to Kanchrapara in the north, and Poddarnagar to Jadavpur in the south.[77] By 1950, 149 colonies had sprung up, placing large areas of both government-owned and private land under occupation. After some time, State refugee camps were also converted into refugee colonies. Refugees within such colonies found themselves in a very precarious state of existence. Because they were considered squatters, they were often forcibly removed and their huts razed to the ground, obliging them to return later to reoccupy the land and start all over again. In this climate of uncertainty and instability, women refugees began to organise women's Samitis, which were involved in coordinating relief efforts, such as the distribution of milk powder and food. In Chittaranjan Colony in Calcutta, for example, the Dakshin Kalikata Sahartali Bastuhara Samiti became very popular amongst refugee women. Amongst the refugees who came into the city were a number of women who had been politically active before independence and they brought their politics and their organising

[75] G. Chakravartty, *Coming Out of Partition: Refugee Women of Bengal* (Sage, New Delhi, 2005), pp. 52–54.

[76] Ray, *My Reminiscences*, p. 161. The recollections and experiences of Renuka Ray as a West Bengal Rehabilitation official support the argument presented by Joya Chatterjee in *The Spoils of Partition*. They agree that rehabilitation of Bengali refugees was largely self-rehabilitation rather than being State-driven.

[77] Sen, 'Spinster, Prostitute, Pioneer?', p.10.

skills with them.[78] Drawing on a longer tradition of organising around relief work and political activism that had developed with the Bengal Famine of 1943, these women took the lead in the creation of these new Samitis.

However, relief provisions could not be distributed if they were not readily available. The invisibility of non-camp refugees and the failure of the West Bengal government to tackle the problem as a long-term one of resettlement and rehabilitation compounded the scale of the influx. The population density of the region and overcrowded nature of the economy meant that refugees desperately needed food, clothing, shelter and basic municipal services, such as clean water, which were often not forthcoming. These Samitis had to extend their activities to protesting, lobbying and demanding municipal and state governments for adequate assistance, with women refugees arranging processions and meetings to 'ventilate their grievances on the scarcity of food, cloth, house accommodation and eviction'. Furthermore, refugee communities increasingly realised that relief would remain short-term and ineffective if it was not backed up by proper resettlement and rehabilitation policies. If refugees had formal and secure housing and access to livelihoods, their more immediate needs of food, shelter and security could be sustainably addressed. In this way, these women's Samitis came to be drawn into the larger movement against evictions and the demand for the formalisation of colonies and the recognition and provision of proper facilities.[79]

In addition to being drawn into the public sphere through the agitational politics of the broader refugee movement in Calcutta, the struggle for relief and rehabilitation brought established women's organisations in the region into contact with these relatively informal women's Samitis. Working side by side with these Samitis, existing women's organisations, such as MARS, played an important role in providing voluntary relief services, and later rehabilitation programmes for women refugees. Over time, considerable interaction and overlap between established women's organisations and new refugee Samitis

---

[78] Chakravartty, *Coming Out of Partition*, pp. 52–59.

[79] Chakravartty, *Coming Out of Partition*, pp. 52–63.

occurred, in terms of membership and agenda. Refugee women found themselves involved with local women's organisations in West Bengal as the latter took up the demands of these communities of women and offered support and practical help with petitioning state assistance.[80] Grassroots refugee activism also led to the emergence of a new set of woman leaders within MARS, other women's organisations working in West Bengal, and the CPI.[81]

A two-way exchange between the socio-economic concerns and needs of refugee women and the national gender politics of the NFIW was fostered. And it was the campaign for the Hindu Code Bill that provided a platform for interaction between these two very different kinds of struggles: one for socio-economic rights and services at a municipal level, and the other for legislative equality at a national level. The Indian social reform movement had been lobbying for the reform of personal laws in India since the nineteenth century, through a discourse of social reform which was paternal in emphasis and aimed at the protection of women from culturally backward practices. In the twentieth century, the campaign for women's franchise in India provided added incentive to the reform of civil laws. Geraldine Forbes notes that activists increasingly began to realise the connection between political rights and civil rights, which determined women's status in the home and family. 'As organised women gained experience in the public arena, they became more aware of their dependent status. They were excluded from new representative structures because they did not own property or were not married to men with property.'[82] From the 1920s onwards, with the emergence of all-India women's organisations, such as the WIA and the AIWC, women campaigners began to take up the reform of civil laws themselves, drawing on

---

80 These women's organisations were building on an earlier history of women's organising; where relief work during the devastating Bengal Famine of 1943 was used by communist women, working within the AIWC, to mobilise and expand the membership of the organisation by bringing in new constituencies of peasant and working-class women. See Renu Chakravartty's account of the Mahila Atmaraksha Samiti in *Communists in the Indian Women's Movement.*

81 Chakravartty, *Coming Out of Partition,* p. 62.

82 Forbes, *Women in Modern India,* p. 113.

older social reform discourses of welfare and paternalism, but also increasingly on the emerging discourse of rights and equal inclusion in the body politic.

In 1929, after considerable campaigning and collaborative efforts, the Child Marriages Restraint Act was passed under the colonial government.[83] Following on from this, in the 1930s, the government, favouring a piecemeal approach towards the reform of civil laws, introduced a number of different acts covering various aspects of family and marital life. It was only with the passing of the Hindu Women's Right to Property Act (Deshmukh Act) in 1937 that a renewed boost was given to demands for codification.[84]

In 1941, the Hindu Law Committee, also known as the Rau Committee, was established to assess the weaknesses of the 1937 Act. The Committee recommended a comprehensive code of marriage and succession which led to the establishment of a second Hindu Law Committee in 1944, to prepare a draft Code. This was revised, becoming known as the Hindu Code Bill[85] which was introduced to Parliament in 1947, with the intention of becoming a law on 1 January 1948, but the project was temporarily suspended because of ongoing post-Partition and post-independence operations.[86] In 1948, under the leadership of Nehru, this draft Code was referred to a Select Committee under the Chairmanship of Dr Ambedkar, Law Minister and Chairman of the Constitution Drafting Committee.

Ambedkar incorporated several important changes to the draft Code Bill, including equal property rights for women, the abolition

---

[83] Ibid.

[84] The Act secured for the widowed daughter-in-law legal rights equal to those of her son to enjoy her husband's share in the joint family property but did not give her absolute and alienable rights of ownership. See R. Som, 'Jawaharlal Nehru and the Hindu Code: A Victory of Symbol over Substance?' in *Modern Asian Studies,* 28:1 (1994), p 4.

[85] For a detailed account of the legislative development of the Hindu Code Bill and previous colonial endeavours to reform personal law in India, see J. Nair, *Women and Colonial Law in India* (Kali for Women, New Delhi, 1996) and F. Agnes, *Law and Gender Inequality: The Politics of Women's Rights in India* (Oxford University Press, New Delhi, 2001).

[86] Ibid, p. 5.

of customary law, and specification of grounds for divorce, before reintroducing it to Parliament.[87] These changes brought the Code closer to the demands of women's organisations for complete equality in the civil law for Hindu women as the starting point, and for the eventual introduction of a Uniform Civil Code. These changes, however, aroused stiff opposition from various quarters, including from President Rajendra Prasad, who argued that they would result in the destruction of the Hindu family.[88] This opposition led to the stalling and obstruction of the Bill in Parliament, with women's organisations who had been closely monitoring the progress of the draft Code, increasingly concerned that the draft Code Bill would be sabotaged as a result. In October 1951, a group of women leaders met in Delhi to form the Women's Fundamental Rights Committee, electing Kamaladevi Chattopadhyay as its President. This committee agreed to review all existing legislation to ensure that it accorded with the fundamental rights as laid out in the Constitution, to take up matters of discrimination and to educate public opinion and galvanise public support in favour of the Hindu Code Bill.[89]

The campaign for the Hindu Code Bill was one of the first legislative struggles taken up by the NFIW, and a site of collaboration and united effort with other organisations, including the AIWC. It was a cross-organisational nationwide initiative that represented a sustained and proactive attempt on behalf of the AIWC and the NFIW to hold the government accountable in terms of its constitutional commitment to equality. Signature campaigns and petitions, which had defined gender politics in the earlier decades of the century, continued to be used as a central tactic in the campaign. Petitioning would start off with a series of local meetings amongst organisations of women, to spread the word and create awareness around the issue in particular constituencies.[90]

---

87 Ibid.

88 See letter from Rajendra Prasad to Jawaharlal Nehru, 15 September 1951, in V. Tagra, *Jawaharlal Nehru and the Status of Women in India: An Analytical Study* (Reliance Publishing House, New Delhi, 2006), Appendix III, pp. 366–373.

89 Hannah Sen, 'President's Circular letter No. 6', 22 September 1951, File 159, AIWC Papers, NMML; The Action Committee of the Hindu Code Bill, meeting minutes, 4 October 1951, File 159, AIWC Papers, NMML.

90 Interview with Chakravartty, 4 November 2011.

This would be followed by a signature campaign with activists going door to door in their neighbourhoods and amongst their social networks to collect support, and at a statewide level mass rallies would be held where resolutions in support of the Hindu Code Bill were passed.[91] The Hindu Code Bill campaign represented a struggle within the constitutional framework of the new State, drawing on the formal political strategies of lobbying. These signature petitions were then used to pressurise the relevant MPs and political parties who represented the constituencies from which the signatures were collected. Campaign leaders threatened that women would withhold their vote if their representatives did not commit themselves to promoting the Hindu Code Bill in the Lok Sabha.

The signature drives were intended as a demonstration of democracy in practice, an exercise in the power and legitimacy of a collective voice. On top of that, there were the aforementioned door-to-door campaigns in neighbourhoods. This drew on one of the biggest strengths of all women's organisations like the NFIW and the AIWC—their outreach capacity and their embeddedness in the communities in which they worked. They made use of personal interaction, talking to and persuading the women from their communities and their families to change prevalent attitudes. The act of signing a petition was, in itself, hugely significant:

> At that time collecting a thousand signatures was something, and sending it to the Collector or the Prime Minister was something great during that period. Because you see, the women were not allowed to even sign. They did not have much freedom to intervene in any such social issues...getting a single signature was in itself a huge task. But managing a thousand signatures...that was a big achievement.[92]

The campaign for the Hindu Code Bill was one of the NFIW's activities that pulled refugee women into the mainstream women's movement in West Bengal. Because the NFIW and its founding organisations were

---

[91] Ibid.; Interview with Raja, 18 November 2011.

[92] Ibid.

already working with these refugee communities, they were one of the communities targeted in signature campaigns, since the refugee women provided a vital source of support. Of a total of 45,760 signatures collected in favour of the Special Marriage Bill by January 1955, 36,000 were collected in West Bengal, indicating the importance of the state as a support base. Likewise, for the Hindu Marriage and Divorce Bill, the majority of signatures—36,000 out of a total 44,437—were collected from West Bengal.[93]

Rallying public support for the Hindu Code Bill was essential for women's organisations and activists; it was a decisive and hard-fought campaign. 'There was so much resistance,' recalled Vidya Munshi.[94] Resistance emanated from across the political spectrum, from the conservative hardliners, from the Hindu Mahasabha, the Sikh groups, and Muslim men.[95] President Rajendra Prasad himself was wary of these proposed legislative changes.[96] This made those in support of equal rights for women in the Assembly feel very frustrated, recalls Renuka Ray.[97] Many women's constituencies also opposed the Bill, such as the Hindu Mahasabha Women's Wing.[98] The Secretary of the CPI Andhra Provincial Women's branch reported the opposition of rural village women to the Bill, on the grounds of destruction of the family:

> We, it seemed, were swimming against the current. A vigorous vile slanderous campaign was organised against women comrades. We were slandered as having trying to disrupt family life, through divorce, impose women-raj in the name of property rights and encouraging debauchery and prostitution.[99]

---

[93] NFIW, 'Report of the Joint Secretaries Mrs Anasuya Gyanchand and Mrs Hajrah Begum', 4 January 1955, File 99, AIWC Papers, NMML.

[94] Interview with Munshi, 22 December 2011.

[95] See Som, 'Jawaharlal Nehru and the Hindu Code: A Victory of Symbol over Substance?'

[96] R. Prasad to J. Nehru, 15 September 1951 in V. Tagra, *Jawaharlal Nehru and the Status of Women in India* (Reliance Publishing House, New Delhi, 2006), pp. 366–373.

[97] Ray, *My Reminiscences*, p. 139.

[98] Interview with Chakravartty, 4 November 2011.

[99] M. Suryavati (Secretary of Andhra Provincial Women's Fraction), Report on Agitation concerning the Hindu Code Bill, 24 December 1952, File 1953/14, CPI Papers, Joshi Archives.

Eventually, the Bill was passed between 1952 and 1956 as four separate Acts: the Hindu Marriage Act, the Hindu Succession Act, the Hindu Minority and Guardian Act and the Hindu Adoptions and Maintenance Act.

The campaign for the Hindu Code Bill encouraged the inclusion and mobilisation of new communities of women in the NFIW's politics of gender equality. 'While working with them, they collected signatures and that became a base, a platform,' Gargi Chakravartty emphasises.[100] Refugee women began to enter the structures of the NFIW, and formed a visible presence in the 'spectacular demonstration of women' who marched through the streets of Calcutta from the University Institute as part of the opening of the first NFIW Conference in 1954.[101] According to *New Age*, refugee women from 15 colonies in and around Calcutta attended this first conference. By the second conference, three years later, in June 1957, the organisation reported that its affiliated organisations working with refugee colonies in Bengal had 'grown and stabilised'.[102]

Through the process of collecting signatures, NFIW campaigners were able to introduce abstract national-level issues, such as gender rights and equality in an accessible and meaningful way that engaged the day-to-day domestic struggles of women refugees. Visiting households and talking to women and their families gave campaigners an opportunity to broach and challenge the predetermined notions of what a lady should be. They were able to challenge the idea that 'she should be confined to the four walls of the house and she should look after her children, her parents and in-laws, she should prepare food for the husband and family on time...she should not look at what is happening outside'.[103] 'We wanted to increase awareness amongst women and the people at large; women ought to know at least what they were entitled to,' stresses Manikuntala Sen, a Calcutta-based NFIW leader during this period. 'Earlier even when I noticed women with marks of violence on their

[100] Interview with Chakravartty, 4 November 2011.

[101] S. Munsi, 'National Conference of Women in Calcutta', 13 June 1954, *New Age*, copy located in CPI offices, Ajoy Bhavan

[102] NFIW, 2nd National Conference Report, June 1957, Vijayawada, p. 28.

[103] Interview with Raja, 18 November 2011.

bodies, inflicted by their husbands, there was little I could do to help them. Now I might actually be able to do something.'[104]

Leaders, such as Sen, were making connections between freedom and equality in the private sphere of the household, and freedom and equality in the public sphere as the 'sexless citizen'. The campaign for the Hindu Code Bill carried enormous meaning and significance for women's organisations because it was an articulation of the idea of equality for women in law. It was about the principle involved, but it also had very practical material implications. It was seen to be a way for women's organisations to make a positive impact on the physical and emotional well being of women. By giving women greater rights to divorce and maintenance, as well as custody over children, it was intended to offer them greater room to manoeuvre, especially within the contexts of abusive relationships or other family disputes, thereby expanding agency and choice in the private sphere. The right to equal inheritance fulfilled a similar function by entitling women whose families had resources to a fairer share of those resources.

As already mentioned, the campaign for the Hindu Code Bill invited the participation of refugee women into the mainstream women's movement. But this was a two-way exchange. Not only did the signature drives associated with the Bill help to conscientise and organise refugee women into the movement, but they led to the infiltration of the immediate socio-economic concerns of these women into the NFIW. 'The struggle of the refugee women from East Bengal for food and shelter is a landmark in the history of the women's movement,' argues Gargi Chakravartty, as these immediate concerns became 'linked to the issues of the larger women's struggle in general, and were consequently incorporated into the mainstream women's movement'. This influence can be seen in the way women's employment as a livelihood and source of personal independence comes to be taken up as a key concern for the NFIW in West Bengal. In 1953, MARS and other women's organisations (which were to form the nucleus of the NFIW in 1954) were already calling on the government to create employment opportunities for women as a rehabilitation and development initiative. The motivation

---

[104] Sen, *In Search of Freedom*, p. 234.

was one of practicality and economic survival. 'The question of economic emancipation, still a distant dream, did not consciously influence the political choices of women in the colonies or camps,' Chakravartty tells us. 'However, the economic needs of those women brought the agenda for employment for women to the forefront of the women's movement.' As a result, '[t]he whole issue of employment for women was taken up by the communist women in Bengal much before their national body took it up.'[105]

This chapter looks at how participation in a range of different kinds of struggles provided the basis for new forms of collective organisation and identity amongst Indian women, by documenting and analysing some of the developments that led to the formation of the NFIW in 1954. The first section traces the roots of this new Federation back to the beginning of the 1940s, looking at the growth of communism in India, the impact of organising around relief work during the Bengal Famine of 1943 and the influence of women's participation in the Telengana and Tebhaga peasant struggles of the late 1940s and early 1950s. The second section outlines two parallel processes; the growth of refugee women's Samitis in Calcutta and the formal establishment of the NFIW, showing how a shared agenda of relief work and rehabilitation brought these two processes together. This, in turn, facilitated the intersection of two very different kinds of struggles, one for socio-economic rights and services at a municipal level, and the other for legislative equality at a national level. The NFIW's Campaign for the Hindu Code Bill provided the grounds for this intersection. The campaign for the Hindu Code Bill encouraged refugee women to think about their socio-economic needs through a language of rights, rather than a language of survival. This, in turn, allowed them to voice an active notion of citizenship. The campaign also provided a space for raising awareness and knowledge about these rights, and the responsibility of the State to enshrine and protect them through legislation. This enabled refugee communities of women to begin thinking about their socio-economic needs, not in terms of welfare and relief, and themselves as victims in need of State assistance, but rather as citizens who were entitled to

---

[105] Chakravartty, *Coming Out of Partition*, p. 37, 69–70.

demand services and facilities, access to living space and livelihoods as rights. The initial plea of women refugees for assistance as victims of circumstance was consequently transformed into a demand based on their rights as citizens. The claim of refugee women to physical space, resources, visibility and recognition through the politics of protest and presence, enabled such communities to become participants in the development agenda of the nation. Protest and agitation become a duty or responsibility for the citizen in the same way that social service or being a 'good' Indian mother did in other contexts. The State has a responsibility to its citizens, but, equally, an individual as a citizen has a responsibility to hold the State to account.

Chapter 6

The Embodied Citizen: Family Planning in Independent India

Today, reproductive rights are internationally recognised as human rights. They are a core component of the claim to inclusive citizenship. Securing these rights through the transformation of law, health policy and social attitudes have been crucial struggles for Western feminism. In India, however, the potential of family planning as a vehicle for achieving women's empowerment has never been embraced with the same degree of consistency and consensus; not for the generation of women who are the focus of this book, nor for their daughters and granddaughters who were a part of the second wave of women's movement that emerged in the late 1970s.[1] In fact, throughout the period of independence, family planning has remained a highly contested subject and one that has never escaped the paradigm of population control that continues to define it as both a planning challenge and a socio-economic problem.

The coercive Emergency era population control policies of Indira Gandhi cast a dark shadow over family planning in India, as does the ongoing complicity of international development aid in the funding of such programmes.[2] New technologies and wealth have brought with

[1] I am in no way claiming that family planning and reproductive rights discourses are inherently liberating and progressive in the West. As Matthew Connelly emphasises in his book *Fatal Misconceptions*, family planning has always been a 'two-edged sword' with the capacity to be used for agendas of empowerment as well as more conservative and coercive agendas. See M. Connelly, *Fatal Misconceptions: The Struggle to Control World Population* (Cambridge University Press, Cambridge, 2008)

[2] Here, I refer again to the analysis presented by Matthew Connelly in *Fatal Misconceptions*. It has also been identified by Betsy Hartmann in her groundbreaking text *Reproductive Rights and Wrongs: The Global Politics of Population Control* first published in 1987. Over the past two years, media in the United Kingdom has included several exposés of DIFD funding sterilisation programmes in India. See 'UK aid helps to fund forced sterilisation of India's poor', *The Guardian* online, 15 April 2012, United Kingdom. Accessed 1 October 2012, at http://www.guardian.co.uk/world/2012/apr/15/uk-aid-forced-sterilisation-india

them new forms of exploitation, such as a growth in surrogacy, where poor Indian women rent out their wombs to the wealthy from India and abroad.[3] Advances in prenatal care, such as the ultrasound that was intended to improve maternal and infant health, have facilitated the rising imbalance of birth gender ratios by allowing couples to choose the sex of their child. According to the 2011 Indian census, 933 girls are born to every 1,000 boys.[4] The legal right to termination of pregnancy, as an expression of a woman's choice and control over her fertility, has been severely undermined by its use for sex-selective abortion. There is an estimated 160 million 'missing' women in India today, as a result of foeticide, infanticide and femicide.[5]

India launched the world's first official population control policy in 1952 when many of Chattopadhyay's generation were beginning to build their public careers and coalesce their developmental and political praxis. Interestingly enough, this generation had a complex and varied perception of, and engagement with, family planning as the predecessor of reproductive rights. Attitudes ranged from the staunch advocacy of Rama Rau and the Bombay AIWC, who sought to institutionalise population control into government policy and to roll out wide-scale family planning programmes, through to Rajkumari Amrit Kaur, India's first National Minister of Health, who opposed the use of mechanical and chemical contraceptives. The outspokenness of Kamaladevi Chattopadhyay, who addressed birth control in terms of equal freedom and rights, was accompanied by communities of communist women who completely rejected the population explosion paradigm. This chapter takes a historical look at how Indian feminists have engaged with questions around the development of family planning in India, by tracing the divergent opinions of two prominent

---

[3] Interview with Raja, 18 November 2011. Raja emphasises that the majority of surrogate mothers in India are tribals and Dalits from the economically weaker sections of Indian society. Both affluent Indians and foreigners are recipients of their services.

[4] Government of India, Census 2011, accessed 14 September 2013, at http://censusindia.gov.in/Census_And_You/gender_composition.aspx

[5] See, for example, M. Hvistendahl, *Unnatural Selection: Choosing Boys over Girls and the Consequences of a World Full of Men* (PublicAffairs, New York, 2012)

individuals who played important roles in shaping the health policy under the Nehruvian government—Lady Rama Rau, founder of the Family Planning Association of India (FPAI), and Rajkumari Amrit Kaur, India's first Health Minister from 1947 to 1957.

Population Control and Family Planning in Colonial India

Population policies are measures or programmes designed to affect the size and growth of a population to enable a State to achieve its economic, social, demographic and political goals.[6] In this chapter, three different terms are used: birth control, family planning and population control. Birth control refers more specifically to education around and provision of methods of contraception, including abortion to reduce the birth rate in a population. Birth control and family planning often tend to be used interchangeably. Family planning is broader, however, in that it also encompasses the systems and institutions surrounding birth control, as well as maternal and reproductive health in general. While the focus of birth control is driven by the intervention itself and the technology, family planning places greater emphasis on changing attitudes and behaviour and empowering couples to control their fertility through the provision of health services and education. Population control is the broadest and most encompassing of the three terms. It covers demographic planning and policy, as well as the implementation of this policy through educational and health institutions and services. The three terms are used differently in various contexts and can sometimes be used interchangeably, making it difficult to distinguish clearly between them. In this chapter, I generally use the joint term 'family planning and population control' as this is the term that is used in the government's first Five-Year Plans (1951 – 56).

The history of family planning in the twentieth century reveals a set of practices broad enough to encompass a wide range of agendas,

[6] P. Demeny, 'Population Policy: The Role of National Governments', *Population and Development Review*, 1:1 (1975), p. 147.

from the support of rights and health, through to social engineering, class control and racism.[7] We can identify these multiple agendas at play within the Indian context. Indian feminists themselves espoused and employed a range of these in their advocacy for, and opposition to, family planning.

In the second half of the nineteenth century, ideas and practices concerned with national health were often expressed in terms of maternal and child welfare. These were shaped by the philanthropy of maternal imperialism[8] and the reforming agenda of the educated middle-class and elite Indian men and women. They were protective and paternalistic in their approach. Emphasis was laid on the provision of maternity hospitals and the training of a small number of lady doctors to tend to the needs of childbearing women. Maternal and child health through social reform, such as through prevention of child marriages, was also stressed upon.[9] Such reformers and Indian nationalists were not concerned with reducing the birth rate to prevent population growth, but rather with improving the health and survival rates of mothers and children, hence enhancing the 'quality' of the population, through healthcare and delayed marriage.

According to Kamaladevi Chattopadhyay, birth control in the modern Indian context was being 'offered to women by private doctors on compassionate grounds' by the 1920s, and a number of philanthropic organisations, such as the Neo-Malthusian League, the Marriage Hygiene Society and the Bhagini Samaj, were running family planning clinics in urban areas like Bombay[10] and in the major towns and cities of

---

[7] Here again, I refer to Connelly, *Fatal Misconceptions*.

[8] For a detailed analysis of the complex dynamics between European women and their Indian counterparts, see B. Ramusack, 'Catalysts or Helpers? British Feminists, Indian Women's Rights and Indian Independence' in G. Minault (ed.), *The Extended Family* (Chanakya, New Delhi, 1981); K. Jayawardena, *The White Woman's Other Burden*, (Routledge, New York, 1995) and A. Burton. *Burdens of History: British Feminists, Indian Women and Imperial Culture 1865–1915* (University of North Carolina Press, Durham, 1994)

[9] Hodges, *Reproductive Health in India*, pp. 12–13.

[10] K. Chattopadhyay, *Indian Woman's Battle for Freedom*, (Abhinav Publications, New Delhi, 1983), p. 83.

Tamil-speaking south India.[11] By the 1930s, international birth control activists, including Marie Stopes, Margaret Sanger, Edith How-Martyn and Eileen Palmer,[12] had visited the country and were establishing a presence through their advocacy for family planning education and by assisting local activists set up services.[13] In 1936, according to Sanjam Ahluwalia, 60 clinics, welfare centres and hospitals, both public and private, were offering birth control information in India, with the majority of doctors trained in the West. These efforts remained largely uncoordinated and were generally sporadic and short-lived. There was no coherent colonial or nationalist policy on population control and family planning. Initiatives tended to come from civil society and the private sector with the colonial State hesitant to intervene, afraid of alienating more conservative groups in Indian society.[14]

By the 1930s, population growth as a developmental concern had entered the vocabulary of the public sphere, with nationalists, businessmen and professionals raising concerns about both the quality and the growing size of India's population. This was accompanied by a movement from compassion and philanthropy as concepts for framing population growth, to social engineering and race, in line with international trends. Eugenics was gaining ground as an increasingly common way of talking about population and patterns of reproduction by the 1930s.[15] In 1939, a report on population was commissioned by the National Planning Committee (NPC),[16] which shows the influence of neo-Malthusian thinking. The report was based on the underlying

---

11 See, for example, S. Hodges, *Contraception, Colonialism and Commerce* (Routledge, Ashgate, 2008), p. 1. The Madras Neo-Malthusian League (MNML) was particularly active in this region, pp. 48–49.

12 S. Ahluwalia, *Reproductive Restraints: Birth control in India 1877–1947* (University of Illinois Press, Illinois, 2008), pp. 147–164.

13 Connelly, *Fatal Misconceptions*, p. 82.

14 Ahluwalia, *Reproductive Restraints*, pp. 160–161, 116–117, 141.

15 Sarah Hodges provides a comprehensive account of the development of eugenics in the Indian context in her chapter 'Indian Eugenics in an Age of Reform' in *Reproductive Health in India*, pp. 115–138.

16 Vijayalakshmi Pandit was one of the eight members of the Population Report Committee although it is unclear how actively she was involved in the research and writing of the report.

theory that a rapid growth in population was occurring and that this was going to place an unprecedented strain on the environment and its resources, leading to poverty, famine and disease, and to a consequent decline in the health and fitness of India's population:

> The pressure on the soil and unemployment of all classes have increased, and in the coming decade, the present piling up of the minor and adolescent groups will add many millions of mouths to feed and employ, enormously aggravating economic pressure and rudely dis-establishing the land-man ratio.
>
> [T]he forecast of the future population based on analysis of the quantitative aspects of the population structure foreshadows a grave economic crisis which is primarily and fundamentally the problem of food planning for the additional 160 millions or so, who, unless fertility changes or some famines or epidemics ravage the land, are sure to come.[17]

In a pattern repeated over and over again in population control documents, women, in this particular case 'the increase in females in age-groups 10–30', were targeted in this report as 'responsible for the recent storm in breeding in the country' divorced from social context and family dynamics.[18] The seeds of a coercive population control policy were already present in this report; it included recommendations for the segregation of lepers and for the legal prohibition of marriage in such cases. The sterilisation of the feeble-minded, insane and criminal 'who are yielding a plentiful crop of abnormal and anti-harvest individuals' was also mentioned as a possibility for consideration:

> There are ample justifications for selectively sterilising the entire group of hereditary defectives; for it is found that due to both tainted hereditary and maintenance of inferior homes...a trail of crime, murder, pauperism, prostitution and illegitimacy is generally the characteristic of the history of defective families.[19]

---

[17] K.T. Shah (ed.), *Population*, National Planning Committee Series (Bombay, 1947), pp. 22–23, p. 31.

[18] Ibid., p. 35.

[19] Ibid., p. 79. The report in fact quotes Germany as example of a country practising sterilisation. See pp. 85, 87–88.

As extreme as such ideas might sound today, the report must be understood as the product of a particular milieu where such ideas were widely accepted, before their devastating application in the Holocaust. Matthew Connelly reminds us that such discourse was evident during the 1930s and 1940s in Denmark, Norway, Finland, Sweden, the United States, Brazil and Mexico, and that an 'interest in ensuring a racially sound citizenry cut across the political spectrum and circled the world'.[20] The proposals made in the National Planning Report were merely reproducing and adapting this discourse.

Nationalist thinking around population by this stage was developing in conjunction with, and in close interaction with, a growing international population control movement. In the nineteenth century, population was generally understood as a national resource. The rapid growth of a population was not a concern, although its health and quality were. In fact, population growth was positively viewed as a sign of strength. In the second half of the nineteenth century, Sanjam Ahluwalia identifies a shift in the way population comes to be understood; it transitions from being a national resource to being seen as a mark of national poverty, of backwardness and overall economic, social and cultural underdevelopment.[21] This change influenced the way in which population growth came to be understood and addressed in India.

The high population density of certain regions of colonial India and the overcrowding, especially in urban centres, easily gave the impression of 'overpopulation' to advocates of the population control movement travelling through the country in the first half of the twentieth century.[22] The 'teeming millions' of India were drawn on in this discourse as the epitome of overpopulation[23] and as a 'warning' to other countries of the route they should avoid. In this international

---

20 Connelly, *Fatal Misconceptions*, p. 80.

21 Ahluwalia, *Reproductive Restraints*, p. 27.

22 This discourse and perception continues to be influential today. See, for example, Paul Ehrlich's *The Population Bomb* (Buccaneer Books, New York, 1971) in which the author describes how he came to the conclusion that overpopulation was the cause of poverty, one swelteringly hot night in a Delhi slum.

23 Connelly, *Fatal Misconceptions*, p. 262.

discourse, having a population control policy, including the provision of family planning, became a marker of modernity and progress. The extensive unplanned family, on the other hand, always shown enmeshed in poverty, was a sign of backwardness.[24] Those within India who were concerned with questions of development used this discourse to articulate their concerns. Simultaneously, this discourse was being shaped by cultural and imperial laden perceptions of India as a nation of underdevelopment and overpopulation. These aspects fed into and reinforced each other.

The growing international movement for population control presented a largely negative perspective of India as a country of underdevelopment and backwardness due to its 'over population'. But there was equal scope for Indian nationalists, social reformers and women's rights advocates to use the discipline of demography to re-imagine and reinvent the nation-state in a positive light. Advocacy for population control became a way of expressing a commitment to development, progress and modernity, and was increasingly voiced as the country moved towards independence.

While the discipline of demography functioned to imagine a future 'modern and progressive' nation-state, it was equally invested in reinforcing class and caste divisions. There are a variety of opinions amongst scholars on the extent to which this occurred, particularly taking into consideration the understanding that birth control encompassed a broad range of concerns that were historically contextual. Ahluwalia argues that the support of birth control, articulated by middle-class Hindu men at the end of the nineteenth century and the beginning of the twentieth in northern India, offered a means for the strict surveillance of the reproductive functions of those seen to be undesirable national citizens—the working classes, lower castes and, in particular incidences, Muslims. For Sarah Hodges, too, birth control in the first half of the twentieth century in south

[24] Ibid., p. 264. Also see Mayo's *Mother India* (1927). As with the debate around sati, women were the 'site' upon which these questions about the nature of Indian society and culture, and the responsibility of the West, in promoting 'development', were debated, but the genuine empowerment of women was often not the primary objective.

India functioned to reinforce class and caste divisions, but not so much through the targeting of lower classes and castes. Rather, it legitimised and protected particular sexual practices associated with Brahmanical identity, such as child marriage, that had been socially as well as legally reclassified from normative to illicit. For these higher castes, the potential of contraception 'was less about governing the social—that of the non-Brahmin masses and women—and more about forging new modes of self-governance under late colonial conditions.' Because class identities often overlap with other socio-economic identities, such as those of caste and religion, birth control as a strategy for reimagining and remoulding the nation-state—targeted at communal and caste groups—could have an inbuilt class dimension as well. In the post-independence era, alarm created around perceptions of Muslim communities in India, as having higher birth rates than their Hindu neighbours, channelled family planning and birth control into monitoring and containing Muslim communities in particular contexts.[25]

The AIWC and the Institutionalisation of Family Planning in Independent India

As an organisation committed to the welfare of women and children through socio-economic and political development, the recently established AIWC took an almost immediate interest in the subjects of population growth and birth control. In 1931, the first resolution on the subject was moved at the annual conference by S. Lakshmibai Rajwade. It proposed the appointment of 'a committee of medical women to study and recommend ways and means of educating the public to regulate the size of their families.'[26] The following year, in 1932, the various constituent branches of the organisation debated the question at their local meetings

[25] See Ahluwalia, *Reproductive Restraints*, p. 35; Hodges, *Contraception, Colonialism and Commerce*, pp. 74–75, 16–18; H. Bannerji, *Demography and Democracy: Essays on Nationalism, Gender and Ideology* (Canadian Scholars, Toronto, 2011).

[26] AIWC, 6th Annual Conference Report, 28 December 1931 to 1 January 1932, Madras, p. 81a.

and the resolution 'was adopted by a large majority.'[27] Over the course of the following two decades, various AIWC branches worked to translate this resolution into action by setting up or taking over small birth-control clinics in their local towns, and by promoting sex education.[28] These efforts, however, remained largely irregular and uncoordinated.

The debate around the AIWC's 1931 resolution on population growth and birth control suggests that at the Conference, family planning was already being contextualised within the looming crisis of population growth, as one of the key obstacles hindering socio-economic development:

> When the births and deaths are equally excessive and the surviving population is weak and unfit and, what is more lamentable, the illusive increase of population puts an undue strain on the economic and physical resources of the nation... If India is to take her place in the comity of nations, she must produce men and women who will be worthy of that name... The physical health of our nation is deteriorating in every generation.[29]

Set against the backdrop of the 1931 census figures,[30] which showed a growth in India's population, this resolution and the debate around it convey a sense of urgency that Matthew Connelly identifies as a defining feature of the post-war international population control movement. It was also intertwined with discourses of eugenics and racial nationalism.

---

[27] Chattopadhyay, *Indian Woman's Battle for Freedom*, p. 84. The subject had been discussed prior to this date in the AIWC, but this was the first conference resolution on the issue.

[28] Basu, *Women's Struggle: A History of the All India Women's Conference*, pp. 95–96; Chattopadhyay, *Indian Woman's Battle for Freedom*, p. 84. The Calcutta branch of the AIWC took over the running of a birth control clinic that had initially been set up by Saudamini Mehta who had met Margaret Sanger during one of her earlier visits to India. The FPAI was to later work through some of the clinics that were still in existence after independence.

[29] AIWC, 6th Annual Conference Report, 28 December 1931 to 1 January 1932, p.81a.

[30] The 1931 census indicated that India's population had increased by 30 million since the previous census of 1921, creating alarm amongst colonial officials as well as certain Indian nationalists and reformers. See D. Arnold, 'Official Attitudes to Population' in S. Hodges (ed.), *Reproductive Health in India: History, Politics, Controversies* (Orient BlackSwan, Hyderabad, 2006), p. 28.

The extensive debate that the resolution provoked did, however, indicate that even at the time of its introduction into the Conference, diverse views existed amongst AIWC members on this matter and how it should be addressed. Mrs Khem Chand, for instance, spoke out in disagreement with the resolution, proposing an alternative point of view, which did not see population growth as inherently negative. She emphasised that India, like other countries such as France, might regret the decision to practise birth control if significant manpower was needed in the future for the defence of the nation. Instead of practising birth control, she recommended that education be improved as 'having more occupation and recreation', 'people were sublimated with art and took to artistic works' and hence would 'naturally and automatically [beget] less children'.[31]

Advocacy for birth control was not necessarily altruistic. As Ahluwalia has shown in her insightful study of the history of family planning in colonial India, support for population control and family planning was motivated as much by concerns with maintaining class and caste hierarchy, as it was by concern for the health and well being of women and children. But this does not mean that family planning as concept and practice could not be drawn on in aid of agendas more directly concerned with the questions of freedom and empowerment. Kamaladevi Chattopadhyay was one of the individuals in the AIWC who spoke in such terms, differing from many of her colleagues by linking birth control with women's sexual freedom and control over their bodies, rather than framing the issue merely in terms of maternal and child health and welfare. In an essay entitled 'Our Cause', she made the connection between female bodily integrity and economic independence.[32] Chattopadhyay recognised how family planning, in fact, worked to perpetuate inequalities between men and women, 'For

---

[31] This range of views reflected public opinion in general. AIWC, 6th Annual Conference Report, 28 December 1931 to 1 January 1932, p. 82. Hodges emphasises that in the 1930s, an understanding of a large population as the root cause of poverty was not yet hegemonic amongst Indians. See Hodges, *Contraception, Colonialism and Commerce*, p. 14.

[32] Ahluwalia, *Reproductive Restraints*, p.105. This point has also been made by Reena Nanda in her biography of Chattopadhyay. See R. Nanda, *Kamaladevi Chattopadhyay: A Biography* (Oxford University Press, Oxford, 2002)

even this field of family planning was beset by devious discriminations against women. For instance, men could get sterilised without any reference to their wives, but no woman could do the same without the permission of the husband.' 'For successful family planning, a basic change in social attitudes and values had to be wrought.'[33]

Lady Rama Rau and the Family Planning Association of India

In the first half of the twentieth century, family planning and population control entered the public sphere in India. There was growing awareness and discussion amongst nationalists, social reformers and women's rights advocates, and it came to be closely associated with ideas of development, Indian nationalism and the imagining of an independent nation. When India gained her independence in 1947, the country had a group of advocates, including women's organisations, nationalists and development planners who saw family planning and population control as essential to the success of the new nation-building project. Lady Dhanvanthi Rama Rau of the Bombay AIWC was one of these advocates.

Rau had a long-standing interest in social work, especially projects concerned with alleviating the social inequalities faced by Indian women. Between 1929 and the late 1940s, she spent a number of years living abroad,[34] where she was exposed to the feminist movement

---

[33] Chattopadhyay, *Indian Woman's Battle for Freedom*, p. 84. There were also other individuals and communities in India who saw the emancipatory potential of birth control. Sarah Hodges's research, for example, documents how the Self Respect Movement formed in 1926 by E.V. Ramasamy embraced contraception as part of an agenda for a radical personal emancipation, because it allowed women to prevent pregnancy while existing as sexual agents. Hodges, *Contraception, Colonialism and Commerce*, pp. 77, 85.

[34] Rau's husband was an important bureaucrat for the colonial government and later a diplomat for the independent State. Rau had spent time abroad in England in the 1930s where her husband was involved in drafting the Simon Commission Report. She also lived in Japan and Washington in the 1940s, after WWII, when her husband took on the role of the Indian Ambassador. They returned to India in the late 1940s, when he was offered the position of the Governor of the Reserve Bank. For a detailed account of Rau's life and work, see her autobiography, D.R. Rau, *An Inheritance: The Memoirs of Dhanvanti Rama Rau* (Harper & Row, London, 1978)

in England and first began to hone her skills as a networker and fundraiser. On returning to India in the late 1940s, Rau contemplated how best she could use her skills to contribute to the development of the new nation. In her autobiography, she describes the moment of her decision to dedicate her social work and philanthropic career to the promotion of family planning whilst visiting a slum housing industrial workers near Bombay. Like many advocates of population control and family planning before her, Rau saw the overcrowding, poverty and lack of facilities in this slum as the product of 'overpopulation' and framed her arguments for the promotion of family planning largely in these terms:

> It was when I thought over these glimpses of slum life that it became perfectly clear to me that, however much our social workers tried to improve conditions, nothing could be accomplished while unlimited numbers of children continued to be born in crowded houses where expansion was impossible...I knew then that I had found a new purpose in life. There was no question in my mind that I should work for family planning single-mindedly and intensively.[35]

Together with fellow AIWC colleague Avabia Wadia, Rau worked to expand the small existing family planning initiatives that were being run by the AIWC in Bombay and encouraged AIWC branches in other parts of the country to set up their own family planning clinics.[36] The AIWC also began importing small numbers of mechanical contraceptive devices for these clinics, with other organisations showing an interest in this endeavour.[37]

Although population control and family planning were being discussed in the public sector, and independent initiatives such as those of the Bombay AIWC were gaining recognition, the provisional government of India did not, at this time, have a clear policy position

[35] Rama Rau, *An Inheritance*, pp. 245, 243.

[36] These early initiatives were later used as pilot models for the FPAI's own initiatives.

[37] See, for example, correspondence from the Indian Conference of Social work to the AIWC head office, requesting an order of diaphragms on its behalf for its family planning clinics, and correspondence between the AIWC President and the National Department of Information and Broadcasting, calling on AIWC assistance for a commissioned documentary on family planning, File 148, AIWC Papers, NMML.

on the matter. Between 1950 and 1952, Rau began bringing advocates and experts in this field together to lobby the PC on the importance of including family planning as a 'priority program' in the first Five-Year Plan.[38] This group sent a memorandum to the PC, the body responsible for preparing this important developmental roadmap, requesting inclusion of family planning in the Plan. Rau wanted the latter to offer a concrete programme of action and advocated for the provision of information and advice on contraceptives, and their widespread availability at all government hospitals and clinics, with the aim of making 'family services a required component part of every health programme'.[39]

In response to these efforts, the Commission formed two panels to research and debate related matters, one on health programmes and another on social welfare. Rau was given a seat on the former together with Rajkumari Amrit Kaur, while Avabai Wadia was a representative on the latter with Sushila Nayar, Kaur's deputy, and Durgabai Deshmukh. In April 1951, the health programmes panel appointed a sub-committee specifically to look at issues concerning population growth and family planning, placing Sushila Nayar and Rama Rau together on this sub-committee.[40]

In this context, Rama Rau and Avabai Wadia found themselves in conflict with Rajkumari Amrit Kaur, the new Minister of Health, and her deputy, Sushila Nayar, over the relevance and application of population control and family planning in the development praxis of the new state. Kaur opposed the use of contraceptives during her tenure as national Health Minister, and according to Connelly, waged 'a rearguard action against birth control' together with Sushila Nayar.[41] Kaur was not opposed to family limitation as a concept, but she disagreed with the use of any pharmaceutical and mechanical contraceptive methods. She made this position clear in an address to the Parliament in 1956:

[38] This nucleus of experts and advocates were to form the core of the FPAI in 1952.

[39] Connelly, *Fatal Misconceptions*, p. 146.

[40] B.L. Raina, *Population Policy* (B.R. Publishing, New Delhi, 1988), p. 5.

[41] Connelly, *Fatal Misconceptions*, p. 146.

> Time and again I am approached to solve the problem of over-population by what our so-called educated women call mechanical contraceptives. It sounds so simple but it is wholly impracticable.[42]

Kaur's objections were both practical and moral. She argued that the effective distribution and use of pharmaceutical and mechanical contraceptives was totally impractical in the Indian context due to lack of resources, infrastructure and trained personnel.[43] This was particularly the case in India's vast rural hinterlands, where the majority of Indians lived. She advocated delayed marriage and self-restraint as appropriate alternatives that aligned with Gandhian principles and values:

> After all, the God-given remedy of self-restraint is given to us. Are we going to be weak enough to say that no self-restraint can be practised, and that we have to resort to other methods? We are quoting the Father of the Nation again and again...but should we forget him in this vital thing?[44]

Unlike Rama Rau, Kaur did not view population growth as the root of the problem. She tended to be critical of the rhetoric of 'population explosion', arguing that it was not the real cause of India's lack of development and that it was receiving a disproportionate amount of attention. For her, family planning and access to contraception were not developmental priorities, and the implementation of wide-scale family planning as part of a policy of population control was, therefore, considered misdirected. Kaur was not the only official within the government with such views. Sushila Nayar, who took over from Kaur as Health Minister in 1957, supported her in her opposition to a family planning programme in the PC, stressing that 'the only proper state policy on population was to promote education and improve living standards'.[45]

---

[42] See Rajkumari Amrit Kaur's speech 'Resolution on Re-Sterilisation of Adults', in *Rajkumari Amrit Kaur*, p. 260.

[43] Ibid., p. 261.

[44] See Kaur's 'General Budget 1953 – 54' speech in *Rajkumari Amrit Kaur,* pp. 88–89.

[45] Connelly, *Fatal Misconceptions*, p.146.

Adherents of Gandhi, such as Kaur and Nayar, were not the only group opposed to State-sponsored birth control. Communist women, such as Renu Chakravartty, Sarla Sharma and Vidya Munshi, like Kaur, did not consider population control and family planning a developmental priority, a fact which is borne out by the general absence of family planning in the programmes and policy priorities of the NFIW. The CPI was cynical of the threat of 'population explosion', viewing the introduction of family planning programmes by the Nehruvian government in terms of class conflict, as an attempt on the part of the government to control the working classes and rural masses.[46]

In the face of the governmental resistance, Rama Rau continued to collaborate with the informal group of population and family planning experts and advocates that she had brought together. She also called on her networks within the AIWC for additional assistance. In January 1951, the AIWC passed another important resolution which spelt out very clearly the Conference's outspoken support for family planning and for the widespread availability of contraceptives in the State sector. It urged the government to back a specific type of action in this regard. It furthermore called on its own membership to take action and become a part of the solution by studying the issue and establishing clinics:

> This Conference is strongly of the opinion that the Central and state governments should accept the principle of family planning in the interest of national economy and the health of women and children, and encourage study and research in birth control appliances. In view of the fact that production of food, health services, educational facilities and other schemes of progressive development lag far behind the needs of the people, it is desirable that every measure be devised to maintain a stable population. The Conference, therefore, urges government and municipal health services to provide birth control clinics in hospitals and health centres. Further, it directs its branches (a) to study the question of family planning in towns and villages, (b) to establish private clinics, and (c) to encourage the work of clinics run by other organisations.[47]

---

[46] 'Our Tasks among the Peasant Masses', Resolution adopted by CC in its meeting held in April 1954, File 1954/23, CPI Papers, Joshi Archives.

[47] AIWC, 22nd Annual Conference Report, p. 22.

The intention behind this resolution was to give additional weight to the pro-family planning and population control contingent in the PC. It was followed up in August 1951, by the All India Conference on Family Planning, coordinated by Rau and her colleagues in Bombay as part of their efforts to raise the profile of the subject as a planning and developmental priority. The organisers were surprised, yet greatly encouraged, when this Conference received coverage in the international press. This was followed by a request from Margaret Sanger to host the third International Planned Parenthood Conference, which was held in Bombay in 1952.[48] Significantly, it was out of this gathering that the International Planned Parenthood Federation was established, with Rama Rau as one of its honorary presidents, and the FPAI was officially launched.[49]

Although Rama Rau set up the FPAI as an independent voluntary body, it used the networks of the AIWC to further its propaganda and advocacy work. FPAI established its first consultation and advice centre in Bombay within an AIWC clinic building that had already been established under the direction of Rama Rau and Avabai Wadia. This connection is reinforced in the AIWC's own organisational history, which claims the initiative for laying the foundations of India's family planning policy through the establishment of the FPAI, as this extract from the AIWC's official history *Women's Struggle: A History of the All India Women's Conference* (2002) suggests:

> A few members of the AIWC had advocated family planning from as early as the 1930s. After Independence, some of them formed the Family Planning Association of India (FPAI) under the presidentship of Dhanvanti Rama Rau.[50]

---

48 Rama Rau tells us in her autobiography that Margaret Sanger had read about the Conference in Paris newspapers. See Rama Rau, *An Inheritance*, pp. 225–226. Connelly offers a slightly different perspective on these events. While Rau gives the impression of being eager and enthusiastic to host the third International Planned Parenthood Conference in India, in her autobiography, Connelly stresses that Sanger pushed for this arrangement even though the FPAI was not a member of the International Committee and that Rama Rau accepted with some trepidation. See Connelly, *Fatal Misconceptions*, p. 66.

49 Connelly, *Fatal Misconceptions*, p, 168. The AIWC lists the 1952 International Planned Parenthood Conference as an international event organised by the AIWC in its organisational history, suggesting how closely interconnected the AIWC in Bombay and the FPAI were. See Basu, *Women's Struggle*.

50 Basu, *Women's Struggle*, p. 119.

With renewed international attention to population growth in India, the Indian government began to take note. Rau's advocacy, combined with the high profile official launching of the FPAI, and the International Planned Parenthood Association, is likely to have encouraged the Indian government to finally announce official support for a population limitation policy in December 1952, making it the first country in the world to implement an explicit policy of population limitation. This was then incorporated into India's first Five-Year Plan.[51] As president of both FPAI, and the International Planned Parenthood Federation, Rau worked closely with Margaret Sanger and other international associates and foundations to leverage influence and resources for the work of the FPAI. India and the development of its national population control policy were tied into international networks of funding and policy thinking from the moment of its conception.

Family Planning and Population Control in Independent India

With an official policy commitment confirmed, family planning and population control were integrated into Chapter 32 on Health in the first Five-Year Plan (1951 – 56). They were combined as a single category and listed together with a number of other health priorities, including the provision of water supply and sanitation, control of malaria, preventive healthcare for the rural population, health services for mothers and children, education and training and self-sufficiency in drugs and equipment.[52] Despite this official commitment, a clear working definition of 'family planning and population control', and what it would entail in practice, remained lacking. The tension between those resistant to the wide-scale use of mechanical and chemical contraceptives versus influential advocates, such as Rau and Durgabai Deshmukh, was evident in the ambiguous and contradictory positioning of population control and family in the first Five-Year Plan. The document employed the

---

[51] Connelly, *Fatal Misconceptions*, p. 168.

[52] See Chapter 32: Health, Priorities, point 8, in the First Five-Year Plan 1951–56, Government of India, accessed 15 July 2012 at http://planningcommission.nic.in/plans/planrel/fiveyr/default.html

rhetoric of population growth as a developmental threat, advocating measures for its management and control, yet remained extremely vague and uncommitted to further state intervention, reflecting the ambiguity of the subject within state policy itself.

Family planning and population control was introduced in relation to the context of a looming crisis of demographic growth and finite resources, and put forward as a required response.[53] However, although its application was initially emphasised as a prerequisite for socio-economic growth, 'to stabilise the population at a level consistent with the requirements of national economy', later this same introductory paragraph stated that 'the main appeal for family planning' stemmed from 'considerations of the health and welfare of the family'.[54]

The internal contradictions reveal themselves again in the way the Plan initially stresses 'the need for family limitation on a wide scale by the people'.[55] When it comes to translating this into action, it only advocates mechanical contraceptives on grounds of maternal health, not to encourage smaller families to reduce population growth or within the framework of giving women the choice to control their fertility:

> Medical officers working at hospitals and health centres like maternity and child welfare clinics should give advice to women regarding family planning when such advice is necessary for health reasons. If a doctor feels that a woman patient cannot undergo again the strain of pregnancy and parturition without danger to health, it is obviously the duty of the doctor to give such advice as is necessary to enable the person to prevent conception. In these circumstances, the doctor would be justified in suggesting any chemical, mechanical or biological methods of contraception or sterilization as may be indicated for the individual case.[56]

---

53 Chapter 32, Health, Family Planning, point 105 in the first Five-Year Plan 1951 – 56.

54 Ibid. Despite the emphasis in the Plan on the welfare of the family as one of the core agendas of its policy, family planning and population control was not integrated into the earlier section of the Plan's chapter on Maternal Child Health (MCH). Rather, it was placed at the very end, after the section on vital statistics, reinforcing a framing of the subject within the larger parameters of demographic growth and crisis. Such an approach has been heavily criticised by latter heath planners and reproductive rights activists for encouraging a top-down, impersonal approach, driven by abstract targets and figures, rather than the needs and rights of those seeking these services.

55 Chapter 32, Health, Family Planning, point 105.

56 Ibid., point 107.

The Plan is careful to emphasise the urgency and importance of resolving this issue, but at the same time, it provides very little detail about a specific course of action, speaking in one voice with urgency and a need for immediate and decisive action, but in other with hesitancy and cautiousness. First, it advocates family limitation on a wide scale, then it steps back, stating that further 'groundwork' must first be done before any action can be taken.

The rhythm method is advocated but even this is suggested only once its social acceptance has been established:

> From the point of view of avoiding enormous expenditure, as well as that of securing the ethical values that community life would gain by the self-imposed restraint which the rhythm method involves, it would seem desirable to try out this method fully and thus ascertain its practicability. Whether the rhythm method is capable of wide application in the community with adequate results or not, actual experimentation alone can tell.[57]

Furthermore, while acknowledging the urgency of the matter, the plan is very careful not to commit the State to this responsibility. Instead, it leaves it to voluntary organisations to take up the required action by asserting that 'There are numerous voluntary agencies which are currently propagating the spread of information on family planning and the use of chemical and mechanical contraceptives. Their activities would need support.' It is interesting to contrast the national government's response to population control and family planning, with its maternal and child health (MCH) programme. With regards to MCH, the government assumed a key role in the provision of such services, 'Voluntary organisations have played an important role in the past... But the responsibility for providing such services rests upon the government,' states the first Five-Year Plan.[58] This stands in opposition to population control and family planning in the Plan, where the government makes it clear that the voluntary sector will take the lead.

---

[57] Ibid.

[58] Ibid., point 67.

The disorientated positioning of population control and family planning in this Plan document reveals how a range of discourses, from economic planning and social nationalism, through to the sanctity of the family and maternal and child health, continued to be utilised to describe and justify such a policy. This ambiguity offered a way of resolving the conflict and disagreement over this issue in the PC by placating both sides without making a clear commitment to either those in favour of a wide-scale roll-out of family planning, such as Rau, or those resistant. Consequently, despite the rhetoric of family planning and population control in early planning documents, the national government took little practical action towards implementing a programme during the time frame of the first Five-Year Plan, limiting its activities to preliminary behavioural and attitudinal studies.

Rajkumari Amrit Kaur's Resistance to Birth Control

How can a historian understand and make sense of Kaur's resistance to the use of mechanical and chemical contraceptives? Kaur was strongly influenced by Gandhian thinking and values. Recommending self-restraint and delayed marriage as appropriate alternatives to birth control reflect this influence on her development praxis. A Gandhian influence is also discernible in her focus on primary healthcare and preventative medicine, through which she sought to address the underlying socio-economic causes of ill health.[59]

Despite the fact that Rau had spent much of the last 20 years of the Indian nationalist struggle outside of the country, while Kaur had been at the heart of the nationalist movement, Kaur and Rau had much in common. Both had been executive members of the AIWC, with Rau holding the presidentship in 1946, following in the footsteps of Kaur who had held this position 12 years earlier in 1934. Kaur did not remain part of the official leadership of the Conference

---

59 K. Kumar, 'Rajkumari Amrit Kaur: Her Life, Work and Ideology' in *Rajkumari Amrit Kaur*, p. 71.

once she became Union Minister of Health, but she continued to attend meetings in an informal capacity and her role and influence in the organisation continued to be recognised.[60] Kaur, like Rau, had spent a number of years abroad and had, in fact, trained in Britain as a doctor.[61] More significantly, both Kaur and Rau had a passionate interest and belief in challenging women's social and economic inequality.

Kaur became politically conscious in the 1930s when she joined the nationalist movement, a decision which required a drastic change in her previously affluent and aristocratic lifestyle.[62] After going to live with Gandhi at his Wardha Ashram she became one of his personal secretaries, a position which she occupied for 16 years. She soon became known in the nationalist movement 'as a right-hand man of Gandhi in many ways'.[63]

Gandhi opposed any form of contraception in both principle and practice because he viewed it as an obstacle to the achievement of the political goals of the nationalist movement, as well as a hindrance towards self-mastery, factors which he viewed as intricately co-dependent. To the Mahatma, sexuality was dangerous because it was a form of self-indulgence that showed weakness and was draining of vital life energy. Self-realisation required control and mastery over all sexual desires. This required *brahmacharya* or celibacy, a practice he advocated and struggled with himself for the latter part of his life. He opposed contraception because it worked against his promotion of self-mastery, but also because divorcing sex from procreation was seen to encourage promiscuity, which was dangerous for the individual and society, in his

[60] Renuka Ray emphasises that 'in some countries other than the United States of America (U.S.A), more than one illustrious person had said that Rajkumari was the AIWC and the AIWC was her'. See R. Ray, 'India's First Woman Cabinet Minister' in *Rajkumari Amrit Kaur*, p. 47.

[61] Kaur spent part of her childhood in England.

[62] Kaur was born in 1889 into the princely family of the Kapurthala State of Punjab. Her family, however, lost the right to the throne when her father converted to Christianity, although their family continued to be part of a social elite. See K. Kumar, 'Rajkumari Amrit Kaur: Her Life, Work and Ideology', p. 71 and Ray, 'India's First Woman Cabinet Minister', p. 44 in *Rajkumari Amrit Kaur.*

[63] Ray, 'India's First Woman Cabinet Minister', p. 45.

eyes. This was a belief that incorporated elements of Hindu philosophical and religious traditions, as well as Victorian Puritanism. In his text, *Self Restraint V Self Indulgence* he argues that, contraception

> ...removes all prudential motives for self-restraint and makes it possible for sexual indulgence in marriages to be limited only by the diminution of desire or the advance of age...It opens the door for irregular, promiscuous and unfruitful unions, which from the point of view of modern industry, sociology and politics, are full of dangers...It is sufficient to say that by contraception, inordinate sexual indulgences both in and out of marriage is facilitated and, if I am right in foregoing physiological arguments, evil must come to both individuals and the race.[64]

For Gandhi, self-mastery was essential for achieving self-realisation and self-realisation was, in turn, essential for being able to transform the world around oneself.[65] This was a philosophy that saw the personal and moral as having direct implications for the political and public. Any kind of sexual relationship, even within marriage, was a distraction. It limited the ability of nationalist and constructive workers to devote themselves completely to the cause of *purna swaraj*. In *Yeravda Mandir*, he explained the logic behind this thinking to his readers:

> The man, who is wedded to Truth and worships Truth alone, proves unfaithful to her if he applies his talents to anything else. How then can he minister to the senses?... we find that the fulfilment of ahimsa is impossible without utter selflessness. Ahimsa means Universal Love. If a man gives his love to one woman or a woman to one man, what is there left for all the world besides?[66]

In line with this belief, he often discouraged his constructive and political workers from getting married, as he did in the case of Sucheta and Acharya Kripalani when they announced plans to marry

---

[64] Appendix I: Generation and Regeneration by William Loftus Hare, reprinted from the Open Court, Chicago, March 1926 in M.K. Gandhi, *Self-Restraint V. Self Indulgence*, 3rd ed. (Navajivan Publishing House, Ahmedabad, 1947), p. 120.

[65] J. Lelyveld, *Great Soul: Mahatma Gandhi and his Struggle with India* (Vintage, New Delhi, 2011), p. 272.

[66] Chapter Sixteen: Brahmacharya or Chastity, (Reprinted from *Yeravda Mandir*, Chapter III) in M. K. Gandhi, *Self-Restraint V. Self Indulgence*, p. 50.

in 1936.[67] His advice to those already in matrimonial bonds was abstinence:

> ...every husband and wife can make a fixed resolution from today never to share the same room or the same bed at night, and to avoid sexual contact, except for the one supreme purpose for which it is intended for both man and beast...Every woman can decline to have anything to do with contraception. Both man and woman should know that abstention from satisfaction of the sexual appetite results not in disease but in health and vigour, provided that mind co-operates with the body.'[68]

Gandhi's philosophical and developmental worldview was also affected by his personal experience and his understanding of sexuality and relationships between men and women. Madhu Kishwar explains that Gandhi saw marriage as a burden for women and celibacy as a kind of freedom.[69] Viewing women primarily as passive and men as active, 'He saw sexuality as almost synonymous with aggression towards women.'[70] All these factors inclined Gandhi against contraception, which he perceived as a vehicle that enabled the further sexual exploitation of women. According to such a philosophy, birth control or contraception would have no place and purpose. Gandhi held a completely different world view and approach to sexuality compared to Margaret Sanger, who visited the Mahatma at his Ashram in Wardha in 1936.[71] She debated with Gandhi on the subject, stressing

---

[67] Acharya was the General Secretary of the AICC at the time. Sucheta stood up to Gandhi and married Acharya despite Gandhi's opposition. See S. Kripalani, *Sucheta: An Unfinished Biography* (Navajivan Publishing House, Ahmedabad, 1978), pp. 21–22.

[68] Chapter 15: Startling Conclusions, (Reprinted from Young India, 27th September 1928) in Gandhi, *Self-Restraint V. Self Indulgence*, p. 50.

[69] For a comprehensive analysis of Gandhi's understanding of Indian women and their social and political position, and his personal gender politics, see M. Kishwar, 'Gandhi on Women', *EPW*, 20: 40 (5 October 1985) and 20:41 (12 October 1985).

[70] Kishwar, *Gandhi and Women* (Sage, Delhi, 1986), p. 43.

[71] For an account of the meeting and discussion between Gandhi and Sanger, see A. Aryee, 'Gandhi and Mrs. Sanger Debate Birth Control: Comment' in S. Hodges (ed.), *Reproductive Health in India: History, Politics, Controversies*, (Orient BlackSwan, Hyderabad, 2006).

the 'life enhancing nature of sexual intimacy for women as well as men' and arguing that to achieve peace women must be able to have control over their own bodies.[72]

Gandhi has been criticised for placing women on moral and social pedestals, pushing them into idealistic and sacrificial roles that denied their human desires and needs. In the process, he reinforced stereotypical gender divisions between men and women.[73] In reality, Gandhi's approach towards women's sexuality had both negative and positive consequences. As Kishwar points out, it facilitated a much greater and more relaxed interaction between men and women, and for a number of his women devotees, celibacy indeed offered a new form of freedom, enabling them to travel and interact amongst their male colleagues.[74]

Kaur's emphasis that family limitation should be achieved through lifestyle and discipline of the self, rather than through an external and institutional approach, shows a definite element of Gandhian thinking. She sought to demarcate the boundary between the public space of governance and the private space of family, albeit very differently from Rama Rau, who lobbied to expand the boundaries of the public space by making the family and the regulation of sexuality a public concern through the institutionalisation of family planning. But Kaur was not a blind adherent to Gandhian thinking. Her extensive political career in the nationalist movement had shown that she was prepared to disagree with the Mahatma on strategic issues, as she had done in the early 1940s when she supported the women of the Congress and their continued participation in the Hindu Law Committee (later to become known as the Rau Committee) against

---

[72] Lelyveld, *Great Soul*, pp. 257, 50–52.

[73] Gandhi has also been validly criticised for the contradictions between his theories and actions. While he preached sexual abstinence, he continued to maintain intimate emotional relationships and domestic life with women in his ashrams. As a consequence, he was accused of hypocrisy, and also of exploiting these female followers without consideration of how his actions might affect them.

[74] M. Kishwar, 'Gandhi on Women', *EPW*, 20:41 (12 October 1985), pp. 1753–1754.

the wishes of the Congress. This had put her political career and personal friendships on the line.[75]

Kaur's developmental approach, like that of Kamaladevi Chattopadhyay, suggests the influence of Gandhian thinking on her politics and praxis. Yet it equally shows how Gandhian thinking was transformed and integrated with other schools of thought in conjunction with her life experience, enabling her to construct a unique development philosophy. Her world view acknowledged the fluidity and dynamism of new ideas and concepts, their potential for evolution, and their application in new contexts. While discussing the objections of certain members of the Lok Sabha to the introduction of a new Red Cross Bill, on the basis of it being 'too modern' and 'too Western', Kaur put forward the following counter perspective: 'I do not understand what Western and modern mean—for surely in the world in which we live, we must take everything that is good from every part of the world. We certainly cannot live to ourselves.' Later in the same speech, she goes on to give her opinion that 'more and more I feel, that the future doctor has to come into line with modern medical practices and India cannot possibly stay away from the steady progress and development that is taking place in other parts of the world'.[76]

Kaur recognised the value of biomedicine as an effective and practical system and discipline. More specifically, for Kaur, it was the capacity of biomedicine to evolve, its reflexive nature, and its rigorousness as a discipline, that made it an effective tool for improving people's lives. But

---

75 At this stage, the Congress was boycotting the government as part of its Quit India Campaign and did not support any endeavours by co-operation. The view of Congress leadership was that the Hindu Law Committee was intended as a distraction from more serious political issues and that any recommendations were unlikely to be acted upon in the near future. Rajkumari Amrit Kaur, however, wanted women to be able to participate in the Committee and voiced her opinion, as she felt that the AIWC had invested so much effort and time lobbying for a review of the legislation, that any change even if was only incremental would be valuable. See Correspondence from Mridula Sarabhai to J.B. Kripalani (Secretary of the AICC), 14 and 22 March 1941, File P9 1940–1941 and P7 1941, AICC Papers, NMML.

76 See Rajkumari Amrit Kaur's speech 'All India Institute of Medical Sciences Bill 1956', in *Rajkumari Amrit Kaur*, p. 155–156.

it was ultimately the ability of biomedicine to fulfil particular ends. These were essentially the same ends shared by the Mahatma: holistic health, the well being of India's people, and consequently a more just society:

> Science is a search for truth. Medical science is not less a search for truth than any of the other vital sciences. In fact, it is much more vital because it touches the human being in a special way. It means life or death; it means enjoyment or suffering; it means illness or well being; it means pain or lack of pain. Therefore, we have to approach medical education in a very, very scientific manner.[77]

On this basis, Kaur embraced the benefits of technology and Western biomedicine. In her role as Minister of Health, she worked consistently to promote primary healthcare and to develop a new infrastructure to facilitate medical research, technology transfer and medical training, with the intention of establishing India as a regional leader.[78] She fostered close professional associations with other international health and development agencies, such as the Ford and Rockefeller Foundations, WHO and UNICEF, as well as national voluntary associations, in an effort to leverage the resources and support necessary to build this infrastructure.[79] Under her ministership, the internationally recognised All India Institute of Medical Sciences (AIIMS) in New Delhi, a centre

---

[77] Ibid., p. 172.

[78] Kaur's efforts to develop medical research facilities in India were coupled with efforts to establish India as a regional leader in the area of medical research, training and technology transfer. In the early 1950s, Delhi was chosen as the headquarters for a regional bureau of the WHO for South East Asia, incorporating India, Ceylon, Afghanistan, Burma, Thailand and Indonesia. Through the Colombo Plan, a technical cooperation scheme, India was to provide technical assistance to neighbouring countries on a bilateral basis. See Directorate General of Health Services (1956) Report of the Activities of the Ministry of Health 1951–1952 and programme for 1952–53 for further details.

[79] The Indian Ministry of Health's Quadrennial Report 1949–1952 acknowledges the 'progress made on account of the assistance received from international organisations, namely the WHO and UNICEF, emphasising that aid from these two organisations had 'contributed to a rapid stepping up of services'. See Directorate General of Health Services Report (1960) and Report for the Quadrennium 1949–1952, p. 7.

for the training of medical staff and experts, was established with funding secured from New Zealand and the United Nations.[80]

When she retired from her portfolio in 1957, President Rajendra Prasad wrote to her, expressing an appreciation for her work as Health Minister and mentioning 'How valuable your contacts in foreign countries have been not only in securing assistance for many of our health projects but also generally in making our efforts appreciated.'[81] Dean Rusk of the Rockefeller Foundation thanked her for her 'inspiration, leadership and steady support' in developing 'the basic research upon which Indian medicine must ultimately rest'.[82]

As an advocate of biomedicine and the many benefits of medical technology, it was, therefore, not moralism or idealism that led Kaur to dismiss a family planning programme for India based on the widespread distribution of birth control. Instead, it was a nuanced understanding of the complexity of interactions between communities and State structures of authority, such as medical institutions, clinics and doctors, and an awareness of the potential tyranny of technology and the Western trajectory of progress, when imposed as a 'silver bullet' solution.

Family Planning in India: a Controversial Legacy?

Despite the rhetoric of prioritising family planning and population control in independent India, government efforts to address the issue in the second and third Five-Year Plans, and the advocacy and work of the FPAI achieved little success in reducing birth rates during the first 20 years of the Republic. The failure of these early family planning and population

[80] The Bhore Commission Report of 1946 had recommended a training institute, such as AIIMS to tackle the shortage of qualified medical personnel in India but the idea had initially been put on hold due to a lack of resources. See 'Rajkumari Amrit Kaur: Her Life, Work and Ideology' in *Rajkumari Amrit Kaur*, p. 74.

[81] Rajendra Prasad to Kaur, 6 May 1957, Correspondence with Rajendra Prasad, Rajkumari Amrit Kaur Papers, NMML.

[82] Rusk to Kaur, 14 May 1957, Correspondence with Dean Rusk, Rajkumari Amrit Kaur Papers, NMML.

control initiatives in the 1950s and 1960s encouraged government and civil society advocates, such as the FPAI, to seek alternative and more effective measures that would be easier to implement.[83] Such measures tended to be increasingly invasive and aggressive, shifting the agenda even further from the health and choice of the individual patient, towards a mass scale top-down approach. This, coupled with the fact that such programmes were largely funded by international development organisations driven by an agenda of population control rather than rights and health, pushed family planning policy in India in a specific direction. From the 1950s onwards, India had been a significant recipient of international aid directed towards family planning programmes and, as Connelly argues, this aid has had a significant impact on shaping the discourse and agenda of family planning within the country. One of the consequences of this has been that Indian family programmes have remained trapped within a policy framework driven by the concerns of population control, rather than that of rights and health. In claiming a leading role in the establishment of a policy which was to ultimately result in the population control programme of the Emergency era, the AIWC and the leading figures who worked through the Conference to promote family planning, such as Lady Rama Rau and Avabai Wadia, could easily be called to account. What role did they inadvertently play in the promotion of a policy ethos that facilitated such brutal and invasive treatment of its citizens' bodies, where eight million Indians, mostly men, were sterilised?[84] This challenges the organisation's claim to have played a leading role in the establishment of institutions and policy frameworks that were inherently progressive and emancipatory for Indian women. One could, however, equally make the argument that Kaur, through playing a key role in building some of these relationships with international development foundations and First World governments, was equally responsible for such a trend.

[83] The Khanna Study conducted in the Punjab in the 1950s, with Rockefeller Foundation aid, is one such case study. For a more detailed analysis, see M. Mamdani, *The Myth of Population Control: Family, Caste and Class in an Indian Village* (Monthly Review Press, United States, 1972)

[84] Connelly, *Fatal Misconceptions*, p. 279.

The shift towards population control policy is evident from the mid-1960s, when a new group of government planners and ministers, including Ashok Mehta, Minister of Planning, began to push a more aggressive population control policy based on the use of IUDs and sterilisations, administered through mobile centres and camps. This was accompanied by the increased use of the metaphor of 'war' on population growth in policy discourse. Rama Rau had initially been hostile to sterilisation but by this time her opinion on the matter had changed. Its promotion as a birth control solution was gaining widespread acceptance and approval, even from those working in the social welfare and reform sectors in post-independence India. Rama Rau, therefore, became part of a group of individuals who helped to promote a governmental approach that emphasised incentives and targets. These were to become standard practice under Emergency era population control programmes.

These developments unfolded against the backdrop of the political rise of Indira Gandhi, an outspoken advocate for family planning. She emphasised her policy position immediately by renaming the Ministry of Health, the Ministry of Health and Family Planning, the day after she was sworn in as Prime Minister. Rama Rau, together with others in Indira Gandhi's government, pushed for the expanded use of both incentives and disincentives under her leadership and pressurised Sushila Nayar, who had become Health Minister by this stage, to pay women to accept IUD insertion. By the late 1960s, a number of Indian states were denying maternity benefits to state employees with three or more children. All this was occurring at a time of a food crisis in India, and under Indira Gandhi's Prime Ministership, United States development aid came to be directly linked to population control.

This expansive and aggressive birth control programme proved unrealistic. India lacked the infrastructure and manpower for proper follow-ups, pre-treatment counselling and the effective management of complications. Major problems with IUDs began to emerge, but the healthcare system did not have the capacity to deal with these. These were the very same concerns that Kaur had raised earlier in the 1950s to justify her Ministry's reluctance to implement a widespread family planning programme.[85] Could Kaur's approach, if she had continued as Health Minister, have enabled a more sensitive policy response? Could her hesitancy represent an alternative path for India in terms of the history of population control policy? Would her Ministry have been able to resist both the national and international developments that facilitated Indira Gandhi's forced sterilisation campaigns of the 1970s?

In 1952 and again in 1953, motions were raised in Parliament for the introduction of Bills for the 'Sterilization of the Unfit', which would have given the State power to sterilise the diseased and insane, with the intention of eradicating diseases such as syphilis, leprosy, 'insanity' and 'imbecility', which were deemed to render such individuals 'unfit' and a danger to society.[86] In both cases, Kaur argued strongly against these Bills 'with all the emphasis at my command because I looked upon it from the point of view of science as wholly unscientific, from the point of view of ethics as wholly unethical and from the point of view of practicability as wholly impracticable.'[87] In rejecting these Bills, Kaur did not reject science and technology itself. In fact, in both cases, she drew on sociological and medical understandings of these diseases, to put forward her counter-arguments:

> Would they like people with congenital blindness to be sterilised? As I said, these are things that require a very scientific mind to be brought to bear on them. Please remember that the growth of population will not be stopped by a Resolution of this kind or by sterilising those who are suffering from these diseases or those who are insane.[88]

Kaur also stressed that those putting forward the Bill were really using it as a cover for a 'quick fix' population control solution. The main object of those advocating for these measures, according to Kaur, was

---

85 Connelly, *Fatal Misconceptions*, pp. 207, 218–225, 246–247.

86 See 'Sterilisation of the Unfit Bill', in *Rajkumari Amrit Kaur*, p. 255. In July 1952, a private members Bill arguing in favour of preventing procreation amongst 'human being[s] of undesirable physical and mental conditions' was raised by Shri. S.V. Rameswamy in the Rajya Sabha. The motion was later negated. In August 1953, Shrimati Lilavati Munshi raised a similar resolution, calling for the 'sterilisation of adults suffering from incurable diseases or insanity', tuberculosis and venereal disease.

87 Ibid., p. 257.

88 Ibid., p. 259.

'to try and stem the tide of the growth of population rather than to help those people and also help me and my other colleagues who are Health Ministers in the various states to stem the tide of the growth of infection... I ask you, is this fair? Is this the only way to stop disease? Is sterilising people the only way?'[89] Kaur's response shows an awareness and understanding of the human impact of such interventions. The end could not justify the means. A quick fix, such as enforced sterilisation, would not solve the poor health of the population. The ethical application of science and technology had to be equally considered together with the end result:

> I would also request the members of this honourable House to remember that sterilisation has got a great psychological effect, especially if it is compulsory on the victim. What are you going to do if a leper refuses to get sterilised? Are you going to prosecute him? I tell you that I would be very sorry to be part and parcel of a government that indulges in violence of this nature.[90]

Kaur's words here preempt the harsh critique that was to emerge 25 years later with the Shah Commission's investigations into the abuses of power in the implementation of population control programmes under Indira Gandhi. But it must also be acknowledged that Emergency era population policy was the outcome of a longer set of discourses, approaches and strategies going back to the beginning of the twentieth century, evident, for example, in the 1939 National Planning Committee Population Report.

One of the many commonalities between Rama Rau and Rajkumari Amrit Kaur was the fact that they both were successful internationalists, moving in international circles and drawing ideas, resources and support from these circles, to implement their visions of healthcare and development in India. In her efforts to build a medical research and training infrastructure for India, Kaur also played a vital role in securing international funding to develop programmes and expertise for India's health sector. With the close connection

---

[89] Ibid.

[90] Ibid., p. 260.

between international development aid and the international population control movement, Kaur's legacy could equally be seen to have facilitated the latter Emergency era population policies.

In light of these factors, did Kaur's proposed alternative approach really help or benefit ordinary Indian women and their reproductive rights? Maybe the Health Minister's moral opposition to mechanical and chemical contraceptives was counterproductive, polarising debate on the uses and benefits of this new technology? The argument could be made that in their polar perspectives and responses to the potential of family planning for India's development, Rau and Kaur reveal alternative faces of a women's movement out of touch with the socio-economic dynamics of the working-class, agricultural Indian family, where large families offered security in old age and provided vital household labour. The divergent approaches adopted by Lady Rama Rau and Rajkumari Amrit Kaur towards the idea and practice of family planning and population control in independent India reveal the multifaceted and diverse nature of the developmental praxis of this generation. What is shared between these two distinctive approaches is the fact that neither drew predominantly on the language of women's empowerment, equality and rights.

Family planning, although inherently gendered, has, in the Indian context, largely not been conceptualised by advocates or opponents in terms of women's health or rights, reminding the historian of the importance of the 'ongoing historical constructions of feminist histories' in their local contexts. Instead, frameworks of development and poverty have dominated. Although Rau did sometimes draw on the language of rights to talk about the potential of family planning in her advocacy, this language was largely subsumed by the more dominant 'emergency' discourse of population explosion, its impending threat, and the need for immediate action. The solution Rau argued was to harness the technology, resources and skills of the West to prevent such an outcome. Kaur, in contrast, influenced by Gandhian thinking, adopted a more cautious and tempered approach, emphasising the importance of modifying technology to the specific context and social norms of the Indian environment. An analysis of the stances taken by Rama Rau and Kaur towards family planning and population control proves most insightful when it is used to explore how this cohort of women engaged with and viewed three things: the potential of modernity, technology and biomedical science in the nation-building project; the shifting boundaries between the public and the private; and the legitimacy of State intervention and authority in the sphere of the family and interpersonal relationships.

Chapter 7

The Indian Woman as a Global Citizen: Vijayalakshmi Pandit, Hansa Mehta and the United Nations

The transition from colonial subjecthood to independence unlocked new spaces within which the Indian woman as a citizen found scope for emergence and redefinition, reconfiguring possibilities for both being and belonging within the postcolonial state. This was set against a broader backdrop of transformation, as an international arena defined by the United Nations (UN) and the concept of human rights emerged. This book has shown how this generation of women's rights activists sought to influence the nationalist project, and the making of Indian citizenship, by building a clearer definition of, and commitment to, equality into its founding principles. The international arena provided an uncharted space into which this project could be expanded. This chapter focuses on the careers of Hansa Mehta and Vijayalakshmi Pandit at the UN during its earliest years. It illustrates how this generation engaged with the new international context, negotiating the channels of power and influence that it opened up, in tandem with the new independence-created networks of power and civic identity at home, to pursue a multifaceted political agenda.

Chapter four of this book, centering on the rescue and recovery of abducted women, exposed how the 'fixing' of Indian citizenship along the lines of social belonging within the family, religious community and territorial boundaries failed to resolve some of the uneasily competing layers of being and belonging in the postcolonial state. These tensions came into sharp focus in cases of 'doubtful and resisting' women, such as Nissa or Shanti of Alwar. In our increasingly mobile and multicultural world, the challenge of finding ways to reconfigure the link between the claim to rights, entitlements and protections, and political nationhood has become ever more relevant. Pragna Patel of the advocacy group Southall Black Sisters[1] explains how immigration issues, such as migrant rights and refugee status, often overlap with those of domestic violence in her organisation's work, which seeks to find innovative legal and human rights avenues for protecting Indian women as they move within the diaspora.[2] A growing comprehension of this reality is reflected in the engagement of the first generation of Indian women activists and public figures with the emerging international context after WWII. They did so through participation in the early development of the United Nations, regional Asian and Afro-Asian networks of solidarity, international women's peace movements and the struggles of various communities in the Indian diaspora. As nationalists, internationalists and advocates for women's equality, Pandit and Mehta saw the potential of being able to use the new global space to push for a number of interconnected agendas. Firstly, they wanted to gather added legitimacy and force for the campaign for women's rights in India, and secondly, to promote the presence of women within international bodies, giving their cause access to the channels of power that were shaping diplomacy and international development policy. Thirdly, they sought to push for the liberation of other communities of people from colonial domination. The ability of Mehta and Pandit to interlink these different agendas, so that they reinforced each other, enhanced the depth and influence of their message internationally and at home.

---

1 Southall Black Sisters is a London-based NGO focusing on the rights of Black and other ethnic minority women. See their website for further details, accessed 25 October 2013, http://www.southallblacksisters.org.uk.

2 For example, the organisation has confronted cases of female British residents taken back to India or Pakistan or even murdered by their families. The assumption being that the law and its implementation in these countries offer greater leniency and sympathy. The organisation works to find ways to ensure the more rigorous legal protections that women as British residents enjoy are extended outside the country. They have also attempted to assist women who are brought from the Indian sub continent to the United Kingdom, married, and then abandoned here, without having residential status. One of Southall Black Sisters successes has been as part of a campaign to lobby for the domestic violence rule in the United Kingdom, which enables women in such circumstances to remain in the country. See Pragna Patel, Founder and Director of Southall Black Sisters, speaking at a conference entitled 'Women in the New India: The Impact of Growth in India on Women and their Rights', 12 June 2013, Merton College, Oxford.

The evolving concept of human rights within the UN at this moment was appealing to Pandit and Mehta precisely because it spoke to the inclusive language of rights and citizenship that they were drawing on in India. On one level, they took on a symbolic role in the international sphere, embodying the values of assertive independence, moral conviction and leadership of India's Nehruvian foreign policy. But they also participated in these international forums as individual feminists and as representatives of the Indian women's movement. They lent their experience and insight as women, and as former colonial subjects, to some of the most influential debates of the organisation during its early years. Their role as nationalists and feminists in the Indian context enabled them to contribute to the establishment of a set of parameters for human rights. It also defined them as part of a small but strategically placed contingent of women's rights activists pushing to expand the definition of equality and access to equal rights within an international sphere and consequently renegotiating citizenship for women within the Indian nation-state.

Becoming Internationalists

The opportunity to travel beyond India's borders in the inter-war years allowed this generation to experience India in the world, and what it meant to be an Indian woman in this new world. For Vijayalakshmi Pandit, in particular, the international sphere offered scope for a self-made career where she was able to distinguish her contribution from that of her famous nationalist family, the Nehrus. Being a diplomat, firstly as leader of the Indian delegation to the UN, and later as Ambassador to the Soviet Union, United States, Britain and Spain, played on one of her greatest personal strengths: her capacity to bridge both East and West.

Interaction and travel across the world provided new and innovative ideas for approaching India's social and developmental challenges, and for thinking about India from a comparative perspective. Renuka Ray, for example, talked of her cosmopolitan time at the London School of Economics in the 1920s as a vibrant experience which 'opened many doors' and exposed her to many new schools of thought. It was during this time that she began to think about how to achieve economic regeneration in India.[3] Kamaladevi Chattopadhyay described visiting co-operative farms in Sweden in her autobiography and how this exposure 'opened up new vistas for cooperative work in India.'[4] Travel to other countries provided opportunities for networking with a range of individuals, organisations and governments, which, in turn, gave this generation ample material and intellectual leverage.

Links with the international women's movement were strategic for this generation. They fostered solidarity and inspiration and, conversely, resistance and differentiation.[5] They offered valuable lessons about the power of collaboration and the strategic use of international perceptions in nationalist politics. However, they equally exposed the need for the development of a position from which Indian women, and their colleagues from other colonial nations, could speak both as women and as former colonial subjects.

The United Nations and a New World Order

Emerging from the devastation of WWII, the United Nations was formed to encourage international stability through global governance and the peaceful resolution of conflict.[6] The cornerstone document of the new organisation was its Charter, signed in San Francisco in June 1945. In it, the peoples of the UN reaffirmed their 'faith in human rights and the dignity and worth of the human person and in the equal rights of men and women, and of nations large and small', and committed themselves to 'promoting and encouraging respect for human rights and

---

[3] Ray, *My Reminiscences*, pp. 34, 39.

[4] Chattopadhyay, *Inner Recesses Outer Spaces*, pp. 131, 231.

[5] As can be seen with the controversy over Katherine Mayo's book *Mother India* (1927). In their interactions with American and British social reformers and feminists over how to 'uplift' Indian women, this generation increasingly began to establish a clear position for themselves; firstly, that Indian women had to achieve such transformation of society and upliftment for themselves, and secondly, that in order to do so, they would need to forge their own path based on an understanding and sensitivity to their society.

[6] D. Jain, *Women, Development and the UN: a Sixty-year Quest for Equality and Justice* (Indiana University Press, Bloomington, 2005), p. 11.

for fundamental freedoms without distinction as to race, sex, language or religion'.[7] The UN advanced the concept of global governance and cooperation that its predecessor, the League of Nations, had pioneered. The latter had failed in its mission to avoid an international conflict, but the UN offered a fresh chance for peace.

Literature on the United Nations offers a range of diverse interpretations of the development and impact of this new organisation. Much of the historiography focuses on the UN as an arena for playing out of Cold War tensions. There are laudatory accounts which tell the story of the birth and evolution of a new era of international diplomacy revolutionised by its commitment to the principles of human rights. More contemporary histories, such as those produced by Mazower, Normand and Zaidi, offer a more critical interpretation of the intentions behind the new international order and the discourse of human rights underpinning it.[8] For Mazower, the UN, regardless of its rhetoric, was like its predecessor, the League of Nations, designed 'for interstate cooperation and stability in a world of empires and great powers'.[9] For Normand and Zaidi, it came to operate merely as an extension of the United States and Western hegemony.[10]

The UN embodied its member nations' ambitions for a better world, but it was, from the beginning, a highly political organisation, constrained by internal tensions and driven by conflicting national agendas.

7 Document 1: Charter of the United Nations (extract), signed 26 June 1945 in *The United Nations and the Advancement of Women 1945-1995*, Blue Book Series, Vol. VI (UN, New York, 1996), p. 93.

8 See A. Iriye, P. Goedde and W. Hitchcock (eds.), *Human Rights Revolution: An International History* (Oxford University Press, Oxford, 2012); United Nations, *The United Nations and the Advancement of Women 1945-1995* (UN, New York, 1995) and M. A. Glendon, *A World Made New: Eleanor Roosevelt and the Universal Declaration of Human Rights* (New York, UN, 2001) for a congratulatory interpretation of the history and development of the United Nations as a vehicle for universal human rights. For a more critical interpretation, see M. Mazower, *No Enchanted Palace: The End of Empire and the Ideological Origins of the United Nations* (Princeton University Press, Princeton, 2009); R. Normand and S. Zaidi, *Human Rights at the UN: The Political History of Universal Justice* (Indiana University Press, Indiana, 2008) and S. Moyn, *The Last Utopia: Human Rights in History* (Belknap Press, Cambridge Massachusetts, 2012)

9 Mazower, *No Enchanted Palace*, p. 151.

10 Normand and Zaidi, *Human Rights at the UN: The Political History of Universal Justice*, p. 33.

Dominant member countries, such as the United States and Britain, claimed moral ownership of human rights and its principles of democracy and independence. However, they were cautious when it came to the application of such principles in their colonial empires. There was a split between political and civil rights and socio-economic rights. The United States and other Western nations stressed the former as paramount, while socialist countries argued for greater emphasis on the latter in the UN's declarations and conventions. There was debate as to whether the UN should be an organisation wielding the soft power of moral authority and public opinion, or if it should hold concrete power which could ensure implementation and if so, how could such structures for implementation be agreed upon and built into its institutions?

From the moment of its emergence, the United Nations was profoundly shaped by the bipolar politics of the Cold War. The ideological division between the two superpowers, the United States and its allies as champions of capitalism, and the communist Soviet Union, played itself out in the UN, where these powers frequently found themselves in opposition. Newly independent countries like India were caught in the middle and under pressure to show unambiguous allegiance. Nehru and the leaders of other formerly colonial powers, including Sukarno of Indonesia and Nasser of Egypt, refused to be pressured into either of these camps. Instead, they developed a third way, known as Non-Alignment.

Non-Alignment employed the structures and influence of the UN to pursue a foreign policy agenda which sought to neutralise both camps and mould an independent and united 'One World.' The development of human rights at the UN, with its consequent split into both positive and negative rights, was conceptually important for this project. It offered a way of bridging the ideological differences between East and West, capitalist and communist, combining and validating both world views.[11]

Non-Alignment was a core component of Nehru's ambitious foreign policy agenda for India, which sought to challenge the unequal power dynamics of the colonial empire and replace these with a new era of

[11] M. Bhagavan, *India and the Quest for One World: the Peacemakers* (Palgrave Macmillan, Hampshire, 2013) pp. 1, 103–106.

social justice. It offered the possibility of greater independence for previously colonial countries in a bipolar world, while the term 'Third World' provided a new collective identity; a new positional platform from which the people of India, together with the peoples of Africa, Asia and Latin America and their nationalist leadership, could come together in their fight against colonialism. The United Nations gave these 'Third World' nations advocating Non-Alignment a forum through which they could articulate their grievances and demand political freedom.[12] The early years of the UN were, therefore, a period when 'The world was full of hope' in the words of Vijayalakshmi Pandit. 'The Charter of the United Nations was a challenge to the most cynical, and it was a moment in time when it seemed possible to remould the world to a design in which justice, equality and opportunity would help to establish the peace for which the exhausted humanity yearned.'[13]

Vijayalakshmi Pandit, like Jawaharlal Nehru, was a powerful advocate of this 'One World' vision[14] and when she gave her debut speech to the first General Assembly on the 25 October 1946, she carried the weight of this ambitious foreign policy agenda on her shoulders. She opened her speech by affirming 'the adherence of my country to the principles and purposes of the United Nations Organisation' and 'the determination of our people to help make it a reality'. Quoting Jawaharlal Nehru, head of the new provisional government, she went on to stress that towards the UN Charter,

> India's attitude is whole-hearted cooperation and unreserved adherence in both spirit and letter....to that end India will participate fully in its varied activities and endeavour and assume that role in its councils to which her geographical position, population and contribution towards peaceful progress entitle her—in particular, the Indian delegation will make it clear that India stands for independence of all colonial and dependent peoples and their full right to self-determination.[15]

---

12 V. Prashad, *The Darker Nations* (The New Press, New York, 2008), pp. xv-xvi.

13 Pandit, *The Scope of Happiness* (Crown Publishers, New Delhi, 1979) p. 209.

14 Bhagavan, *India and the Quest for One World*, p. 26.

15 Vijayalakshmi Pandit, speech delivered at the General Assembly of the United Nations, 25 October 1946, File 4: Speeches and Writings, Vijayalakshmi Pandit Papers, 1st Instalment (hereafter V.L Papers), NMML.

Pandit's words were immediately able to harness the authority of the UN to India's foreign policy agenda. She had committed her nation to the principles of the UN, while simultaneously, though subtly, stamping India's interpretation of these principles. The nascent Indian nation could, therefore, claim legitimacy in the international sphere as a committed follower of the UN when, in fact, it sought to play a leading role in shaping its priorities. Once this legitimacy had been established, Pandit went on to introduce what were to become the defining concerns of Indian international relations over the following decades: political freedom and independence as a precondition for international peace, the right of formerly colonised nations to participate equally in newly established international organisations and the importance of India as a key role player in international affairs.

Pandit laid out India's commitment to challenge colonial domination, and the government's support for the independence of colonised peoples across the globe and their right to political, economic and social equality. Her country's experience of such domination and its prolonged nationalist struggle for independence gave her message an added conviction and resonance. Less than a year later, on 15 August 1947, India would achieve its long fought-for freedom under the leadership of the Congress. The country's early years of nation-building occurred in parallel with the development of the concept of global governance within the United Nations, and its allied organisations. In fact, the inaugural session of the General Assembly and the first sitting of the Indian CA took place only months apart in the aftermath of the WWII.

Pandit's speech makes the connection between universal political freedom and international peace. But it also refers to a specific case of injustice—the discriminatory treatment meted out to resident Indians in the Union of South Africa:

> We...have for this reason and as a demonstration, that we look to the United Nations to implement in practice the principles and basis of civilised life which has been embodied in the Charter, brought before this Assembly the treatment of Indians in the Union of South Africa, a member state and signatory to the Charter.[16]

[16] Ibid.

In 1946, the union government of South Africa passed the Asiatic Land Tenure and Indian Representation Act. This relegated Indians in the province of Natal to second-class citizenship by restricting their franchise—through educational and property qualifications—and by legalising segregated residential areas.[17] When the Act came into force in June 1946, the Natal Indian Congress launched a civil disobedience campaign and called on the Indian government to raise the issue at the UN. The Act 'galvanised Indian sentiment' and left Indians angered. According to Mazower, Nehru seized on this issue to push his wider foreign policy agenda. The new Prime Minister was eager for India to assume a leadership role in the anti-colonial movement and sought to challenge the hypocrisy of the Allied powers in their selective application of the principles of self-determination and democracy.[18] This matter was by no means 'a narrow or local one', Pandit argued. The Union of South Africa was a member state of the United Nations and a signatory to its Charter and could, therefore, not get away with such 'a gross and continuing outrage' to its fundamental principles.[19] Claiming 'equal and honourable treatment for our people wherever they may go', she emphasised that the South African issue had global significance because of the interconnectedness of freedom and rights as laid out in the Charter.[20]

The rights of Indians living in South Africa had first brought Pandit into the political space of Indian nationalism 30 years previously as a teenager in 1916. Gandhi, recently having returned from South Africa, had re-entered Indian politics and brought an awareness of the struggles faced by indentured labourers in South Africa to the public eye. Pandit decided to attend a women's meeting organised by her aunt Rameshwari Nehru in her hometown of Allahabad to publicise the issue. At the time, she did not understand the broader significance of these events, but the experience gave her 'a feeling of participation in the cause' and was followed by her attendance at the 1916 Indian National

---

17 Pandit, *The Scope of Happiness*, pp. 205–206; Mazower, *No Enchanted Palace*, p. 171.

18 Mazower, *No Enchanted Palace*, pp. 175, 173, 170.

19 Pandit, 'Speech delivered at the General Assembly of the United Nations', 25 October 1946, Subject File 4: Speeches and Writings, V.L. Pandit Papers, NMML.

20 Bhagavan, *India and the Quest for One World*, p. 58.

Congress session in Lucknow.[21] Stepping onto the podium at the first General Assembly at Lake Success in 1946, Pandit had come full circle. This time she confronted the subject with considerable experience and acumen, shaped by the cut and thrust of Indian nationalist politics.

By 1946, Pandit had already begun to make a name for herself in America. At the beginning of 1945, she had undertaken a lecture tour of the United States to raise public awareness for India's independence struggle.[22] This tour proved to be a highly successful public relations exercise, receiving favourable media coverage, and enabling Pandit to begin cultivating influential networks and contacts.[23] During the course of the tour, she was persuaded by the nationalist leadership to head an unofficial Indian delegation to San Francisco in April 1945, where the Charter of the UN was being drafted. Here she was tasked with voicing nationalist disapproval of the official Indian delegation, who, the Congress believed, had been selected for their loyalty to the Raj, rather than as representatives of the interests of the Indian people. She was also to emphasise how the British refusal to commit to a specific schedule for withdrawal from India was undermining the nationalist demand for independence.[24] Although India's voice of protest at San Francisco had little impact on determining the policy behind the Charter, it proved another public relations success. 'India Delegates Challenged by Nehru's Sister,' reported the *New York Herald Tribune,* describing Pandit as setting 'off the first fireworks here today'. *The Tribune* described her efforts as a 'spearing' attempt on the part of

---

[21] Pandit was too young to join at the time, but she became a volunteer and recalls being thrilled at being able to meet the various well-known politicians present. The oratory of Annie Besant and Sarojini Naidu mesmerised her and she became a 'devoted fan' of Besant. See Pandit, *The Scope of Happiness*, pp. 61–62.

[22] Bhagavan emphasises that this tour also provided an opportunity for Pandit to articulate the idea of the new international framework of 'One World'. See Bhagavan, *India and the Quest for One World*, p. 26. Pandit had a personal interest in the United States as well, having sent both her daughters to Wellesley College shortly prior to her trip in 1945.

[23] One of the reasons this tour was well received was that public opinion in the United States was sympathetic to the cause of Indian freedom. See Mazower, *No Enchanted Palace*, p. 166.

[24] Pandit, *The Scope of Happiness*, p. 195.

the Congress 'to bring the cause of India's freedom to the attention of conference delegates'.[25] Reflecting back in her autobiography, Pandit acknowledged how this initial American experience marked 'a new and very important beginning' in her life by paving the way for her later diplomatic roles.

Returning to the United States for the second time at the end of 1946, Pandit was tasked this time with bringing the discrimination of Indians in South Africa to world attention by getting the issue inscribed on the UN's agenda.[26] To this end, the Indian delegation forwarded a Resolution criticising the South African government's passage of the Asiatic Land Tenure and Indian Representation Act on the grounds of discrimination.[27] The issue of domestic jurisdiction lay at the heart of the debate that followed and would dominate future discussions, remaining an internal weakness for the international organisation. The UN was in the process of developing a set of international declarations and conventions intended to protect the human rights of all people across the globe. However, the international body was itself constituted by the powerful post-WWII states of Britain, France, America, the Soviet Union and China. Vital to their authority was their sovereignty and independence, which was protected in Article 2(7) of the UN Charter, under the domestic jurisdiction clause. This clause stated that legislation implemented within the boundaries of member states was an internal issue, beyond the purview and mandate of global governance. Field Marshal General Smuts, leader of the South African delegation and Prime Minister of South Africa, argued on this basis that the petition put forward by the Indian delegation was invalid, and, therefore, could not even be inscribed on the agenda in the first place. The still embryonic and nebulous concept of human rights and its jurisdiction gave Smuts another piece of ammunition in his case. Although the Charter promoted and emphasised upon the importance

[25] 'India Delegates Challenged by Nehru's Sister', *New York Herald Tribune*, Press Clippings 2, V.L Pandit Papers, 27 April 1945, NMML.

[26] Pandit, *The Scope of Happiness*, p. 197, 209.

[27] M.P. Bradley, 'Approaching the Universal Declaration of Rights' in Iriye, Goedde and Hitchcock (eds.), *Human Rights Revolution: An International History* (Oxford University Press, Oxford, 2012), p. 332.

of human rights, it did not offer a concrete legislative definition. Smuts was, therefore, able to argue that Indian criticism was void because there was no international legislative basis to it. As Hansa Mehta reported in one of her briefs to the Indian government as a delegate on the CHR,

> [t]he attitude taken up by SA during the discussions on the race bias resolution in the General Assembly, was that there was not a violation of human rights in South Africa because there was no written definition of human rights as such within the ambit of the United Nations.[28]

The counter-argument put forward by India's advisors was that any violation of the Charter contravened Article 14, which allowed the General Assembly to act, regardless of the origin of the concern. The Indian delegation emphasised that the Preamble of the Charter held significant judicial weight. Consequently, all member states were bound by its conventions, as if by a constitution. India stressed that this was not a matter that should be determined by legal formalities. It needed to be addressed because it violated the principles upon which the UN was founded. All governments of member states should be required to show their commitment to such principles through the willing implementation of these. The Indian delegation based their argument on a universal understanding of human rights, claiming that such rights were 'to be guaranteed for all by the United Nations, on the basis of being human, rather than on the basis of being citizens of nation states or subjects of empires'.[29] The racial prejudice underpinning the Asiatic Land Tenure and Indian Representation Act violated the 'dignity and self-respect' of all Indians and threatened peace, a priority at the heart of the new organisation.[30]

Smuts proved a formidable opponent in this debate in the First Committee, which lasted several weeks. The Indian nationalist leadership hoped to raise the profile of this issue on the international stage, but was uncertain how it would be received. As Pandit recalls in her

---

[28] Human Rights Commission Press Release, Soc 20: Second Meeting, 27 January 1947, File 14, Hansa Mehta Papers, NMML.

[29] Bhagavan, *India and the Quest for One World*, pp. 57–58, 87–88.

[30] Pandit, *The Scope of Happiness*, pp. 209–210; Mazower, *No Enchanted Palace*, p. 179.

autobiography, 'my brother was hesitant and Gandhi warned me that I should expect the worst, at best, he said, a few lip service votes.'[31] It was, therefore, unexpected yet encouraging when the Indian motion was voted through the committees, and when India achieved a two-thirds vote for a Resolution on South Africa, in the General Assembly. The Resolution asked 'South Africa to undertake negotiations with India and Pakistan for a better deal for the citizens of those countries in the Union.'[32] The moral authority and mandate of the United Nations had swayed member countries in their voting, rather than the legal nature of the issue. 'The strict reading of the domestic jurisdiction clause was set aside; legal niceties were ignored' and 'the letter of the Charter' was trumped 'by the spirit of human rights and moral anger'.[33] It was another success for Pandit, who made a powerful impression.[34] She had spoken with 'the greatest and clearest voice', according to Elsa Maxwell, a political commentator for the *Washington Post.*[35] '[A]nd what a voice,' proclaimed *The Sphere,* describing Pandit's 'indignation against South Africa's apartheid policies in the United Nations'.[36] For Pandit too, it was a moment in which she became aware of the power of being an articulate and passionate speaker with the world listening: 'It was a truly exhilarating experience to watch the effect of my speech. I, an unknown woman from an as yet nonexistent country...'[37]

---

[31] Taya Zinkin, 'International First Lady', *The Guardian*, date unknown, Press Clippings 2, V.L. Pandit Papers, NMML.

[32] Mazower, *No Enchanted Palace*, p. 179; Pandit, *The Scope of Happiness*, p. 210. Also see press clipping from *The Sphere,* 5 August 1961, Press Clippings 2, V.L. Pandit Papers, NMML.

[33] Mazower, *No Enchanted Palace*, p. 179. Bhagavan points out that Pandit's connections in the United States, especially with the National Association for the Advancement of Coloured People (NAACP), helped give her the support she needed at this UN session to win the vote on the Resolution.

[34] Other notable Indian personalities at the UN during its early years included Rajkumari Amrit Kaur who attended the UNESCO Paris conference in 1946, making a notable impression where she was elected Vice President on the second day. Kaur was also elected President of the WHO in 1950. See 'Indian women's bulletin' and Mrs Grace Lankester to Hansa Mehta, 28 January 1946 File 7: 1944-47, Hansa Mehta Papers, NMML.

[35] Elsa Maxwell, 'Elsa Maxwell's Party Line: On the State and Behind the Scenes', 29 October 1946, Press Clippings 3, V.L Pandit Papers, NMML.

[36] See article in *The Sphere,* 5 August 1961, Press Clippings 2, V.L. Pandit Papers, NMML.

[37] Zinkin, 'International First Lady'.

This was a symbolic victory for India, but it was hollow in terms of its capacity to improve the citizenship rights of Indians in South Africa. The Smuts government ignored the censure of the UN Resolution and two years later, in 1948, the Nationalist party was voted into power. Under the Apartheid state, the 'dignity and self-respect' of all black South Africans would be systematically stripped away with a brutal system of racial segregation. Nevertheless, the vote had set a precedent and opened up the UN as a vehicle for challenging the old, unequal power relationships of the colonial empire. This was highly significant. Although the Union of South Africa refused to withdraw the Act, it was a subject to which UN General Assembly would return in more than a decade.[38]

In 1916, after attending her first women's meeting to publicise the South African issue, Pandit had thought to herself that 'South Africa was very far away—it was a pity Indians were being discriminated against, but what good could result by some women getting together and talking about it in Allahabad?'[39] By the 1940s, she and other members of the AIWC and future NFIW were becoming increasingly conscious of the leverage created for pursuing struggles closer home through such connections. In the nineteenth century, with the abolition of slavery by Britain and the abrogation of the Code Noir by France, Indian labour had become a lynchpin in the economies of the colonial empire. An extensive network of indentured labourers developed, which saw large numbers of Indians being transplanted across the globe. It was this process that had brought Indians to South Africa in the 1860s to work on the sugarcane plantations of Natal. By the time of Indian independence in 1947, four million Indians were living abroad as a result of transportation, in British Guiana, Trinidad, Jamaica and Surinam, Mauritius, Kenya, Tanganyika, the British Protectorate of Uganda and South Africa as well as Burma, Ceylon and Malaya. These communities were created at the 'request and for the benefit of governments of the countries concerned'. India saw the UN as a platform from which it could advocate for the equal treatment and

38 Mazower, *No Enchanted Palace*, p. 185.

39 Pandit, *The Scope of Happiness*, pp. 61–62.

respect of such communities, as part of its larger agenda to undermine the entrenched power inequalities of the old world order. As Hansa Mehta reminded her audience during one of her early addresses before the CHR in January 1947,

> [n]umerous cases of the denial of rights faced by these communities of Indians, and complicated questions like nationality and citizenship and of dual nationality, have got to be straightened out within the meaning of the terms of reference of the Human Rights Commission and of the principles and purposes of the Charter of the United Nations.[40]

The intense concern over the legal status and rights of South African-Indians across the globe reflected the way in which citizenship in India was being redefined in relation to the Indian diaspora and other contexts of colonial and racial oppression. This connection was being made not only by nationalist leaders but also by other Indian subjects with a political awareness. In this way, a powerful imagining and sense of connection with other struggles were being woven into the texture of Indian freedom. Take, for example, the life story of Subbalaxmi, a friend of Kamaladevi Chattopadhyay, who was a middle-class Indian woman, born in 1897 in Tamil Nadu, and whose life has been reconstructed in Uma Chakravarti's sensitive documentary, 'A Quiet Little Entry'. As the wife of a Salt Inspector, Subbalaxmi was unable to openly articulate her growing commitment to the nationalist cause so she sought out more discreet ways of resisting. In the 1920s and 1930s, she wore *khaddar* and sent money to various nationalist causes. In the 1940s, with widespread media coverage of the discrimination and hardships faced by Indians in Natal and the Transvaal, Subbalaxmi wrote in her diary about a recurring dream. In this dream, a Tamil indentured woman labourer beseeched her for freedom. Haunted by the image, Subbalaxmi imagined her 'cries and laments'. She wondered how this woman and her compatriots had felt, so far from home and family in a strange land; 'Did they think of their native land? Will that day ever come when [they will] return? 'Will they think of their mother's homes?' she agonised. Uma Chakravarti

[40] Hansa Mehta, Speech before Commission on Human Rights, 27 January 1947, Subject File 15(ii), Hansa Mehta Papers, NMML.

suggests that Subbalaxmi's intense imagining and anxiety around the oppression of indentured labourers in distant South Africa reflected not only a collective pain and sense of anguish in the face of colonial oppression in India but also her own lack of personal freedom. She was in a young marriage and had failed in her efforts to secure an education for her daughter, and prevent her premature marriage.[41]

Subbalaxmi's story hints at the growing importance of contexts and lives beyond the territorial nation-state, in constructing the texture and possibilities of freedom within the imagined nation-state. In her first speech to the United Nations, Pandit develops this connection further. It commenced by emphasising India's commitment to the independence and equality of subjugated peoples across the globe, but it closed with her expressing 'my own hopes' and those of her fellow countrywomen for the greater participation of women in public life, particularly within the UN. As an example of how this could be achieved, Pandit held up India where 'our women have equality of opportunity with men,' and where 'caste, creed or sex are not recognised' as a barrier to progress.[42] Her words echoed the message of Eleanor Roosevelt's 'open letter to the women of the world', delivered a few months earlier at the UN Inaugural Session in which she called for the increased involvement of women in both national and international affairs.[43] Pandit's words drew actively on the symbolic association between gender empowerment and political empowerment, developed within the context of Indian nationalism. They conveyed the message that just as the ushering in of a more peaceful and equitable world required the ending of relationships of colonial domination, it also called for the smashing of another kind of relationship of domination, that between men and women, in India and across the globe. This should especially be the case in the new institutions of diplomatic power. Pandit built this cause into India's foreign policy agenda by linking the right of women to equality within their nation-states, with the right of colonised and formerly colonised

[41] See 'A Quiet Little Entry' (2009). Directed and written by Uma Chakravarti, Magic Lantern Films.

[42] Speech delivered at the General Assembly of the United Nations, 25 October 1946, Subject File 4: Speeches and Writings, V.L. Pandit Papers, NMML.

[43] United Nations, *The United Nations and the Advancement of Women 1945-1995*, p. 69.

nations to political equality within the international sphere. When Pandit stated, 'We do not recognise caste, creed or sex as a barrier to progress and our women have equality of opportunity with men,' she spoke to an international audience, as well as directly to her political colleagues and the provisional government back at home. She held them to account by quoting Congress's famous Karachi Resolution.

Committee on the Status of Women and the AIWC's Indian Woman's Charter of Rights and Duties

Although the UN Charter affirmed support for human rights and for the equal rights of men and women, it did not provide a definition of these terms. With this need in mind, the Commission on Human Rights (CHR) was constituted in February 1946 by a resolution of The Economic and Social Council (ECOSOC) under the chairmanship of Eleanor Roosevelt.[44] The CHR was responsible for drafting a Universal Declaration of Human Rights (UDHR) and International Bill of Rights, providing a definition that could be written into law. This was to be followed by a convention or covenant which would act as an agreement between states, as well as a contract between the state and the UN, for the protection of the human rights of persons within the jurisdiction of that state.[45] Another grouping of delegates and experts known as the Sub-committee on the Status of Women was formed along with the CHR in February 1946, and placed under the CHR. In June 1946, this sub-committee was elevated to the status of an independent commission. The Committee on the Status of Women (CSW) was tasked with applying the principles of human rights, which would be defined by the CHR, to the position of women in society by making recommendations

[44] A. Black, 'Are Women "Human"? The UN and the Struggle to Recognize Women's Rights as Human Rights' in Iriye, Goedde and Hitchcock (eds.), *Human Rights Revolution* (Oxford University Press, Oxford, 2012), p. 135.

[45] Fifth session of the Human Rights Commission, 9 May to 20 June 1949, File no 15(ii), Hansa Mehta Papers, NMML.

on the legislative and policy action that was needed to elevate the 'status of women to equality with men in all fields of human enterprise'.[46]

When Jawaharlal Nehru, leader of Congress party and head of India's provisional government, asked Hansa Mehta to represent India on the UN's Human Rights Commission, she saw the potential of this new posting immediately.[47] 'It is a great honour that an Indian woman will have a say in the future of the women of the world...Women have played a great part during the world crisis and it is but in the fitness of things that they should demand to have a place in the world of the future,' she wrote.[48] Mehta sat on the CSW prior to her appointment to the CHR. As a delegate with a specific interest in gender equality issues, she continued to follow the CSW's work once she was appointed to CHR and encouraged interaction and exchange between the two Commissions, in the development of their respective documents. In fact, two of Mehta and Pandit's fellow AIWC organisers, Shareefah Hamid Ali and Hannah Sen, were delegates to the 15-member CSW, making contact and the sharing of ideas increasingly viable.[49]

According to Normand and Zaidi, chairman of the CHR, Eleanor Roosevelt did not actively seek out the views of the CSW in the drafting of the International Bill of Rights at first and even suggested that it might have been best to exclude women's rights completely from the work of the CHR. Mehta, together with the Indian and Soviet delegates, disagreed, arguing 'that the status of women was an essential part of the international Bill and that it needed to continue to be part of the CHR mandate'.[50] Consequently, CSW members regularly attended the meetings of the Commission on Human Rights as it worked through the long and arduous process of drafting the Universal Declaration of Human Rights (UDHR), and articles of the draft declaration were sent

46 UN, *The United Nations and the Advancement of Women*, p. 69; A. Whittick, *Woman into Citizen* (Abc-Clio Inc, London, 1979), pp. 152–153.

47 Hansa Mehta was not the original delegate chosen to represent India on the CHR. Nehru offered her the position after Mr K.C. Neogi withdrew.

48 Handwritten statement by Hansa Mehta, undated, File 58, AIWC Papers (2nd Instalment), NMML.

49 Jain, *Women, Development and the UN*, p. 16.

50 Normand and Zaidi, *Human Rights at the UN*, p. 278.

to the CSW for comment.[51] The CSW, in turn, used the UDHR as an instrument to combat political and civil discrimination against women, drawing on the principles of the Declaration as a foundation for the 1952 Convention on the Political Rights of Women.[52] Throughout this period, Mehta provided an important bridge between the two Commissions.

Just as Pandit brought her experience as a woman and as a former colonial subject into debates around the mandate of the United Nations, Mehta brought her insight as a feminist and a nationalist into these Commissions. When called to represent India at the Human Rights Commission, she was involved in the work of the AIWC and was completing a term as the organisation's President. With negotiations for independence and the formation of provisional national and provincial governments well underway, and the writing of the new Indian Constitution about to commence, this was a crucial moment for the AIWC to ensure that the meaning of women's equality was adequately articulated and guaranteed, and that representatives of the women's movement were able to participate fully in this process of nation-building. Although the nationalist movement supported women's equality in theory, the Conference realised that translating this abstract principle into substantial equality would be a challenge. It would require a clear spelling out of meaning and implications of such equality and active lobbying on the part of the women's movement.

The Executive Body of the AIWC at this stage included Rajkumari Amrit Kaur, Hansa Mehta, Lakshmi Menon, Kamaladevi Chattopadhyay, Renuka Ray, Kitty Shiva Rao and Hannah Sen. They drew up an *Indian Woman's Charter of Rights and Duties*, together with a Memorandum on Planning for National Welfare, as part of the organisation's strategy to secure the inclusion of equal rights for women in the drafting of the Indian Constitution, and the development of national economic and social policies. Mehta took a copy of this Charter to Lake Success, where she was meeting with the Human Rights Commission in May 1946. When the Sub-commission on the Status of Women found

[51] Jain, *Women, Development and the UN*, p. 19.

[52] Black, 'Are Women "Human"?', p. 141.

itself struggling to define its own mandate, as well as the meaning and implications of women's equality, both at a national and international level, she offered this Charter as a guideline.[53] A comparison of the wording of the principles of the Sub-commission[54] with the Preamble of the AIWC's Charter suggests the significant role the Charter played in shaping the Sub-commission's mandate. Coverage of this session in the *New York Herald Tribune* described the event with the following headline: 'Women of UN unite in vote of full equality: Mrs Roosevelt is Leader at second Sessions; India's Formula Wins Support'.[55] The first three paragraphs of the Sub-commission's Resolution were taken word for word from the *Indian Woman's Charter of Rights and Duties*:

> Whereas, Freedom and Equality are essential to human development, and whereas woman is as much a human being as man and therefore, entitled to share with him.
>
> We believe that woman has a definite role to play in the building of a free, healthy, prosperous and moral society and that she can fulfil this obligation only as a free and responsible member of society.
>
> In order to achieve this ideal the purpose of this commission is to raise the status of women to equality with men in all fields of human endeavour.[56]

The AIWC's *Indian Woman's Charter of Rights and Duties* was being used as a policy document to lobby for equal rights within the Constituent Assembly over the same period that it was being integrated into the CSW's principles. The movement of the Charter from the Indian context into the United Nations encourages a rethinking of human rights as a West-centric concept. It provides a concrete example of the impact of ideas and 'lived experience' from the margins, in the development of the history of human rights. The influence of the AIWC Charter, and the contribution of Mehta and Pandit to discourses

---

[53] Chattopadhyay, *Indian Woman's Battle for Freedom*, pp. 123–124.

[54] See Document 8: Report of the CSW to ECOSOC on the first session of the Commission held at Lake Success, New York from 10 to 24 February 1947 in *The United Nations and The Advancement of Women 1945-1995*, pp. 103–110.

[55] See article from *New York Herald Tribune*, 2 May 1946, File 58, AIWC Papers, NMML.

[56] See Document 8: Report of the CSW to ECOSOC on the first session of the Commission.

concerning women's equality within the UN, furthermore suggests that there is a need for a renewed focus on the contribution of women from developing countries to the UN.

Human Rights: Remaking the Bounds of Sovereignty

Among the important contributions both Mehta and Pandit made to debates on human rights and women's equality at the UN was their emphasis on the indivisibility of women's rights and their lobbying for the positioning of women's equality within the broader framework of human rights. Their experience as nationalists and feminists, struggling against both the yoke of colonial subjecthood and the restrictions of foreign and indigenous patriarchies, had given them an understanding of this intersection. Mehta and Pandit spoke out during debates on human rights, emphasising that women's rights should not be treated as a separate category.

This emphasis was evident, for example, in the changes pushed for by Pandit, Mehta and Bodil Begtrup[57] to the language of the UDHR that would set the terms for the International Bill of Rights. An earlier draft of Article One of the International Bill of Human Rights had read, 'All men, being members of one family...shall regard each other as brothers.' Mehta and Begtrup objected strongly to the gendered nature of the term 'men', launching a discussion which eventually led to an agreement to use the term 'human beings' instead.[58] Mehta and Roosevelt also asked for the deletion of the word 'woman' in an early draft of the Charter as 'everyone includes women' and mention specifically of the term might 'by inference, mean their exclusion where it is not mentioned.'[59] The notion of the human being, inclusive of all categories of identity and indistinguishable on the basis of race, gender, class or nationality, spoke directly to the identity of the sexless citizen articulated in the Karachi

---

[57] Danish national Bodil Begtrup was chair of the Sub-Commission on the Status of Women.

[58] Normand and Zaidi, *Human Rights at the UN*, p. 187.

[59] A. Whittick, *Woman into Citizen*, p. 164.

Resolution and the democratic Indian Constitution. In this way, the voices and ideas of Mehta and Pandit together with those of the other members of the CSW, helped to shape the language of the UDHR, which formed the framework of the International Bill of Human Rights adopted in December in 1948.

Through their part in these debates, especially through the sharing of the AIWC's *Indian Woman's Charter of Rights and Duties* in the CSW, Pandit and Mehta show how India played a significant role in the development of ideas and structures within the UN during its formative years. But the United Nations experience also enabled Mehta and Pandit to rethink the boundaries and connections between citizenship, rights and nationality through the notion of human rights.

The Indian freedom struggle offered the promise of citizenship and the claim to rights on the basis of a new nation founded on the principles of a secular liberal democracy. However, as Nivedita Menon stresses, democracy took a different shape in the postcolonial world compared to countries of its origin. In the societies of Asia and Africa, democracy entered before the notion of the individual took root. Nationalist leaders, therefore, tended to construct national identities 'not through the idea of individual citizenship but through that of communities'. As a consequence, liberal individualism has never become 'the uncontested core of anti-imperialist struggles or post-independence politics.'[60] This tension between the community versus the individual as the bearer of rights proved problematic for the egalitarian functioning of the relationship between Indian nationalism and feminism. In the Indian context, mediating rights through the framework of community identity has often worked to undermine claims to equality, as the fourth chapter of this book has illustrated by documenting the workings of the Abducted Persons (Recovery and Restoration) Act of 1949.

Furthermore, just as certain powers in the UN limited their commitment to human rights to support an abstract ideal, there were those within the new Congress-led provisional government who supported equality only in principle. They recognised it as part

[60] See N. Menon, 'Elusive 'Woman': Feminism and Women's Reservation Bill', *EPW* 35:43/44 (21 October to 3 November, 2000).

of the making of a progressive modernity, but continued to resist its application in practice. The newly drafted Indian Constitution guaranteed equality on the basis of sex, religion and ethnicity, but, as the fifth chapter documented, a persistent battle, waged by the AIWC and NFIW in the face of ongoing resistance, was needed to ensure that this abstract principle was translated into legislation through the Campaign for the Hindu Code Bill. While the particular national context of India constrained the contours within which an identity for women as citizens could be envisioned, human rights unhinged the claim to rights through nationhood. The debate over South Africa introduced the idea that rights could be broader than claims to both imperial subjecthood and national citizenship. When actions or legislation violated the equality and freedom of the individual, then state sovereignty could be trumped in the name of a global sense of belonging and entitlement, enabling the 'remaking of the bounds of sovereignty'.[61] In the United States, examples of how the local reach of the human rights norms, developed through the UN Charter and the Declaration of Human Rights, could be harnessed to challenge entrenched practices of racial segregation provided evidence that this could indeed be done.[62]

The category of human rights that developed within the UN during this period provided a useful way for thinking about the claim to rights, equality and citizenship itself, beyond the nation-state. This enabled Pandit and Mehta to reframe their demands for Indian women's equality and empowerment within a broader framework of global governance and social justice. Through this process, their demands for equality within the national sphere took on greater momentum and added significance. The UN's focus on promoting the rights of women added an incentive to the Indian government's national commitment to women's equality, but it also offered a concrete benchmark to measure progress. UN Conventions, such as the Convention on Political Rights

[61] Bradley, 'Approaching the Universal Declaration of Rights', p. 332.

[62] The Rice v. Sioux Memorial Park Cemetery Inc case was one such example. The case was brought against the State when the body of a deceased man was removed from a "Caucasians only" cemetery in Sioux City, Iowa, when it was discovered that he was a Native American. See Bradley, 'Approaching the Universal Declaration of Rights', pp. 332–333.

of Women (1952), the Convention on the Nationality of Married Women (1957) and the Commission's Convention on the Consent to Marriage, Minimum Age for Marriage and the Registration of Marriage (1962), offered a practical means of exerting external pressure on the newly established Indian government to implement its constitutional commitment to equality. During its first decade, the key concerns of the CSW mirrored those of the Indian women's rights activists, including ensuring the exercise of equal political rights, legislating for legal rights within marriage and the family, and putting measures in place to prevent the exploitation of women in situations of vulnerability. In 1952, the General Assembly of the UN adopted the CSW-crafted Convention on Political Rights of Women, the same year India held its first democratic elections in which a record number of women voted. In 1957, the Convention on the Nationality of Married Women was drafted and adopted by the General Assembly, supplementing Article 15 of the UDHR. This was followed five years later in 1962 by the adoption of the CSW's Convention on the Consent to Marriage, Minimum Age for Marriage and the Registration of Marriage.[63] Between 1952 and 1956, legislation guaranteeing similar rights for women within marriage and the family was also passed in India, in the form of the Hindu Code Bill.[64] Furthermore, the 1949 UN approval of the Convention on Suppression of the Traffic of Persons and of the Exploitation of the Prostitution of Others assisted Rameshwari Nehru, Lady Rama Rau and a few other organisations in pushing through the Immoral Traffic (Prevention) Act of India in 1956.

---

[63] A. S. Fraser, 'Becoming Human: The Origins and Development of Women's Human Rights' in M. Agosín (ed.), *Women, Gender and Human Rights: a Global Perspective* (Rutgers University Press, New Jersey, 2001), p. 45.

[64] Between 1952 and 1956, the Hindu Code Bill was passed as four separate Acts: the Hindu Marriage Act, the Hindu Succession Act, the Hindu Minority and Guardian Act, the Hindu Adoptions and Maintenance Act.

Conclusion

A History of Doing

Reflecting back on her career, Kamaladevi Chattopadhyay concludes, 'Mine has been an eventful life.'[1] The projects and ambitions undertaken by this generation of nationalists and feminists suggest that this was never the 'quiet period' that historiography tends to define it as.[2] This was an active era, with the crafting of new documents, such as the *Indian Woman's Charter of Rights and Duties*, the AIWC's civic education drives and the Campaign for the Hindu Code Bill. For communist women, in fact, the real 'women's movement' only started in the mid-1950s[3] with the formation of the NFIW in 1954. This was accompanied by the entry of refugee women into agitational politics in Calcutta and the struggle for socio-economic rights.

The establishment of the CSWB; the growing collaboration between the AIWC and other voluntary associations in the conceptualisation and implementation of welfare services and community development projects; the founding and development of new kinds of public-private institutions, such as the Cancer Institute of Madras and the National Council of Child Welfare; and the formation of influential policy-making bodies, such as the FPAI, encourage a re-orientation of the State-centric historiography of nation-building, shifting the focus onto civil society as the agent of change and social justice, and presenting

---

[1] Chattopadhyay, *Inner Recesses Outer Spaces*, p. 1.

[2] See Neera Desai, 'From Accommodation to Articulation' in M. John (ed.), *Women's Studies in India: a Reader* (Penguin, New Delhi, 2008), p. 23. Radha Kumar devotes only one page in her book *The History of Doing* to the period of the 1950s and the dynamics between the women's movement and the newly formed Indian government. Also see Samita Sen, '*Towards a Feminist Politics: The Indian Women's Movement in Historical Perspective*', Policy Research Report on Gender and Development, Working Paper Series No. 9, (2000), pp. 4–5.

[3] Interview with Raja, 18 November 2011.

an alternate picture of Nehruvian India more open to both civil society and the influence of international development.

Belonging

Through these projects and activities, this generation of activists continued to wrestle with the question: how do women 'belong' to the nation-state? In the halls of the CA, Kaur, Mehta and Ray deliberated upon the meaning and possibilities of constitutional and legal citizenship for women. In the towns and villages of India, AIWC branches strove to give middle-class women a sense of purpose and belonging as the agents of development and experts in the field of welfare.

Through serving, educating and mobilising, Chattopadhyay and her colleagues in the AIWC and the NFIW sought to develop an inclusive sense of 'belonging'. However, the segmented nature of these projects kept their ambition of a broader national movement beyond reach. An inability to engage constructively with questions of difference in the body politic was one of the major obstacles that hindered the achievement of this aim. Entangled in a social milieu dominated by communal politics and defined by the destructive hierarchies of caste, identity politics was intrinsically a source of tension and undermined national cohesiveness. In their advocacy for the 'sexless citizen' of the Karachi Resolution, equality was mistakenly equated with homogeneity, and homogeneity misinterpreted as a sign of consensus.[4] The consequence of this was the imposition of homogeneity from above, which left this generation unable to recognise the value and contribution of a politics of difference and the role that such a politics of difference could play in challenging the operation of power in Indian society.

The struggle of integrating questions of difference into a collective politics was also reflected in the ongoing tension between the 'gender-based celebrations of the feminine' and the 'desire for equality which opposed sex-based differentiation'. Radha Kumar identifies this tension as a characteristic of feminism in India.[5] The balancing of rights with

---

[4] Devenish, 'Performing the Political Self', p. 292.

[5] Kumar, *The History of Doing*, p. 5.

duties in the AIWC's *Indian Woman's Charter of Rights and Duties* represented an attempt to resolve this tension by reconciling the feminine through duty with equality through rights. However, this, unfortunately, did not allow for the accommodation of other kinds of difference.

The experiences of this cohort reveal that this generation spoke from various subject positions and with many kinds of voices. Perhaps, this in itself calls for the necessity of multiple kinds of belonging. This leads the scholar back to the perplexing and unanswered question of how a claim to citizenship can accommodate multiple layers of identity, both individual and collective.

Being

Internationalism and the universalising language of human rights was one of the ways that this generation sought to belong beyond the nation-state, enabling them to surmount some of the inherent communal underpinnings of the post-colonial state in Asia. The shared experience of 'being' offered another possibility for collective belonging. As women, experiences such as gendered violence cut across divisions of class, caste and religion, fostering a common platform of 'belonging' built around a shared concern. Feminist history has demonstrated the value of a study of 'being' through theoretical frameworks, such as 'lived experience' and 'embodiment'. The centrality of the experience of 'being', in turn, enables the scholar to think about the meaning, possibilities and limitations of the nation-state and the exercise of freedom and democracy in new and alternative ways.

Revisiting the Bengal Famine of 1943 and the rape and abduction of women during Partition and their recovery by the Indian state through the narratives of Chattopadhyay and her colleagues reveals significant insights. It illustrates how the political, geographical, social and economic processes that facilitated and accompanied decolonisation and nation-building found resonance and expression in the physical bodies of the nation's citizens, and how these processes played themselves out on these physical bodies, gendering these bodies in particular ways. These new areas of focus suggest that in order to grasp its full implications and potential, citizenship needs to be understood not only as an idea and abstract bundle of rights but as a process and experience. 'Being' creates subjectivity, and subjectivity allows for the expression of agency, which lies at the heart of the notion of citizenship.

Institutions and discourses of the State and of civil society created new possibilities of 'being' for Indian women. This widened the horizons and possibilities of citizenship, as can be seen in the AIWC's discourse of citizenship through service, and the NFIW's ambitions for a citizenship through struggle. But by limiting 'being' in particular ways, institutions and discourses of the State and of civil society could just as easily curtail the possibilities of imagining women as agents and citizens, restricting their position in the world to that of subjects and victims. This is most evident in the implementation of the Abducted Persons (Recovery and Restoration) Act of 1949, and the stories of Nissa and Kumari Khan's girl from Lahore.

Becoming

For Chattopadhyay and her colleagues, resources, education and family support, combined with their own self-determination and creativity, enabled them to develop to their full potential. They could come fully into being as intellectuals, professionals and personalities. In this process of 'becoming', citizenship was perceived not simply as a status, something that could be granted, but rather as an attribute that had to be earned through particular kinds of participation in the nation-state, through learning, action and behaviour.

The life stories of Chattopadhyay and her colleagues, however, remain exceptional. Despite the vision and efforts of her generation to facilitate a process of 'becoming' for all their fellow sisters, significant socio-economic inequalities have kept the full meaning and possibilities of citizenship beyond the reach of the majority of women who lived through the transition to independence with them. For these excluded communities of women, who continue in their struggle to become full citizens, the making of an inclusive and egalitarian politics in India remains an ongoing process.

Index

Note—The letter '*n*' following locators refers to footnotes.

ABOUT THE AUTHOR

Dr Annie Devenish (Researcher, African Ombudsman Research Centre [AORC] School of Law, University of KwaZuluNatal, South Africa) is a South African historian working on the history of feminist politics and organisation in India and South Africa. She is particularly interested in the intersections between gender, development and democracy in the Global South, and identity politics in the context of political transition.

A graduate in history from the University Natal (2001), Devenish finished her PhD from the University of Oxford (2015) under the supervision of Dr Faisal Devji. Her research focused on the interaction between gender, citizenship and identity in independent India.

Prior to commencing her PhD, Dr Devenish spent two years teaching undergraduate history at the University of Cape Town and subsequently taught history for a short while at the University of KwaZulu-Natal. Her publications, both forthcoming and present, focus on gender, the informal economy, traditional health practitioners in Southern Africa, and feminism and development in India and South Africa.

Dr Devenish currently works as a researcher at the African Ombudsman Research Centre within the School of Law at the University of KwaZulu-Natal.